Praise for
Breakout Strategies for Emerging Markets

"If every global marketing company applied the principles in this new and important book, I have no doubt that millions of consumers in emerging countries will achieve a higher standard of living and the global marketing companies will all achieve increased sales and profitability."

> **Philip Kotler,** S. C. Johnson & Son Distinguished Professor of Marketing, Kellogg School of Management, Northwestern University

"Sheth, Sinha, and Shah have developed a highly practical and comprehensive guide to navigating the complex challenges and achieving growth in emerging markets. Their book is a must read for anybody who is working in or wanting to enter emerging markets."

> **Cynthia Kantor,** Senior Executive, Global Product Line Leader, GE Power Services

"This is an essential compass for navigating the enormous possibilities and the many pitfalls of emerging markets. This is a well-researched and thoughtful guide-book to the challenges of converting nonusers to users at scale. The authors emphasize an outside-in approach that puts the reader in the shoes, boots, and sandals of the potential consumers before taking action."

> **George Day,** Geoffrey T. Boisi Professor Emeritus, Wharton School of Business, University of Pennsylvania

"Having had the extensive experience of leading a global division operating in over 100 countries, I know first-hand the challenges companies face when they enter emerging markets. The authors have uniquely developed an approach that will prove to be beneficial for those seeking success in emerging markets."

> **Javier C. Goizueta,** Retired Vice President, The Coca Cola Company and President of the Global McDonald's Division

"Despite the volatility in markets, which is greater for emerging markets, the fact is that every multinational company has to master the nuances of working in the different emerging markets. The variance between emerging markets is greater than that observed between different developed markets. As a result, adaptation across the emerging markets becomes important for success. The book provides an excellent approach for doing so."

> **Nirmalya Kumar,** Member—Group Executive Council at Tata Sons, Visiting Professor of Marketing at London Business School and Distinguished Fellow Emerging Markets Institute, INSEAD at Singapore

"Jagdish Sheth, one of the world's leading experts on emerging markets, has done it again! In *Breakout Strategies*, he and his colleagues offer a practical road map for how to gain traction and achieve rapid growth in emerging economies. The book puts flesh on the bones of the 4 A's model that Sheth pioneered some years back. It is a treasure trove of practical strategies and tactics illustrated with numerous real-world examples. It fills a void and is destined to become a classic on the topic."

> **Ravi Ramamurti,** D'Amore-McKim Distinguished Professor of
> International Business, and Director, Center for Emerging Markets,
> Northeastern University

"This book is a refreshing combination of strategic thought and practical application for operating in emerging markets, applied comprehensively and made robust with examples from Africa, Asia, and Latin America. Having lived and worked in each of these geographies, I see great value in the frameworks the authors have created to identify and commercialize opportunities in a responsible manner."

> **Vinita Bali,** Global Business Leader, formerly with Cadbury
> Schweppes, The Coca-Cola Company, and Britannia Industries Ltd.

"Jagdish Sheth, Mona Sinha, and Reshma Shah have created an all-encompassing step-by-step model for engaging relevant stakeholders in emerging markets such as leaders, communities, employees, suppliers, and, of course, customers in their book, *Breakout Strategies for Emerging Markets*. Such a treatment of emerging markets takes this book from the common way of doing business—sourcing from emerging markets or selling commoditized products in emerging markets—to a level of engagement that benefits both emerging markets and those who engage with them. This is a sustainable and long-term viable way of strategizing about emerging markets."

> **Tomas Hult,** Professor and Byington Endowed Chair in
> International Business, Broad College of Business, Michigan
> State University, and Executive Director, Academy of
> International Business

"A must-read book for companies that are searching for growth opportunities. This book very succinctly articulates how to tap into market opportunities in developing/ emerging markets. Concepts like Breakout Strategies and 4 A's marketing are simple yet very powerful and pragmatic concepts that companies can benefit from. This book is a brilliant blend of simple frameworks and well-articulated examples that brings the story to life very effectively and another marketing blockbuster on the anvil from Dr. Sheth."

> **Stan Sthanunathan,** Executive Vice President,
> Consumer and Market Insights, Unilever

"Despite the recent economic slowdown in China and some other emerging markets (EM), it is indisputable that companies everywhere still need to sell much more to these EM consumers if they wish to grow. The framework and examples in this book should be of great help. Not only is it chock full of terrific insights and examples—it weaves these together into a new and very useful conceptual framework that has great managerial relevance. It brings together many new and useful points about how to sell to low (bottom of the pyramid) and middle income consumers, and the crucial youth market, in a multitude of geographical locales—not just China and India but also Latin America and Africa. Marketers everywhere need to read this book."

Rajeev Batra, Sebastian S. Kresge Professor of Marketing, Ross School of Business, University of Michigan

"A 'must read' book for managers seeking growth in emerging markets! Breakout strategies are new, large-scale ways to convert nonusers to users. The 4 A's provide a powerful framework that starts from what a market offers: culture, values, systems, and needs. Companies grow by leveraging what the market lacks: technologies, processes, products, and brands. The authors' offer compelling stories about how companies have overcome challenges to succeed in Africa, Asia, the Middle East, Europe, and South America."

Dr. Ruth N. Bolton, Professor of Marketing, W.P. Carey School of Business, Arizona State University

"Never have I seen the underlying drivers of success in emerging markets uncovered and communicated more effectively. The consumer and environmental factors discussed are the most often overlooked when setting strategy in emerging markets. The strategies advanced are real-world applicable and capture critical learning for success in emerging markets."

Mike Shattuck, Former President Focus Brands International and Owner, Global Franchising and Brand Building

Breakout Strategies for Emerging Markets

Breakout Strategies for Emerging Markets

Business and Marketing Tactics for Achieving Growth

Jagdish N. Sheth
Mona Sinha
Reshma Shah

Associate Editor: Kim Boedigheimer
Senior Marketing Manager: Stephane Nakib
Cover Designer: Chuti Prasertsith
Managing Editor: Sandra Schroeder
Senior Project Editor: Tracey Croom
Project Manager: Maureen Forys
Copy Editor: Rebecca Rider
Proofreader: Nancy Peterson
Indexer: Valerie Perry
Compositors: Maureen Forys and Kate Kaminski

Published by Pearson Education, Inc.
Old Tappan, New Jersey 07675

For information about buying this title in bulk quantities, or for special sales opportunities (which may include electronic versions; custom cover designs; and content particular to your business, training goals, marketing focus, or branding interests), please contact our corporate sales department at corpsales@pearsoned.com or (800) 382-3419.

For government sales inquiries, please contact governmentsales@pearsoned.com.

For questions about sales outside the U.S., please contact intlcs@pearson.com.

1   16

ISBN-10: 0-13-443495-1
ISBN-13: 978-0-13-443495-7

Pearson Education LTD.
Pearson Education Australia PTY, Limited
Pearson Education Singapore, Pte. Ltd.
Pearson Education Asia, Ltd.
Pearson Education Canada, Ltd.
Pearson Educación de Mexico, S.A. de C.V.
Pearson Education—Japan
Pearson Education Malaysia, Pte. Ltd.

Library of Congress Control Number: 2016941560 [2]

To my grandchildren (Rehna, Maya, Anya, and Arya) whose love keeps me going.

—Jagdish Sheth

To my three special people, Nuri, Sridhar, and Papa for celebrating your milestone birthdays this year.

—Mona Sinha

To my parents, Jagdish and Madhuri Sheth, for showing me the world and enabling me to appreciate all its diverse aspects.

—Reshma Shah

Contents

Acknowledgments

This book has been inspired by the dozens of companies in emerging markets all over the world whose stories we have had the privilege of sharing. There were many more stories that we wish we could have shared. We gratefully acknowledge our many contributors whose profiles are at the back of this book. We also thank our student assistants, Alaina D'Anzi, Ebenezer Osunlalu, and Innocent Djiofack for their help with the in-depth research this book required. In addition, our thanks to Aarya Budhiraja (BBA research assistant at Emory University) and Anthony Koschmann (PhD candidate at Emory University) for assisting in our research. Special thanks to Isha Edwards for editing and organizing the citations for each chapter. We are also grateful to Nicole Smith, Jagdish Sheth's personal assistant, for providing administrative support for the book. Finally, we are deeply appreciative of the support and guidance from the team at Pearson including Jeanne Levine and Kim Boedigheimer, and the team at Happenstance Type-O-Rama including Maureen Forys, Kate Kaminski, Rebecca Rider, and Nancy Peterson.

Breakout Strategies for Emerging Markets

1

Converting Nonusers to Users

Emerging markets offer the biggest growth opportunity in the history of capitalism. Unfazed by the ups and downs of the global economy, many former developing nations have transformed into lucrative markets with potential annual consumption estimated at 30 trillion USD (U.S. dollars) by 2025 (Atsmon et al. 2012). Eyeing nearly 10 trillion USD of annual revenue from just India and China, businesses have been spending billions of dollars to understand and market to consumers in these emerging economies (Silverstein et al. 2012). Emerging economies are not only transforming marketing, but they are also transforming markets all over the world by attracting multinationals, shoring up domestic firms, and launching local brands onto the global stage.

The case for entering and competing in emerging markets is certainly a strong one. As The Coca-Cola Company's CEO Muhtar Kent concisely explained, "About 3.5 percent to 4 percent of the population of the world lives in the U.S., and we're a consumer goods company. So we sell where the people are. It's just math" (Nisen 2012). Further, as affluent nations aged, consumption levels and patterns changed, and consequently companies began to look for growth in emerging markets that were getting liberalized. No longer were they just ex-colonies with predominantly rural, agrarian, bottom-of-the-pyramid (BoP) consumers, but they also comprised a burgeoning middle class and a growing affluent class that was becoming increasingly brand conscious and driving growth in consumption (Sheth 2011).

Multinationals were not prepared for heterogeneity when they first entered these new markets in the early '80s. With almost 50 percent of consumers at the BoP and a fragmented market of largely unbranded domestic products from a large number of small enterprises, many emerging markets were similar to preindustrialization-era farming economies. Vast swathes of the population were illiterate and traditional means of communication were ineffective in reaching them, which meant that marketers often needed to rethink their marketing mix. Many parts of these markets lacked or had poor quality of even basic infrastructure, such as electricity, clean drinking water, banking, telecommunication, transportation, and communications. Resources were chronically in shortage. Branded goods and services were relatively new entrants in emerging markets, which even now tend to be largely dominated by unbranded regional or local commodities. Governance in these markets is influenced predominantly by sociopolitical institutions based on religion, government, local community, business groups, or nongovernmental organizations, leaving new entrants struggling to navigate complex and unfamiliar regulatory structures (Sheth 2011). Further, even though consumers have accepted many aspects of global brands, they also show strong preferences for their traditions and cultures. Multinationals need to be attuned to sociocultural–driven heterogeneities that frustrate unquestioned acceptance of global brands (Strizhakova, Coulter, and Price 2012).

The conceptual foundations as well as the practice of marketing are predominantly based on the study of branded goods and services from the developed parts of the Western world. However, in emerging markets, an estimated 65 percent of consumption is unbranded and much remains unknown about how these consumers and markets are different from or similar to developed ones (Sheth 2011). Douglas Daft, who preceded Muhtar Kent as CEO of Coca-Cola from 2000 to 2004, noted that Coca-Cola's standardization strategy had run its course, "The world had changed, and we had not. The world was demanding greater flexibility, responsiveness, and local sensitivity, while we were further consolidating decision-making and standardizing our practices" (Ball 2003). Companies like Unilever had successfully taken a long-term position in emerging markets, even when they were not yet in a growth surge. Eventually these companies became so ingrained in the fabric of local society that they were perceived more as local rather than global companies. However, for most companies, their foray into emerging markets remains a hit-or-miss experience with as many failures as successes. Thus, the next big evolutionary step of "going global" is not just "going local" but seamlessly blending elements from the developing and developed world.

Despite the realization that entering emerging markets is a competitive imperative and requires a fair amount of rethinking, multinationals, as well as local companies, foraying into branded competition falter because they lack an explanatory framework and practical guidelines. Given that the size and unique consumption needs of emerging markets require investments running into billions of U.S. dollars, the failure to understand the key to succeeding in these markets is a critical and significant knowledge gap in business strategy. While recently much attention has focused on what is wrong with developing or emerging nations and the unreliability of these nations as investment destinations, we focus instead on what is *right*—the opportunities that exist, and those that can be created despite or perhaps even because of the challenges in these markets. We examine not just how brands overcome challenges, but also why those actions help them succeed. We propose breaking out of traditional marketing thought, which is normally centered on differentiation, segmentation, positioning, and the marketing mix to compete against other branded goods and services, to propose new ways of marketing aimed at converting the large numbers of non users in emerging markets to users.

The first step in this process is to acknowledge that as standards of living rise across the world, emerging market consumers are increasingly exposed to products previously used in developed nations or restricted to higher socio-economic groups. The obvious examples include cell phones and flat screen televisions, as well as basic products, such as shampoo and detergent. But, simply bringing in Western products, or even adapting them to emerging markets, is not sufficient because getting consumers to use products that they have not previously considered requires more than just making the products available. In fact, most products sold in emerging markets are typically unpackaged and unbranded so there is great opportunity in branding and organizing them.

Breakout marketing is the way companies can use what a given market offers (e.g., culture, values, systems, and needs) and introduce what it lacks (e.g., technologies, methods/processes, products, and brands), thereby transforming both themselves as well as the market. Notably, although brands usually begin their journey in emerging markets by converting light users into heavy users, the great market expansion that marketers aspire to really comes from large-scale conversion of nonusers to users. Nonusers include those who do not consider the product category itself and also those who may be accustomed to the category but have previously used unbranded or noncommercial options. Consumption of unbranded products in emerging markets offers a huge, untapped potential to marketers, which can be leveraged if companies succeed in providing access, creating acceptability and building awareness at affordable price points.

Our in-depth observations of companies in emerging markets across the world led us to develop the eight key breakout strategies that we recommend in this book. These strategies are based on four key criteria, coined the 4 A's of Marketing and developed into a framework by Jagdish Sheth and Rajendra Sisodia (2012) after they spent years watching and learning how companies succeed. The 4 A's framework, comprising acceptability, affordability, accessibility, and awareness, combines a theoretical approach with the actual practice of marketing. More importantly, it is an outside-in customer-centric approach that begins with customer benefits instead of the inside-out product-centric approach that starts with firms' actions, objectives, and the traditional marketing mix. Marketers can use this framework to align their actions with the four essential values that customers seek. These values can be summarized as follows:

1. **Acceptability.** The extent to which the firms' total product offering meets and exceeds customer expectations. Acceptability has two key dimensions—functional acceptability and psychological acceptability.

2. **Affordability.** The extent to which customers in the target market are able and willing to pay the product's price. Affordability can also be characterized by two dimensions—economic affordability or the ability to pay, and psychological affordability or the willingness to pay.

3. **Accessibility**. The extent to which customers are able to readily acquire and use the product. Again, there are two dimensions to accessibility—the availability of goods and services, and their convenience.

4. Awareness. The extent to which customers are informed regarding product characteristics, persuaded to try a new product or service, and, if applicable, reminded to repurchase it. Awareness includes both brand awareness and product knowledge.

The 4 A's framework helps to eliminate much of the guesswork that goes into marketing, because it lets managers work with a set of objectives that are focused on the consumer versus the marketer. This framework derives from a customer-value perspective based on the four distinct roles that customers play in the market: seekers, selectors, payers, and users. For a marketing program to succeed, it must achieve high marks for all four A's, using a blend of marketing and nonmarketing resources. The 4 A's framework helps companies create value for customers by identifying what they want and need, as well as by uncovering new wants and needs. For example, none of us knew we needed an iPad until Apple created it.

We traversed a creative path between this theoretical framework and the practice of marketing in an emerging-market context in order to develop our eight strategies. Our strategies will help companies build awareness among consumers as well as other stakeholders and gain acceptability for products and services by pricing them affordably and making them convenient to access. This book represents our combined years of experience in marketing, including in emerging markets. We use insights from global primary and secondary research; our work in academia, corporate practice, consulting, and case-writing; as well as our numerous presentations to industry audiences all over the world. Our brand stories range from Africa to Asia, passing through the Middle East to reach western Asia. We also step briefly into Europe and stretch down into South America with our examples. By using a story-telling approach to illustrate the success of these eight strategies, we provide real-world evidence for creative and contextual marketing in emerging markets. We hope that by bringing you the voices of numerous organizations and managers, we show you a way to grasp an unparalleled opportunity offered in the history of the world–the ability to transform the practice of marketing by including scores of new consumers from across the world, and thereby the ability to write new rules to drive strategic thought in marketing. According to the organizing framework developed at the end of this chapter in Figure 1, this book is laid out so that each chapter describes a breakout strategy that operates within the context of the 4 A's framework. We offer two strategies for each A of marketing, and each strategy provides paths by which companies can convert nonusers to users.

The strategies in Chapters 2 and 3 discuss ways of creating *acceptability* by being mindful of special functionality needs and adherence to cultural norms. Chapters 4 and 5 offer strategies for *affordable* solutions, both at the base and at the top of the pyramid. Chapters 6 and 7 are focused on providing *accessibility* by leveraging existing distribution set ups and introducing new ones. Finally, Chapters 8 and 9 focus on creating *awareness* by building brand identity and then going beyond a customer focus to serve the needs of various stakeholders, such as supply chain members, communities, and government and nongovernment agencies. All these strategies are primarily aimed at expanding the market by converting nonusers to users. Here's a snapshot of what the chapters ahead have in store.

Chapter 2, titled "Creating Functional Fusion," speaks to the highly heterogeneous needs and expectations across different emerging markets; these are based on factors like local climate and the genetic makeup of local people that necessitate functional adaptation to make products acceptable (Sheth 2007). For example, the hot and dusty climate of northern India required Panasonic to rethink its air conditioning systems. Variations in skin types and hair texture compel product adaptations in several markets in Asia. Similarly, genetic and health predispositions also require product reformulation. For example, over 90 percent of Chinese consumers are lactose intolerant, so Cadbury Schweppes PLC had to reformulate its chocolates with less milk and, as a result, they also had to use less cocoa to avoid a bitter taste.

The lack of critical infrastructure, such as water and electricity, in many emerging markets also calls for out-of-the-box thinking for product modifications or innovations. For example, Whirlpool Corporation's washing machines for such regions are fully automatic, top-loading machines that restart the washing cycle from the point that a power outage occurred instead of restarting from the beginning of the cycle. They also conserve by reusing water. Companies incorporate local ingredients/components for cost efficiencies. This is especially the case for food companies since ingredients are prone to spoilage if the supply chain is too long. Often companies retain/employ local talent for better leveraging on-the-ground knowledge. The ability to negotiate regulatory requirements of a country may also compel product and process modifications. IKEA's current domestic sourcing in China and future sourcing as it contemplates entry into India are based on government regulations.

In Chapter 3, "Designing Cultural Fusion," we turn our attention to making products culturally acceptable. If products or services do not take the totality of the customers' lived experience into account, then despite superior functional performance, they may fail due to lack of psychological acceptability. In other words, cultural fusion involves closing the gap between the marketing practices of advanced and emerging markets to improve their psychological acceptance. Cultural fusion includes a holistic view of consumers' local traditions, the history of their consumption experiences, and their aspirations to be contemporary.

Food and beverage companies have been at the forefront of cultural fusion by adapting their menus to local palates. Kentucky Fried Chicken's (KFC's) strategy in China reflects their focus on psychological acceptance. Their menu includes items specifically created for the unique tastes and preferences of Chinese consumers. Extensive market research led to the inclusion of lo mein and other noodle dishes that would not typically be found at KFCs in other countries, but several items incorporated Western elements as well, creating fusion cuisine. Disney's feng shui–influenced theme park design for Hong Kong is also an example of fusion because they leveraged aspects of local culture to make their brand more relevant to the local culture while they also retained Western design elements. Integrating new product categories into the local consumption culture often involves community-level assimilation to minimize the social risk of new product adoption. An example of this is Sula Vineyard's marketing efforts in India where they built the wine market from scratch by creating a wine culture and lifestyle that was a whole new concept for the Indian market. Adapting products to accommodate religion- or faith-based considerations is an important element of psychological acceptance. The rise of Islamic banking, which reflects an ingenuous combination of Western banking and the religious considerations of Islam, reflects the power of cultural fusion.

In Chapter 4, we move on to affordability considerations. Titled "Democratizing the Offer," this chapter delves into ways to innovate to achieve low-priced, affordable solutions. Marketers have long acknowledged that, despite a rise in per capita income, consumers in emerging markets have far lower disposable incomes than consumers in developed economies, even after accounting for purchasing power parity. However, determining creative ways of making purchases financially feasible for the BoP can be profitable for companies while also drawing millions into the consumption fold (Prahalad 2006). These large and attractive markets can be targeted by addressing both economic affordability, that is, the ability to pay, and psychological ability, that is, the willingness to pay (Sheth and Sisodia 2012).

Product development in emerging markets is often spurred by the needs of low-income consumers. For example, in Argentina, Sistema Ser/CEGIN transformed healthcare at the BoP by offering a subscription model. Similarly, GlaxoSmithKline came up with vaccines at multiple price levels for a range of middle- to low-income Latin American countries. Going beyond price, Capitec Bank began offering unsecured credit in South Africa, thereby drawing in non-users by helping them overcome noneconomic barriers to purchase. Such products often find markets for similar low-income consumers or those with reduced needs in the developed world; this concept is called *reverse innovation*, and was made famous by General Electric (GE). Levi Strauss & Co. created low-priced Denizen jeans for China, which were eventually launched in the United States, and the brand is now doing very well across segments. Such innovation opportunities are a way for companies to develop critical new skills that are applicable in affluent countries as well.

Managing products throughout their lifecycle is another way of offering affordable solutions. This includes options such as facilitating the sale of used goods, whether in an indigenous street market for, say, home appliances or clothes, or at a higher end, like Manheim's auction-based market for used cars. Creative financing solutions are another way of democratizing the offer, such as by offering small business financing or even by offering the core product for free and earning revenue with add-on services or advertising.

In Chapter 5, we present an idea contrary to popular perceptions that emerging market consumers only want low-priced products. In "Upscaling the Offer," we draw attention to the changing shape of the income pyramid in emerging markets as the ranks of the middle class swell and turn the triangle into a diamond. The neo-rich segments in these countries are expanding and creating an opportunity for luxury players to make an impact as well. The Asia-Pacific region is estimated to have more high-net-worth people than North America, though the total value of wealth held in the United States may be higher (Lorenzetti 2015). Thus, emerging markets present huge financial opportunities for companies that can serve upper echelon consumers.

Moreover, affordability means something is within one's financial means, so the large and growing segments of middle class consumers in emerging markets imply that brands can also be "upscaled" to match the increasing paying capacity of their customers. It is worth noting that many products and brands that are nonluxury in the West are considered luxury products in emerging markets. So as consumers upgrade their consumption, introducing new products and brands to them opens up exciting new prospects for many companies. Since most consumption in emerging markets is of unpackaged, unbranded goods, simply adding packaging, as in the case of Moroccan dates, can transform a commodity into a well-recognized brand that can display/position its country of origin positively. In addition to the inclusion of packaging, accurately positioning, as well as adding services and benefits, adds to the value proposition. Brands like Sundrop in India or Rapoo in China have been able to leverage their success in low-price segments to eventually enter high-priced, value-added segments, effectively reversing their brand lifecycle. Higher prices can become attractive to an affluent audience in emerging markets by emphasizing the brand's country of origin, which creates a halo effect if it is from the developed world. Several foreign luxury brands have discovered this phenomenon and feature their products on websites like Alibaba's Tmall in China.

In Chapter 6, we present marketers with a strategy we title "Managing Reach" where we suggest ways of leveraging traditionally available distribution methods to increase access. *Accessibility* refers to the extent to which customers are able to easily acquire and use the product. Not only does this include ensuring the right amount of product availability (it is neither under- nor overproduced), but it must also be convenient to access the product so the time and effort required to get the product is reduced (Sheth and Sisodia 2012). Distribution is an important challenge for companies to overcome in providing accessibility, given that most emerging markets often lack basic infrastructure, have multiple middle men, and face regulatory as well as scalability hurdles that hamper the physical movement of products to end consumers, especially at the BoP.

Chapter 6 also notes the many existing distribution systems in emerging markets that companies need to adapt to in order to create access. Often companies find that their traditional conceptualization of retailing must change because typical neighborhood stores can just be homes that double as stores with living areas at the back and store counters up front. There are also indigenous channels like street markets, pushcart vendors, and traditional bazaars. Some of these channels such as the Gold Souk in Dubai are fairly organized and increasingly famous international jewelers are setting up shop there. Another way of expanding reach is by collaborating with a variety of partners. Setting up or improving distribution systems in these countries often require partnerships similar to the way Sberbank of Russia partnered with its employees to transform its service quality and delivery. Similarly, SANY in China partnered with its distributors to shoulder some of the risks involved in marketing a relatively new brand. When making channel ownership decisions, businesses must consider the source and level of control they desire, like the way Grupo Los Grobo in Argentina rethought land ownership in order to transform the agro-supply chain.

In Chapter 7, titled "Reinventing Reach," we propose using technology and other innovative ways for reaching out to consumers. Modern retail formats, like China Resources Vanguard Co. in China, and co-exists with "old" (for the developed world) technologies like vending machines and mobile vans are being used in interesting ways and for unusual products. For example, the South African Revenue Service (SARS) used mobile vans that are being used to fan out to rural areas for increasing citizens' compliance with tax filing norms. Likewise, ATMs in Africa or India are like multipurpose kiosks dispensing phone recharges as well as agriculture and weather information.

E-commerce websites like Alibaba are huge online market-places in the business-to-consumer (B2C) as well as the business-to-business (B2B) space, whereas OLX, which offers free classifieds, has first-mover advantage over Craigslist in emerging markets. Online payment systems such as M-Pesa in Kenya are also revolutionizing ways of providing access to consumers in other emerging markets like India. Indeed, emerging markets are leapfrogging landlines and desktops to using mobile platforms for mobile commerce (m-commerce). Microfinance, another way of increasing reach for financial products, is also discussed in Chapter 7.

Chapter 8, "Building Brand Identity," addresses the complexities of communicating with consumers in emerging markets. Although multinationals are well-versed in creating brand awareness, they often find themselves floundering when their traditional ways of brand communication do not find favor in emerging markets, such as when content clashes with the local culture, beliefs, and sentiment. Low literacy rates and limited or no access to media further complicate communication. This chapter examines ways in which companies have successfully created awareness about their product categories and increased knowledge about their brands in order to build a strong brand identity. Specifically, we focus on leveraging the source of communication, customizing the messaging, and evaluating the use of either traditional or new channels. Unbranded products can be infused with value by modernizing the packaging as Haldiram's did in India, successfully branding traditional snacks and sweets that had previously been largely sold as commodities. Using celebrities to build credibility is also a way to leverage the power of communication.

Emerging markets have large youth segments, which companies target using multiple touch points. For example, Micromax, a mobile phone handset manufacturer, positioned itself on innovation and speed, and used music, movies, and cricket, which resonate well with young Indians. Companies can tap many consumers' aspirations, such as for luxury or status (e.g., Buick in China) and beauty (e.g., L'Oréal in India). Media choice is also critical. For example, rural audiences may be best reached by indigenous media, such as wall paintings or street theater, but for young, urban populations, new media, such as WeChat in China, is appropriate.

Chapter 9 is appropriately titled "Engaging Stakeholders." Although creating brand awareness increases consumers' knowledge about the brand itself, an equally, if not more important criteria for success in emerging markets is for the brand to become part of the social, economic, and environmental successes of those countries by demonstrating concern for all stakeholders. Paying attention to the triple bottom line (i.e., people, planet, and profit) is an important way of managing varied stakeholder needs, and it helps companies become a causal part of the success stories of these countries rather than outsiders that merely benefit from opportunities that emerging markets offer.

Education is an important way of managing stakeholder relationships. While companies may need to educate consumers about how or why to use a product/brand, they may also need to educate them about modern sanitary habits, health-conscious consumption, and the environmental impact of consumption. This paves the way for increased brand awareness and also for a more vibrant and sustainable community. Such efforts are typically more successful when community members and leaders are also involved. Many pharmaceutical companies like GlaxoSmithKline in Africa and Latin America, and DuPont in India are engaging such stakeholders.

Co-opting employees and suppliers can help create new ways of creating awareness and preference. This is especially true when traditional media may not have the desired reach in large parts of the country. Establishing manufacturing and supply-chain partners is also an important part of stakeholder management. For example, Nestlé trained farmers, built schools, provided clean drinking water, and even partnered with the government and other organizations to tackle the problem of child labor. Stakeholders also include policy makers and community leaders who can be valuable partners. For example, Microsoft's Partnerships for Technology Access (PTA) initiative is developing a model for creating strategic technology alliances among different public and private stakeholders. In Chile, PTA has created a public-private partnership called Mipyme Avanza (translation: my small business grows) to enable small businesses to buy their first computers. Internet and business software is provided by partners such as Microsoft, Intel, and Olidata. Similarly, for-profit and nonprofit companies often collaborate. Thus, this chapter focuses on the various ways that companies can do well by doing good.

Finally, in Chapter 10, "Connecting the Dots," we combine our learning from global cases and conceptual framework to summarize how you can use our eight strategies built around the 4 A's framework. In particular, this chapter details how these strategies help address the inherent challenges that companies face in emerging markets. These are summarized in Table 1 in Chapter 10. We also take this opportunity to encourage you to promote mindful consumption as you implement your business strategy. This book plugs the knowledge gap in our understanding and practice of marketing with how to compete in emerging markets by offering a strategic marketing toolkit that managers can deploy in complex, heterogeneous markets.

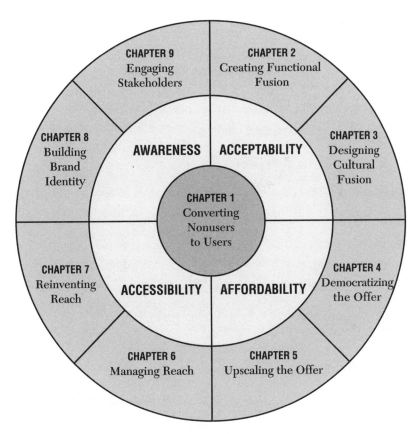

Figure 1: Breakout Strategies for Emerging Markets

Globalization was once about the dominance of Western culture and concepts and *glocalization* was about making adaptations for local sensibilities. *Breakout strategies* transcends its predecessors because it adapts to the new world view by acknowledging the impact of free trade and technology, and social networks that are increasingly weaving the world together. This new world view combines modernization with old-world culture and urges creative adaptation to resource constraints faced by large parts of the developing world (Sheth 2011). Not only does this entail leveraging what exists, that is, thinking in the box, but it also introduces what does not exist, that is, thinking out of the box. Hence, this book is aptly titled *Breakout Strategies for Emerging Markets: Business Tactics for Achieving Market Growth*. We endeavor to help you think differently in order to market differently.

References

Atsmon, Yuval, Peter Child, Richard Dobbs, and Laxman Narasimhan. 2012. "Winning the $30 Trillion Decathlon: Going for Gold in Emerging Markets." *McKinsey Quarterly*. August. Accessed on August 8, 2012. www.mckinsey.com/business-functions/strategy-and-corporate-finance/our-insights/winning-the-30-trillion-decathlon-going-for-gold-in-emerging-markets.

Ball, Donald A. 2003. *International Business: The Challenge of Global Competition*. Boston: McGraw-Hill/Irwin. 478.

Lorenzetti, Laura. 2015. "Here's How Many People Became Millionaires Last Year." *Fortune*. June 17. Accessed on February 14, 2016. http://fortune.com/2015/06/17/millionaires-worldwide.

Nisen, Max. 2012. "Coke CEO Muhtar Kent Perfectly Sums Up Why the Future Is Outside the US." *Business Insider*. October 1. Accessed on December 7, 2012. www.businessinsider.com/why-the-future-is-outside-the-us-2012-10.

Prahalad, C.K. 2006. *Fortune at the Bottom of the Pyramid: Eradicating Poverty Through Profits*. India: Dorling Kindersley Pvt Ltd.

Sheth, Jagdish N. 2007. "Climate, Culture, and Consumption: Connecting the Dots." The Twelfth Distinguished Faculty Lecture, Emory University. February 6.

————.2011. "Impact of Emerging Markets on Marketing: Rethinking Existing Perspectives and Practices." *Journal of Marketing* 75: 166–182.

Sheth, Jagdish N., Nirmal Sethia, and Shanthi Srinivas. 2011. "Mindful Consumption: a Customer-Centric Approach to Sustainability." *Journal of the Academy of Marketing Science* 39: 21–39.

Sheth, Jagdish N., and Rajendra S. Sisodia. 2012. *The 4 A's of Marketing: Creating Value for Customers, Companies, and Society.* New York: Routledge.

Silverstein, Michael J., Abheek Singhi, Carol Liao, and David Michael. 2012. *The $10 Trillion Prize: Captivating the Newly Affluent in China and India.* Boston: Harvard Business Review Press.

Strizhakova, Yuliya, Robin A. Coulter, and Linda L. Price. 2012. "The Young Adult Cohort in Emerging Markets: Assessing Their Glocal Cultural Identity in a Global Marketplace." *International Journal of Research in Marketing* 29: 43–54.

2

Creating Functional Fusion

Emerging markets are characterized by a large and growing group of middle-class consumers who are fueling the purchase of products such as automobiles, luxury goods, and electronics. Although the strategy of marketing global, standardized products keeps costs and prices down, it can alienate emerging market consumers due to differences in product form, product usage, and brand meaning. Further, variations in rules and regulations across national borders, climate, economic conditions, and political stability can add to perceived differences, making it difficult for the local population to relate to and value companies and their offerings (Calantone et al. 2004). Consumers in emerging markets are highly diverse and value-conscious, so companies trying to reach them successfully must rethink their operations, research and development (R&D), marketing, supply chain, hiring practices, and most importantly, their products. Although minor product modifications and design simplifications to ease manufacturing and lower costs may work, often totally new products may need to be invented (Bredenberg 2013). For this, companies need to generate and utilize insights from a variety of sources, such as end-consumers and suppliers, and factor these into their R&D initiatives. This is especially critical because emerging market environments change rapidly, and customers in these markets tend to be extremely price conscious and demanding (Gudlavalleti, Gupta, and Narayanan 2013).

Product adaptation can be understood as the degree to which the physical product differs across countries (Cavusgil, Zou, and Naidu 1993). When adapting products, companies benefit from blending elements from developed countries with those from emerging markets. They must consider differences such as genetics (e.g., physique, skin/hair texture, overall health), climate (e.g., tropical), infrastructural deficiencies, and regulations (Sheth 2007, 2011). Adaptations can involve product quality and appearance, raw materials or ingredients, manufacturing processes, packaging, and promotion, in addition to meeting the

country's physical, social, and regulatory requirements, and engineering or design standards (Nakra 2015). Further, adaptations can also be
made by hiring local employees, using local supply chain partners, and
conducting research and development (R&D) in the country (Johri and
Petison 2008).

The first element of the 4 A's framework (Sheth and Sisodia 2012)
is product acceptability, or the degree to which a firm's total product
offering exceeds customer expectations, both functionally and psy-
chologically. In this chapter, we recommend the strategy of creating
functional fusion, by adapting for product-based attributes along with
country and people-specific attributes, to make products acceptable.
The five strategies we offer in this chapter for achieving functional
fusion are 1) adapting to climate, 2) considering genetic differences,
3) overcoming infrastructure limitations, 4) incorporating local essence,
and 5) aligning to regulatory requirements.

Adapting to Climate

Climatic conditions have a large impact on what people consume
and also why and how they consume. Warm climates call for lighter,
free flowing clothes made of linen or cotton, whereas cold climates call
for tight-fitting, multilayered, woolen apparel. A sloping roof in northern countries allows snow to slide off, whereas, flat roofs, with gentle
slopes, help drain rain water in countries with warm climates. In warm
countries, fat in the diet is sourced from olives or coconut, whereas, in
colder climates, fat comes from animal sources (Sheth 2007). Over the
centuries, such climatic differences have become ingrained into local
traditions and culture.

Both consumer and industrial products in emerging markets need
to be adapted for local climatic conditions including elements of topog-
raphy, temperature, and humidity. For example, for tropical countries
that have hot and humid climates, cosmetics and toiletries such as
shampoo often have to be reformulated so that they function appropriately. Cars have to incorporate filter and clutch system changes for
dusty, desert types of environments such those in the Middle East.
Heat and lack of refrigeration facilities may require certain foods to
be dehydrated (Nakra 2015). Cooling systems also need to be adapted
because most people in these countries cannot afford air conditioners.

For the middle class in north India, a swamp or desert cooler works well to beat the heat. A *cooler* is a large steel box with bamboo or coir mats on three open sides; water is poured into a tray in the bottom of the unit and is then pumped up and sprayed out through the mats. An electric fan inside also blows out air cooled by evaporation as it passes through the wet mats. Though cost effective at .12 U.S. dollars (USD) a day when compared to an air conditioner at 4.50 USD, a cooler can only work in dry heat climates such as in northern India. As Indian consumers are becoming more affluent and aspirational, coolers are being designed to look more like air conditioners with smaller sizes and with plastic molded bodies (Marquand 1999). In turn, air conditioners are adopting some of the features of coolers. For example, Japan's Panasonic studied the Indian market closely and then launched a Made-for-India air conditioner called Cube in 2011. Cube is very compact (given the space constraints in Indian homes), energy-efficient (to compete with coolers), and has a front intake grill with a wider air discharge to deliver better airflow for a rapid cooling effect; in addition, it is much less noisy than a cooler (Business Standard 2011). Thus products from different countries influence each other to result in the creation of hybrid designs. Such adaptations are especially evident in home construction as is borne out in Habitat for Humanity's design process.

Habitat for Humanity in Thailand

Habitat for Humanity (HFH) builds or repairs simple, affordable houses for low-income families. They use donations to provide financial support to families and, in addition, they partner with the families so that each family makes an initial investment and also volunteers time and labor. Joseph Scaria, area director for development with Habitat for Humanity International for its Asia Pacific region, describes the adaptations that HFH makes for materials as well as designs for each country. Localization of material is a prime consideration from a cost, cultural, and functional perspective. Scaria describes hybrid homes where some parts are made of brick and mortar and other parts are made of local materials like bamboo, clay, or even mud. Contrary to popular perception, these traditional, local materials can be durable and last many years. HFH also has to make weather-related adaptations in countries with heavy rainfall such as Thailand, Cambodia, and Malaysia.

HFH began its operation in Thailand in 1998 and set up its national office in Bangkok in 2007. Since then, it has served over 11,500 Thai families. Although Thailand reduced its poverty level to 8 percent (5.4 million people) by 2009 and met most of its Millennium Development Goals by 2015, it still has a sizeable population of migrants, informal workers, and displaced people. Nearly 7.8 percent of the Thai population is below the poverty line. Natural disasters such as the droughts and flooding in 2011–2012 and the subsequent floods in 2013 devastated many low-income families who lost their jobs and savings. Although the Thai government offered some assistance, many were not able to repair or rebuild their homes. These are the kind of situations where HFH fills a gap. HFH set up many partnerships in Thailand, such as those with the Government Housing Bank, international schools, and companies like Dow Chemical Company, The Coca-Cola Company, Caterpillar, and Bank of America (Habitat for Humanity n.d.).

Scaria describes how many of the homes that HFH builds in Thailand take local construction preferences into consideration, many of which are centuries-old adaptations to the local climate and to the materials that are available. Many Thai homes are built on stilts to protect homes from frequent seasonal flooding. The gables have high ends so that the rooms have enough height for heat convection and the eaves are long and projecting to protect the homes from heavy tropical downpours. Being raised above the ground has the additional benefit of allowing the homes to receive the cooling flow of the breeze and this adaptation also provides added protection from wild animals. Ventilation is further enhanced by the choice of building materials—for example, homes can have bamboo frames with woven bamboo for the sides and a roof of palm or grass. Often homes are open, like gazebos, so they can be ventilated from all directions. Often small enclosures are created in the stilt area for open kitchens, which keeps food smells, such as spices and seasonings like shrimp paste and fish sauce, away from the main living area upstairs. The open kitchen also allows the breeze to push the smoke and soot away from the home. Additionally, the stilt area can have smaller enclosures for storage or livestock. HFH works to integrate these traditional materials and designs with its own modern architectural and building techniques.

Considering Genetic Differences

In addition to climatic considerations, products introduced in emerging markets must take several genetic factors into account such as consumers' physique, hair, skin, and even their overall health. Beauty companies are cognizant of genetic differences that lead to differing consumer needs in the various countries in which they sell. For example, the hair care market is a big opportunity in Africa, which has higher per capita spending on hair care than in the United States or Europe. Unique hair texture and complicated styling makes African hair damage-prone, which in turn means Africans require many different kinds of repair and maintenance products. In many parts of South Asia and the Middle East, people tend to have oily skin, so products for pigmentation and pore problems are in great demand (CosmeticWeb 2015). This problem is also faced by people in South America. La Roche–Posay, a skin care products division of L'Oréal launched in Brazil in 2010, took advantage of the fact that 50 percent of Brazilian consumers have oily skin, which leads to extra shine and the perception of dirty skin. In response, L'Oréal developed a sunblock with Airlicium that worked to control oil for up to nine hours (Cosmética News 2014). Another example of companies taking genetics into consideration involves scooters. Engineers from the Italian company Piaggio designed smaller shaped seats for their scooters and made the footboards lower to the ground and narrower; these changes allow people of shorter stature to reach the ground more easily (Stancati and Chowdhury 2012).

Health is another important functional consideration. China's population is genetically homogenous and over 90 percent of the Chinese are lactose intolerant (Yamamoto 2012); this condition is caused by a deficiency of lactase, an enzyme needed to break down the lactose in milk (Rohrer 2007). As a result, Danone (known as Dannon in the United States) changed its product to a less lactose-based yogurt (Dumitrescu and Vinerean 2010). Similarly, British-based Cadbury Schweppes PLC also modified its chocolate production process in China to use less milk, which meant it also had to reduce the quantity of cocoa to keep the chocolate from tasting bitter. The result is chocolate that tastes less sweet and "milky" (O'Donnell 2014).

In addition to the prevalence of lactose intolerance in China, compared to people in the West, Asians are genetically predisposed to developing diabetes at younger ages, at lower degrees of obesity, and at much higher rates, given the same amount of weight gain. Thus, as Asia has undergone rapid economic development and urbanization, as well as transitions in lifestyle and nutritional status, the number of Asians with diabetes has increased to 60 percent of the population (Hu 2011), which is another factor companies should be aware of when marketing in this region of the world. Marico's example illustrates how this can be done.

Marico in India

A survey in India found that 60 percent of Indians have diabetes, hypertension, or both (*The Times of India* 2011). Taking note of this health challenge, Marico, a 700 million USD consumer product company, developed products specifically for this niche market. Harsh Mariwala, the Chairman of Marico, speaks of Marico's transformation from a traditional commodity business in 1990 into a leading consumer products and services company in the global beauty and wellness space. He says this was achieved by successfully targeting niches and avoiding direct competition with large multinationals like Hindustan Unilever Limited (HUL) and Procter & Gamble (P&G). Marico thus achieved market leadership in 90 percent of the niches it entered. Mariwala says, "Multinationals have a lot of resources and technology so we don't take them head-on. We identify segments that multinationals dominate in. Then we avoid those and enter a small sub-segment and lead in that segment. Our biggest challenge is to find hitherto unidentified segments where multinationals are not present or some are present, but they are not market leaders."

This philosophy helped Marico understand the need for helping Indians control diabetes and identify a new niche in the Indian breakfast market where Kellogg's and Quaker Oats were struggling to persuade Indians to adopt a sweet, cold cereal, or sweet oatmeal for breakfast. In 2010, Marico created a new space for branded breakfast foods by launching savory breakfast oats in flavors such as Tomato, Vegetable, and Masala (meaning spicy). This product offered the low cholesterol health benefits of oats while it leveraged the traditional Indian preference for a hot and salty breakfast. Marico's prior positioning on a health platform—with products like low-cholesterol flour and muesli and rice with a low glycemic index under its Saffola brand—was further reinforced with the launch of oats, which are known for their health benefits. (Marico website n.d.; Bhat 2012).

Overcoming Infrastructural Limitations

Another element that companies must consider is the infrastructure of the markets they want to enter, such as transportation, energy, water, communications, or waste management. In Africa, Heineken operates breweries for beer using its own power and water treatment plants. Companies routinely buy their own power and water sources and pave roads. Since many countries do not have a cold supply chain, food and beverage companies have to be especially mindful of the condition in which their products will reach the end customer. Promasidor, an African dairy, developed Cowbell, a milk powder in which they replaced animal fat with vegetable fat to increase its shelf life and reduce the need for a cold supply chain (Forbes 2012). India faces considerable infrastructural challenges as well, and many multinationals have been innovative in designing their products to address this problem.

Overcoming Infrastructural Deficiencies in India

Whirlpool addressed the water shortage problem in India by making a fully automatic, top-loading washing machine that restarts the washing cycle from the point that it cuts off, instead of restarting from the beginning of the cycle. Its "aqua store" feature allows the washing machine to store water up to the required level for a washing load as a safety measure in the event that there is an inadequate water supply. Furthermore, an "aqua save" feature allows the water to remain in the washing machine after the cycle is finished so that it can be used for the next load of laundry, which also keeps clothes from wrinkling. This machine also senses the amount of laundry detergent and the water level required for each particular load and adapts accordingly (Price18.com 2010).

To address the issue of poor quality road infrastructure and pot-holes in India, the Italian company Piaggio replaced the disk brakes on its Vespa range of motor scooters with drum brakes to make it easier for passengers to change flat tires. Additionally, the horn is louder on the Indian Vespa due to the packed traffic and high congestion in urban areas in this country (Douglas and Craig 2011).

The level of self-sufficiency in energy production and the state of energy infrastructure also influence the extent to which fuel efficiency is important in a country. In India, energy considerations are an important part of consumer decision-making. As a result, the engines on the Indian Vespa are more fuel-efficient when compared to the European Vespa—a liter of fuel lasts for 62 kilometers, rather than just 35 kilometers, at a speed of 50 kilometers per hour (Stancati and Chowdhury 2012).

Nokia, which has been a trailblazer in mobile phone penetration in many emerging markets, developed a mobile phone with features such as an anti-slip grip and a dust-resistant body for emerging markets such as India (BusinessLine 2007). The Nokia 105 is built for challenging environments; it is remarkably tough and has a dust- and splash-proof keypad. It also has an extraordinary battery life of up to 12.5 hours and it has up to 35 days of standby. Further, to help rural consumers who face prolonged power outages, it comes equipped with a flashlight (Nokia n.d.).

Incorporating Local Essence

When multinationals enter an emerging market, local companies with inferior technology tend to falter initially, but soon they begin emulating and adopting the innovative processes and cutting-edge technologies that multinationals bring with them (Khanna, Palepu, and Sinha 2005). By partnering with multinationals or by reverse engineering technologies, local companies raise their quality standards and eventually the standards for the entire industry rise to match the higher consumer expectations set by multinationals. In turn, by competing with local companies to hire local talent, and also via partnerships and emulation, multinationals also learn how to adapt. We believe this two-way interaction of companies as partners or competitors leads to a melding and merging of experiences, capabilities, and strategies, resulting in the creation of hybrid products—another aspect of functional fusion.

An effective way of incorporating the local essence is by hiring local employees, which helps multinationals,speed up their familiarization process for operational set-up and also demonstrates goodwill by creating local jobs. BHP Billiton—a large, diversified business-to-business (B2B) resource company dealing in aluminum, energy, coal, oil, and so on—set up an aluminum smelter in Mozambique, investing over 160 million USD in the local economy. They employed local workers, contractors, and suppliers, but to ensure a well-trained workforce, they also set up training centers for mechanical and electrical maintenance and construction workers that benefitted nearly 10,000 people from the local area (Werhane, Hartman, and Mead 2008).

Although hiring local talent certainly helps create acceptability for companies and their products, we believe a much more intensive effort is required to avoid the negative outcomes from plurality of thought between headquarters and international office or subsidiaries. L'Oréal demonstrates such an approach on a worldwide scale by hiring and training for creating a fusion managerial style, which then reflects in outcomes that are more flexible and adaptable to different countries.

L'Oréal's Multicultural Teams

L'Oréal strikes the right balance in combining its need for global scale—which requires some degree of uniformity across the globe—with its need for local differentiation—which requires it to adapt its products and business models. This balance is critical in the cosmetics business where product development requires complex knowledge that may be tacit and collective. Tacit knowledge, in this case, would be ensconced in employees' knowledge of their own country and its people, in their common language and culture, and also in their pre-established interpersonal networks. L'Oréal operates in over 130 countries and over half of its sales come from emerging markets. Each year over 20 percent of its products are new. L'Oréal's success in new product development rests, in large part, on its unique approach to teams. Instead of having largely autonomous subsidiaries and regional entities, which would have led to higher localization, or global business units, which would have resulted in ignoring local differences, L'Oréal internationalized their entire management team. Instead of function- or project-based global teams or culturally diverse teams, they built multicultural teams that had both global and local expertise (Hong and Doz 2013).

Each of L'Oréal's 40 product development teams works on a different concept and each is made up of three or four people of which two are multicultural. They share an office to enable exchange of ideas. The multicultural managers come from the international subsidiaries, other global companies, or are graduates from leading international business schools. They are trained for a year, spend two to three years in global product development at headquarters, and then they may return to their home region. L'Oréal believes that when its managers are rooted in more than one culture, they are better able to adapt to different mindsets and communication styles (Hong and Doz 2013). Having multicultural managers throughout the organization has helped the company aggressively expand in the Asia Pacific region with a slew of product innovations. For example, its Garnier Fructis shampoo brand in India combines shampoo and hair oil, and its Colossal Kajal under the Maybelline brand is a moisture resistant eye pencil that combines a traditional element of the Indian beauty regimen with a technological touch of Western eye pencil (Nymex Consulting 2015). Indeed, its Colossal Kajal is also popular in Thailand and Indonesia. L'Oréal is growing at 23.3 percent in India and 33.9 percent in Indonesia, and China is poised to play a pivotal role in its strategy of winning 1 billion new consumers with its universalization strategy (McDougall 2013).

Incorporating local essence by adopting local ingredients and raw materials is a well-accepted practice across many industries, such as food and beverage, clothing, and home construction. Using local ingredients also helps companies create products that find a market in a specific country as well as similar countries in the region. For instance, SABMiller developed local crops to brew a sorghum-based beer for Uganda, which was eventually launched in many countries in Sub-Saharan Africa (Tranovich 2011). The success story of the Peruvian drink, Inca Kola, is a well-known example of creating a new fusion product by combining ingredients from different parts of the world. In 1910, a young British couple moved to Peru and started selling a homemade carbonated beverage in their shop. In 1935 for Lima's celebration of its 400-year anniversary, they created a unique, fruity soda by adding carbonation to lemon verbena, which they named Inca Kola. By 1945, with technology improvements, Inca Kola became the leading bottled beverage in Peru and was found in most mom and pop stores. It was positioned on a patriotic platform (since it was named after the Incas), was low priced, and had a sweet flavor that complemented the traditional cuisine. By the 1980s, it had a 35-percent market share as compared to 21 percent for Coca-Cola. Unable to overcome the local challenge, Coca-Cola finally bought it in 1999. Inca Kola's recent market share in Peru stood at 26 percent compared to Coca-Cola's 25.5 percent (Knowledge @ Wharton 2012).

The key reason for incorporating local ingredients is often cultural in nature, which we discuss in Chapter 3, but a behind-the-scenes look at the supply chain reveals compelling cost and procurement reasons that also drive such localization. This is as evident for industrial goods, such as industrial oils and petrochemicals, as it is for consumer products. For example, for their China-based retail operations, Kentucky Fried Chicken (KFC) uses local suppliers for relative ease and to keep costs low. However, in order to maintain quality and process control, they have to closely manage the distribution process. Distribution systems are highly fragmented in China with more than 650,000 small wholesalers in the foods, beverages, and infrastructure sector, and they have an inadequate temperature controlled transportation system. As a result, KFC had to set up 20 of its own distribution centers, even though in the rest of the world it outsources such logistic functions (Finn 2004). McDonald's went a step further in China by replicating its supply chain and even bringing its key potato supplier into the country. In this case, long-term supply contracts distributed the market entry risk between franchisors and the supplier, but typically companies try to source from within the country in which they are marketing.

Aligning to Regulatory Requirements

Though tariff barriers are falling globally, product standards prescribed by foreign governments can become barriers unless companies adapt their products to meet local regulatory requirements for acceptability. For example, the use of the metric system in most parts of the world necessitates changes in labels and instruction/maintenance manuals for companies using the U.S. non-metric system. Other common country-specific changes include adaptation for electrical requirements (e.g., cycles and voltage) and environmental requirements (e.g., use of unleaded fuels in combustion engines). Knowledge of legal and operating requirements is another critical component of competing in such markets. The rules regarding food additives tend to be country-specific and typically require documentation describing quantities and sources (Nakra 2015). Labeling and packaging must also comply with local regulations. Countries have detailed packaging regulations that companies must adhere to, especially for food packaging. However, these differ across emerging markets since they do not have a common market system such as the European Union. China, for example, has standards for many polymeric materials that are commonly used to produce food-contact articles, food additives, and food packaging materials. Indonesia has a Food Law of 2012 that requires food to not only be of certain quality but also be compliant with religions, beliefs, and culture (Clark and Nielsen 2013). Government import restrictions may also restrict the availability, use, or even repair of packaging machinery.

Navigating the regulatory framework can often involve large changes in products that a company offers. In 2013, after years of negotiations, the Indian government allowed Swedish furniture giant IKEA to invest about 1.75 billion USD over 10 years in single-brand retail stores for home furnishings. Although IKEA can sell most food and beverages in its in-store cafés (except their famous meatballs, since beef is not acceptable in this Hindu-majority country for religious reasons), it did not receive permission to sell packaged food items (Chu, Girdhar, and Sood 2013). A year earlier the government had rejected 15 out of 30 product lines—such as gift items, fabrics, books, toys, and consumer electronics. Several of IKEAs food items were rejected for violating food policy regulations and their consumer financing program ran into a problem since it would violate local banking regulations. The government also required IKEA to source 30 percent of its supplies from small Indian manufacturers, which was later amended so that the quota requirement remained, but the size of the manufacturer was not necessarily small (*The Local* 2012). IKEA has been navigating the regulatory landscape in India for several years now and is only expected to open its first store by 2017, even though it has been sourcing products from India for over 28 years. Building sustainable, long-term sources to fulfill government requirements has taken it longer than anticipated (Business Standard 2016). Similarly, in China, IKEA built several factories since it sources nearly 30 percent of its products from China for its stores all over the world. However, for its stores in China, IKEA was required to source 65 percent of its products domestically in order to avoid high import taxes (Chu, Girdhar, and Sood 2013). Naturally, this has transformed its offerings in China as compared to its stores in other parts of the world.

Capital Markets and Banking in Emerging Markets

Although emerging markets account for 50 percent of the global economic output, they only account for 22 percent of the global equity market capitalization. Over the next decade or so, these markets are expected to liberalize further and both domestic and foreign investors are likely to enter the market. In China, for example, The Shanghai-Hong Kong Stock Connect program was launched in 2014, a significant step toward helping China's capital markets integrate with global markets. In the same year China also announced increased market access to foreign banks. Up until 2013 they had been restricted and had been able to control just

1.7 percent of the total banking asset (Langridge and Valle 2015). Many restrictions have recently been eased on the operations of multinational banks in China. Banks can now build branch networks and offer certain products, and they no longer need to have a representative office in China for two years before opening their first branch. Yet many restrictions still remain, such as on foreign shareholding structure and foreign investment in domestic banks (Hong 2015; Wildau 2014).

EY (Ernst & Young), the consulting firm, studied several rapid growth markets (RGM)—those considered the next wave of emerging markets—and noted several characteristics of these financial markets. In *Frontier RGMs*, including countries like Kenya, Nigeria, and Vietnam, the economies are just beginning to monetize, and demand for financial services is in the initial stages; common financial products are microfinancing-based and community-based savings for the poor, whereas commercial banks focus on the more affluent. In addition, deposit and savings accounts are limited. In *Transitional RGMs* like Colombia, Egypt, and Indonesia, there is greater financial inclusion, and so over 30 percent of the population have bank accounts. With the growth of consumer financing and capital markets, the demand for deposit and savings accounts, retail credit, credit cards, debit cards, mortgage products and bank loan products have also increased. Large companies in these countries have started using bond and equity financing. Although commercial banks have widened their reach and credit card companies and non-banking financial institutions have entered the market, microfinance institutions still serve the poor. In *Established RGMs* like Chile, Malaysia, Mexico, South Africa, and Turkey, there is high demand for individual credit with growth in capital markets, and so businesses seek long-term, complex financial products. Formal bank loans, project finance, hedging products, and capital markets financing have become popular. Although commercial banks dominate the financial sector in these countries, microfinance institutions still work with the poor (EY 2014).

Thus, financial markets in these emerging economies are in varying levels of development, much of which is dictated not only by economic growth but also by government regulations. Many countries are seeing an increase in banking regulation, such as Chile and Indonesia. In Turkey, bankers expect tighter regulations on credit card payments and individual consumer loans. In Nigeria, the cash reserve requirements on public sector deposits was raised to 75 percent in 2014. Due to such government regulations, multinational banks have had to work around the restrictions, such as by establishing separately capitalized local subsidiaries. In Indonesia, foreign banks had to set lending quotas that mandated institutions to directly lend to certain borrowers such as small- and medium-sized enterprises (SMEs). In India, the rules required banks to hold total capital of 10 percent. This increased the capital required for banks to operate in these markets (EY 2014). Thus, these restrictions vary across geographies and shape the financial service products that can be made available. In Islamic countries the financial sector has had to almost entirely reinvent itself and launch Islamic banking, which demonstrates that country-level regulations and socio-cultural considerations can result in the creation of hybrid products. This is described in greater detail in Chapter 3.

References

Bhat, Harish. 2012. "Battle of the Oats." *The Hindu Business Line*. April 18. Accessed on December 4, 2013. www.thehindubusinessline.com/news/variety/battle-of-the-oats/article3324566.ece.

Bredenberg, Al. 2013. "How Manufacturers Can Compete in Emerging Markets." Thomasnet. March 12. Accessed on May 9, 2015. http://news.thomasnet.com/IMT/2013/03/12/how-manufacturers-can-compete-in-emerging-markets.

BusinessLine. 2007. "My Mobile Is Me." *The Hindu Business Line*. October 8. Accessed on April 24, 2016. www.thehindubusinessline.com/todays-paper/my-mobile-is-me/article1679900.ece.

Business Standard. 2011. "CUBE AC, the First of Its Kind in the World Launched by Panasonic India." February 18. Accessed on April 22,

2016. www.business-standard.com/article/press-releases/cube-ac-the-first-of-its-kind-in-the-world-launched-by-panasonic-india-111021800115_1.html.

Business Standard. 2016. "IKEA to Open 1st India Store at Hyderabad in 2017." March 6. Accessed on April 20, 2016. www.business-standard.com/article/pti-stories/ikea-to-open-1st-india-store-at-hyderabad-in-2017-116030600115_1.html.

Calantone, Roger J., S. Tamer Cavusgil, Jeffrey B. Schmidt, and Geon-Cheol Shin. 2004. "Internationalization and the Dynamics of Product Adaptation—An Empirical Investigation." *Journal of Product Innovation Management* 21 (3): 185–198.

Cavusgil, S. Tamer, Shaoming Zou, and G. M. Naidu. 1993. "Product and Promotion Adaptation in Export Ventures: An Empirical Investigation." *Journal of International Business Studies* 24: 479–506.

Chu, Valerie, Alka Girdhar, and Rajal Sood. 2013. "Couching Tiger Tames the Dragon." *Business Today.* July 21. Accessed on October 16, 2014. http://businesstoday.intoday.in/story/how-ikea-adapted-its-strategies-to-expand-in-china/1/196322.html.

Clark, Mitzi Ng, Catherine R. Nielsen. 2013. "The Regulation of Food Packaging in the Pacific Rim." PackagingLaw.com. September 24. Accessed on April 20, 2016. http://packaginglaw.com/special-focus/regulation-food-packaging-pacific-rim.

Cosmética News. 2014. "La Roche-Posay Lança Uma Nova Geração De Protetor Solar Para a Pele Oleosa." October 9. Accessed on October 13, 2014. www.cusmaneditora.com.br/leitura.php?n=la-roche-posay-lanca-uma-nova-geracao-de-protetor-solar-para-a-pele-oleosa&id=5423.

CosmeticWeb. 2015. "Emerging Market Consumer Wants Innovative 'For Me' Formulations." *CosmeticWeb Business Section.* June. Accessed on October 11, 2014. www.cosmeticweb.co.za/pebble.asp?relid=34837&sec=bus.

Douglas, Susan P., and C. Samuel Craig. 2011. "Convergence and Divergence: Developing a Semiglobal Marketing Strategy." *Journal of International Marketing* 19 (1): 82–101.

Dumitrescu, Luigi, and Simona Vinerean. 2010. "The Glocal Strategy of Global Brands," *Studies in Business and Economics* 5 (3): 147–155. Accessed on March 6, 2016. http://eccsf.ulbsibiu.ro/RePEc/blg/journl/538dumitrescu%26vinerean.pdf.

EY.com. 2014. "Banking in Emerging Markets: Investing for Success." EY. Accessed on April 24, 2016. www.ey.com/Publication/vwLUAssets/EY_-_Banking_in_emerging_markets:_Investing_for_success/$FILE/EY-Banking-in-emerging-markets-Investing-for-success.pdf.

Finn, Mark, 2004. *Kellogg on China: Strategies for Success*. Edited by Anuradha Dayal-Gulati and Angela Y. Lee. Chicago: Northwestern University Press.

Forbes. 2012. "How Companies Overcome Africa's Five Great Challenges." April 5. Accessed on April 25, 2016. www.forbes.com/sites/baininsights/2012/04/05/how-companies-overcome-africas-five-great-challenges/#39d13e1f5438.

Gudlavalleti, Sauri, Shivanshu Gupta, and Ananth Narayanan. 2013. "Developing Winning Products for Emerging Markets." *McKinsey Quarterly*. May. Accessed August 5, 2014. www.mckinsey.com/insights/innovation/developing_winning_products_for_emerging_markets.

Habitat for Humanity. n.d. "Habitat for Humanity Thailand." Accessed on April 20, 2016. www.habitat.org/where-we-build/thailand.

Hong, Hae-Jung, and Yves Doz. 2013. "L'Oréal Masters Multiculturalism." *Harvard Business Review*. June. Accessed on April 23, 2016. https://hbr.org/2013/06/loreal-masters-multiculturalism.

Hong, Sun. 2015. "China Banking Restrictions Relaxed: New Rules Further Open Banking Sector to Foreign Investors." Norton

Rose Fulbright. January 30. Accessed on April 24, 2016. www .regulationtomorrow.com/asia/china-banking-restrictions-relaxed-new-rules-further-open-banking-sector-to-foreign-investors/.

Hu, Frank B. 2011. "Globalization of Diabetes: The Role of Diet, Lifestyle, and Genes." June 2011. *American Diabetes Association* 34 (6): 1249–1257. Accessed on April 12, 2015. http://care. diabetesjournals.org/content/34/6/1249.full.

Johri, Lalit M., and Phallapa Petison. 2008. "Value-based Localization Strategies of Automobile Subsidiaries in Thailand." *International Journal of Emerging Markets* 3 (2): 140–162. Accessed on March 24, 2015. http://dx.doi.org/10.1108/17468800810862614.

Khanna, Tarun, Krishna G. Palepu, and Jayant Sinha. 2005. "Strategies That Fit Emerging Markets." *Harvard Business Review*. June. Accessed on March 24, 2015. https://hbr.org/2005/06/ strategies-that-fit-emerging-markets.

Knowledge @ Wharton. 2012. "Branding Lessons from Inca Kola, the Peruvian Soda That Bested Coca-Cola. University of Pennsylvania Wharton School. October 3. Accessed on April 22, 2016. http://knowledge.wharton.upenn.edu/article/branding-lessons-from-inca-kola-the-peruvian-soda-that-bested-coca-cola/.

Langridge, Kathryn, and Paolo Valle. 2015. "The Changing Shape of Capital Markets in Emerging Economies." Manulife Asset Management. May 11. Accessed on April 24, 2016. www. manulifeam.com/Research-and-Insights/Market-Views-And-Insights/The-changing-shape-of-capital-markets-in-emerging-economies/.

The Local. 2012. "IKEA Can't Get the Meatball Rolling in India." November 23. Accessed on October 16, 2014. www.thelocal.se 20121123/44612.

Marico website. n.d. Accessed on August 24, 2013. http://marico.com.

Marquand, Robert. 1999. "For Heat Relief, India Turns to 'Desert Coolers.'" *The Christian Science Monitor*. July 13. Accessed on October 10, 2014. www.csmonitor.com/1999/0713/p1s4.html.

McDougall, Andrew. 2013. "Investments in Asia Key to Universalization Strategy for L'Oréal." April 16. Accessed on April 22, 2016. www.cosmeticsdesign-asia.com/Business-Financial/Investments-in-Asia-key-to-universalization-strategy-for-L-Oreal.

Nakra, Prema. 2015. "Export Marketing Strategies: To Adapt or Not to Adapt?" *Shipping Solutions.* September 14. Accessed October 9, 2015. www.shippingsolutions.com/blog/export-marketing-strategies-to-adapt-or-not-to-adapt.

Nokia. n.d. "Nokia 105." Accessed on January 1, 2014. www.nokia.com/global/products/phone/105.

Nymex Consulting. 2015. "L'Oréal India: Market Penetration Strategy." August. Accessed on April 23, 2016. www.nymex-consulting.com/publication-though2015-24-08.pdf.

O'Donnell, Claudia Dziuk. 2014."The Diffusion and Distribution of New Consumer Packaged Foods in Emerging Markets and What It Means for Globalized versus Regionally Customized Products." Global Food Forums. January 1. Accessed on August 29, 2014. www.globalfoodforums.com/global-information/new-food-products-emerging-markets.

Price18.com, 2010. "Price of Whirlpool Washing Machine Fully Automatic Top Load–6.5 Kg." December 4. Accessed on July 29, 2014, www.price18.com/home-appliances/washing-machine/price-of-whirlpool-washing-machine-fully-automatic-top-load-6-5-kg-3.

Rohrer, Finlo. 2007. "China Drinks Its Milk." BBC News. August 7. Accessed on October 14, 2014. http://news.bbc.co.uk/2/hi/6934709.stm.

Sheth, Jagdish N. 2007. "Climate, Culture, and Consumption–Connecting the Dots." Presented at the 12th Distinguished Faculty Lecture, Emory University, Atlanta, GA, February 6.

———. 2011. "Impact of Emerging Markets on Marketing: Rethinking Existing Perspectives and Practices," *Journal of Marketing* 75 (4): 166–182.

Sheth, Jagdish N., and Rajendra S. Sisodia. 2012. *The 4 A's of Marketing: Creating Value for Customers, Companies, and Society.* New York: Routledge.

Stancati, Margherita, and Anuran Chowdhury. 2012. "Beep! Beep! Here Comes the 'Indian Vespa.'" *The Wall Street Journal.* April 27. Accessed on July 10, 2014. http://blogs.wsj.com/indiarealtime/2012/04/27/beep-beep-here-comes-the-indian-vespa.

The Times of India. 2011. "1 in 5 Indians Have Diabetes, High BP." December 14. Accessed on October 10, 2014. http://timesofindia.indiatimes.com/life-style/health-fitness/health/1-in-5-Indians-have-diabetes-high-BP/articleshow/10650014.cms.

Tranovich, Anja. 2011. "Pioneers on the Frontier: A Look at Africa's Growing Multinationals." Dalberg.com. July 27. Accessed October 4, 2014. http://dalberg.com/blog/?p=101.

Werhane, Patricia H., Laura P. Hartman, and Jenny Mead. 2008. "BHP Billiton and Mozal." Ivey Publishing. Case Study #UV 1162 and 1163. Accessed on April 22, 2016. www.iveycases.com/ProductBrowse.aspx?q=BHP%20Billiton%20and%20Mozal%20&em=0.

Wildau, Gabriel. 2014. "China Eases Rules for Foreign Banks." *Financial Times.* December 21. Accessed on April 24, 2016. www.ft.com/cms/s/0/b0ccedda-88e1-11e4-ad5b-00144feabdc0.html#axzz46mWuHed7.

Yamamoto, Brian. 2012. "Map of Milk Consumption & Lactose Intolerance Around the World." *Foodbeast.* November 21. Accessed on August 29, 2014, www.foodbeast.com/2012/11/21/map-of-milk-consumption-lactose-intolerance-around-the-world.

3

Designing Cultural Fusion

Functional fusion creates acceptability for products and services by adapting for better functionality. However, this is just a necessary, but not sufficient, condition. To win over hearts, minds, and wallets, you also need to pay attention to the psychological aspects of creating acceptability. You can achieve this by becoming sensitive to a host of factors that are ingrained in the local cultures of the people in emerging markets and in their communities at large. *Culture* is understood as a programming of the mind that distinguishes one group of people from another (Hofstede, Hofstede, and Minkov 1991). Thus, cultures collectively hold certain values that then influence common perceptions of actions, emotions, images, objects, or even people. Cultures are created over centuries as people evolve based on the climate and natural conditions of where they live, and these then influence their consumption. For example, for our ancestors, climate determined the type of food and fiber that was available for consumption (i.e., plant- versus animal-based), which then became part of the country's traditions and eventually its culture. Similarly, conceptualizations of time and distance were also determined by climate (i.e., daylight hours, ruggedness of terrain, land availability, etc.)—for instance, more punctuality was required where daylight hours were limited (Sheth 2007).

When companies introduce products or even ideas that are dramatically different from their consumers' original consumption experiences or traditions, they must create what Sheth and Sisodia's (2012) 4 A's framework describes as *psychological acceptance*. This means integrating products with the local culture in some meaningful way by incorporating the local traditions, history, languages, tastes, and preferences of that community. We call this strategy the development of cultural fusion by which new, hybrid products or positioning are created that are neither purely local nor completely international.

Cultural fusion's importance stems from people's natural resistance to change. The more radical the idea or change, the greater the acceptability challenges. Rather than conflicting with set attitudes and habits, our strategy of cultural fusion calls for a mixing of local consumption cultures with those that are new or "foreign" to that land. When companies enter emerging markets with new-to-country products and brands, they can try to adapt them to existing traditions, customs, and habits in order to offer superior solutions to consumer needs. However, they can also find success by adopting local products and infusing them with modern/Western elements. The latter requires a significant attitudinal shift for companies that have, until recently, looked at emerging markets as places and people to be converted to Western ways and have not valued existing offerings from local markets. Companies that successfully absorb (versus adapt to) local cultures then have the opportunity to take these blended innovations to other parts of the world, making these opportunities bidirectional.

Adapting or adopting cultural elements often requires taking an anthropological approach to gain the kind of insights required to understand a society and its people. This must be accompanied by companies' inherent internal willingness and ability to act on such insights. IKEA, for example, regularly has its employees visit consumers' homes, observe their daily life, take pictures, and produce a "Life at Home" report. By doing so, they have discovered new routines, food preferences, and habits and have been better able to satisfy the needs and wants of their consumers across the world. These qualitative insights are then combined with data from an online panel and secondary research to create what IKEA calls a digital "Data Mining Board," which reduces the search for information and enables the detection of patterns and creation of stories that depict the values and cultures they are trying to understand (Yohn 2015). Thus, a holistic understanding of the local culture helps companies appreciate consumers' values and background that provide valuable insights into how best to interact and communicate with them. In this chapter, we describe five distinct strategies for creating cultural fusion: 1) incorporating traditions, 2) using local languages, 3) considering social norms, 4) respecting faith, and 5) understanding sensory preferences.

Incorporating Traditions

One way to create cultural fusion is by infusing accepted traditions and historical context from the local markets into modern products to enhance the core benefits to local consumers while also keeping them aligned with global offerings. Thus, more than simply localizing, cultural fusion creates something new, as illustrated by Disneyland's and Starbucks' efforts to design experiences customized for China.

Disneyland and Starbucks in China

Hong Kong Disneyland's park design was conceptualized to reflect the strong traditions of Disney's storytelling. Featuring the same beloved areas, such as Main Street U.S.A, Fantasyland, and Adventureland, the park also incorporates many Chinese elements in its design and landscaping, creating a fusion of Western and Eastern design. In line with feng shui, there are two large boulders at the park's entrance to represent stability and prevent good luck or energy from flowing out of the park. Fortune and wealth are represented by numerous water bodies, such as lakes, ponds, streams, and the large fountain with Disney characters at the entrance to the park. The park is located in a north-south direction for good fortune. The number 8, which symbolizes wealth, manifests itself in several places, such as in the 888-square-meters-sized main ballroom at the Hong Kong Disneyland Hotel. Meanwhile, the unlucky number 4, which sounds like "death" in Mandarin and Cantonese, is missing from the park's buildings. Clocks and green hats are also missing from the gift shops since these are associated with funerals and marital cheating, respectively. Fashion design for costumes is also mindful of tradition. For example, in Shanghai Disneyland, the opening ceremony has featured Mickey Mouse in a traditional, red, collarless, silk, embroidered jacket with toggle buttons and matching red trousers with cuffs (Tang 2012).

Starbuck's cafés in large cities like Beijing and Shanghai mirror those in the West, but as Starbucks expands into second or lower-tier Chinese cities, they are blending regional design elements into their in-store experience. In Chengdu Taikoo Li, the café features Sichuan-inspired tiles, silk artwork by local craftsmen, and warm colors in the interior (Starbucks 2014). In Taikoo Li Sanlitun, a modern, upscale shopping area, Starbucks features work by local graffiti artists (Burkitt 2012). In Fuzhou, a small town with a population of 7 million, Starbucks drew heavily from the local culture and came up with a local courtyard home design with sliding doors, soaring ceilings, and a screen with black and white pieces of the chess-like Chinese game Weiqi (also known as Go). At the café entry, a large stone, taken from the mountains nearby, bears the Starbucks logo.

Thus, Starbucks has had to create fusion by retaining its basic café design but avoiding its standard white look, which signals affluence in the West but indicates quite the opposite in China—a product no one wants! Such tactical approaches are important as companies move from large, affluent, Tier 1 cities like Shanghai and Beijing, which have optimistic, affluent, more Westernized consumers, toward Tier 5 towns with lower income, thrifty, rural consumers; in these towns, fitting in is more important than standing out, and smaller-sized establishments are steeped in local cultural cues (Wentz 2012).

Both Disneyland and Starbucks incorporated traditional Chinese elements into the physical environment where their experience/service is delivered to the customer. In contrast, the story of Maver, from Chile, illustrates how consideration of tradition can spur product innovation while also fundamentally transforming the business and marketing strategy for an entire company.

Maver in Chile

Contributor: Rodrigo Guesalaga

Maver, a marketer and distributor for international brands, developed its own hugely successful brand by combining western medicine with Chilean traditional remedies. Maver's business is focused on large-scale consumption of personal hygiene and over-the-counter (OTC) pharmaceutical drugs in Chile. Its marketing prowess under the leadership of Alberto Albala, son of the founder, is reflected in the number of international brands that Maver represents in Chile. In the 1950s, Maver obtained the licenses and successfully marketed several renowned brands, starting with a deodorant, Dolipen, an antacid, Eno, and also an analgesic, Anacin. Maver's traditional focus on representing international brands, rather than developing its own brands, ran into problems when several international companies decided to end their licensing agreements with Maver. The termination notice period was just six months. Maver's realization that their main assets were brands that were not in their control prompted Alberto Albala to ask himself why they could not develop their own brands since they had been so successful commercializing international brands that meant nothing to Chileans.

Maver then decided to launch a product in the analgesic-antipyretic category, which was not dominated by any single company. It was one of the most popular products in the OTC segment. In 1996, foregoing the typical tablet format, Maver developed an innovative formula and format for a flu medication they branded as Tapsin. This lemon-flavored powdered mixture of acetaminophen and other anti-flu medications was to be prepared as a hot lemonade and was available in two variants for day-time and night-time usage. At the time of launch, and even now, Tapsin's main competitor, Bayer's Aspirina, is available only in tablet form and is advertised aggressively by Bayer, an international company with vast resources. Other competitors in this industry are GlaxoSmithKline's Panadol, Novartis Laboratories' Zolben, and Laboratorio Chile's Kitadol.

There were three main aspects of the marketing strategy that drove Tapsin's success: the hot lemonade presentation, the communication strategy, and the development of two types of products based on usage occasion (day and night). Tapsin's success with this new format for anti-flu medication was based on how it leveraged tradition— most Chilean was based on leveraging tradition—most Chilean families take hot lemonade or tea with lemon when they have the flu. Maver successfully communicated this in its television ads that featured a grandmother preparing hot lemonade and showing how this preparation was easier because Tapsin came in a sachet. It highlighted the balanced formula and the link with the traditional way to protect the family from flu. The advertising campaign also emphasized a "Chilean" component, by showing different regions and types of people in Chile, the message being that "Tapsin protects all Chileans." Inclusion and closeness were the key concepts on which Maver successfully positioned Tapsin as a local brand that is close to all Chileans. Additionally, offering night and day time variants was also a good move. The "night" product sells better because it is also used to induce sleep.

By 1998, Maver decided to extend Tapsin's product line by launching Tapsin in tablets (with a similar formula). The additional usage for other occasions created an adoption challenge for Maver because consumers perceived the tablet format as a less effective drug compared to the hot lemonade powder. Maver responded to this problem by launching a new advertising campaign that highlighted the attributes and the convenience of the new Tapsin format. Currently, 68 percent of its sales are for the powder and 32 percent are for tablets. Fernando explained, "The big hit was the hot lemonade and Tapsin became the owner of that category. Today there are several other brands with the same presentation but we have a 96 percent market share." In fact, the hot lemonade segment represents approximately 35 percent of the entire analgesic/anti-flu category in Chile.

Maver's Tapsin was a new formulation of an existing, Western medication that was adapted to the format and flavor of the local market. On the other hand, Dabur, a natural healthcare company, had herbal products tracing their origins to Ayurveda, a 3,000-year-old ancient holistic medicinal system that originated thousands of years ago in India. Ayurveda focuses on balancing the mind, body, and spirit with herbs, minerals, and special diets. Established in 1884, Dabur used Ayurvedic formulations to create a number of strong brands in a range of categories from hair-care products to digestives and tonics. Dabur has adopted the business and marketing acumen from the multinationals it competed with competed with in India. It acquired several companies, and in 2007, it even modernized its packaging for its juice products and ventured into its own organized retail through a subsidiary. In 2012, Dabur's turnover reached 1 billion U.S. dollars (USD), a first for an Indian origin consumer goods company (Press Trust of India 2012).

Using Local Languages

History and tradition reflect not only in products but also in communication. The most common adaptation that a company needs when it enters a new market is adapting its communication to the new language(s) of the land. This demonstrates the company's willingness to respect the local culture. But rather than simple translations, companies have to consider the context, and when their products or brands are unfamiliar to the consumers, they have to use their translations creatively to convey their positioning and benefits. For example, the slogan "Red Bull gives you wings" had to be changed to "Drink Red Bull when you feel sleepy or tired" in China (Dudovskiy 2012).

However, translations can pose major problems and several multinational companies have found themselves in an uncomfortable situation following a bad translation or simply one that does not take the local context into account. For example, in 2012, Sony localized their *Call of Duty: Black Ops II* for the large Latin America gaming market and saw a significant 300 percent increase in sales compared to when their product was not localized. The translation effort was intensive since English and Brazilian Portuguese differ in many ways (Werkmeister 2013). But Sony knew that a bad translation could ruin the game experience by diverting a player's attention to the poor translation. For instance, in *Call of Duty: Modern Warfare 2*, one mission was named "No Russian"—in the Japanese translation it was translated as "Kill Them: They're Russian," which was a blunder that had to be corrected (De Souza 2012). Similarly, Pepsi blundered as well when their slogan "Come alive with the Pepsi Generation" translated to "Pepsi brings your ancestors back from the grave" in Chinese. Though translation is an obvious way of localizing, a more interesting and nuanced approach involves fusing languages, as demonstrated by Bollywood (Indian cinema's Hindi language Hollywood) in India.

Blending Hollywood and Bollywood

Hinglish is a term coined to describe a blend of Hindi (the national language of India) with English. For instance, the title of a recent Bollywood movie, *Ek Tha Tiger*, translates as "There Was a Tiger." Hinglish is different from Indian English—which is the way English is characteristically spoken on the Indian subcontinent. It includes novel expressions, some of which originate from the military English of the East India Company, such as "Where are you putting up?" meaning "Where do you live?" (Baker 2015). Similarly, the Hindi phrase for asking a person's name is *"Aapka shubh naam kya hai?"* where the word *shubh* means good. Hence, the Indian English version of "What is your name?" becomes "What is your good name?" Hinglish and Indian English are especially popular among the Indian youth and the number of speakers are pegged at almost 400 million people. This is fueled in large part by media channels like MTV, its Indian competitor, Channel V, and entertainment such as music and movies. Fusion in entertainment is not new—the Beatles incorporated Ravi Shankar's Indian classical music into hits like "Norwegian Wood" and took it to a huge international audience. Now, Bollywood is creating more movies using fusion languages like Hinglish and Indian English. *Slumdog Millionaire* was a hybrid Indian movie filmed in both English and Hindi. It had the emotions and musical appeal of Bollywood with the sensibilities of Western movies, and it used Hinglish as well as Indian English. Previous Bollywood releases, like *Bend It Like Beckham* and *Monsoon Wedding*, also combined Hindi and English themes and languages. Now filmmakers from the West want to make movies about India and Indians (Quereshi 2008). Big production houses such as Fox and Disney have already set up shop there aiming for a share of the Indian film market that launches over 1,000 movies and sells over 3 billion tickets a year. Given that India hasn't been very receptive to English language movies (just 9 percent of the box office), foreign studios are churning out Hindi films for now, but cross-over or fusion films that can find a global audience as well are on the horizon (Crabtree 2013).

Considering Social Norms

Culture is embedded in the social fabric of the land, the linkages across communities, and relationships between people. Typically, companies hire locally and develop local managerial talent to help integrate into the broader community (Joerres 2011). The Coca-Cola Company was able to do this well in Cairo. Coca-Cola's president for the Eurasia and Africa group was from Turkey and used a global functional team with finance, marketing, and strategic capabilities to assist the local marketing teams in local adaptation. Therefore, during the Arab Spring uprisings in Egypt, the team was able to gauge that the youth were struggling with a lot of uncertainty but that they were looking for a bright future. Accordingly, Coca-Cola's advertising message reflected this optimism and aspiration with visuals of people getting together in Tahrir Square in Cairo and ropes falling from the skies, which people used to pull away dark clouds and reveal the sun (Holstein 2011). Even domestic companies that are introducing a new-to-market product need to spend significant effort on product adoption, as the story of wine marketing in India demonstrates.

Sula Wines in India

Alcohol consumption has increased by 55 percent since India's economic liberalization in the early '90s. The local culture has changed as compared to earlier when social norms, religious beliefs, and gender roles restricted alcohol consumption. Although the per capita consumption of alcohol is low, the market has been growing at a compound annual growth rate (CAGR) of about 20 percent, despite high restrictions on companies that consequently have to rely on surrogate advertising (Business Wire 2010).

India has been predominantly a spirits market, but beer has recently become a popular part of social interactions like sports and music. Wine is a nascent category; research indicates that 50 percent of Indians feel intimidated because they don't know how to choose and buy wine, and so they would serve it just as an option during parties. However, this is now changing with the efforts of domestic wine companies, led by Sula Vineyards. This company has been at the forefront of creating this category by hosting events for education and awareness and by setting up specialized distribution systems (D'Souza 2010).

An interview with Rajeev Samant, owner of Sula Vinyards, the largest wine brand in India, provides interesting insights into the process of converting nonusers into users and the subsequent transformation of this category into one of the fastest growing markets, which is now attracting international competitors. As an early entrant in a category defined only by international brands, Sula Vineyards was venturing into an untapped market. Very few Indians preferred or could even afford the limited range of imported, international wines that were available in the market. One of the key success factors for Sula Vineyards was that it never pretended to be French like the other small, domestic manufacturers. Instead, Samant took a very French product and Indianized it. The rising sun on the label prominently declared that the wine was made in Nashik (a city 200 kilometers from Mumbai), and the name "Sula" (Samant's mother's name) also played on national pride. This was a bold move, not just in terms of product category, but also in terms of marketing strategy.

Samant realized the importance of integrating his product into society, so he started tapping into his family's social network to get people to sample his wines. Soon, he moved on to host sampling parties and small, by-invitation-only events sponsored by companies like Merrill Lynch, Yahoo!, and Boston Consulting Group, where the invitee list included rich and affluent venture capitalists and Internet entrepreneurs. He started wine sampling groups at Lions Clubs, Rotary Clubs, and corporate events. He hired talented young people to conduct tastings all over India. Eventually, the media picked up his entrepreneurial story, which brought Sula Vineyards to prominence.

Samant realized early on that wine could not be directly promoted as a beverage for social occasions in India, so he promoted the glamorous, sophisticated "wine lifestyle"—a new concept for India.

He set up vineyard tours, wine trails, tasting rooms, and an Italian restaurant amidst his lush vineyards in Nashik. His tasting room hosts between 500–1,000 visitors every weekend. He has expanded his hospitality business with a resort close to his winery that has its own visitor center. As a result of Samant's social fusion efforts via the Sula Vineyards brand, the wine market is heating up in India.

Respecting Faith

The impact of faith in most countries is undeniable, with 84 percent of the world's population identifying with a particular faith (Seiple 2015), so managing consumers' faith considerations can be a winning proposition for marketers. It is challenging to build a corporate culture that is able to engage consumers in regions where faith has a large, observable, or even unobservable, impact on consumption. However, this engagement is critical for companies so they can avoid mistakes in places where the local religion is important to building trust in brands.

Being cognizant of this, marketers in the packaged goods industry adhere to translations and also ensure display of information related to religious requirements such as *halaal* certification. Even product innovation must consider local religious practices. For example, in India, which has a majority Hindu population but also a sizeable Muslim population, eating beef for the former, and pork for the latter, goes against their respective religious beliefs. Thus, McDonald's menu in India has no beef or pork items and half the menu is vegetarian. Its flagship Big Mac has been replaced by a chicken Maharaja (where Maharaja means King in Hindi) Mac. Going a step further, McDonald's has launched completely meatless restaurants in two cities that host a large number of pilgrims— first since the chain was founded in 1955. McDonald's has plans to leverage this to double its presence in India (BBC News 2012). Product innovation based on religion can extend beyond line extensions and become transformative for the entire industry, as demonstrated by the rise of Islamic banking.

Islamic Banking in Emerging Markets

Islamic banking, a growing trend since the 1960s, is based on Sharia law as well as Islamic principles under which speculative trading or trading in risk is forbidden or *haram*. One major prohibition is charging interest, known as *riba* in Arabic. In addition, any excess payments or premiums on loans, including interest, is considered unjust, as it is a form of exploiting the borrower while the lender makes a profit, which is considered usurious. Only investment and purchasing, as determined by religious Islamic principles, is considered acceptable.

The main difference between conventional and Islamic banks is the emphasis on profit and loss-sharing concepts, including their approach to lending money. In Malaysia, for example, Islamic banks and conventional banks with Islamic counters practice an interest free banking system that includes guaranteed custody for demand and savings deposits, and profit sharing for investment deposits. Thus, Islamic banks mobilize the deposits for entrepreneurs for various business investments.

Unlike conventional banks, Islamic banks do not guarantee a fixed interest rate in return for investments regardless of the performance of the bank. Instead, the customer's return is based on the performance of the bank so that if the bank makes a profit, then the reward is called a *hiba*, meaning voluntary gift. On the other hand, no *hiba* is offered if the bank does not generate a profit. However, the principal amount is always guaranteed. In the case of an Islamic savings account, *hiba* is replaced by a profit-sharing ratio based on the performance of the bank. In this way, larger investments generate higher returns when the bank profits and higher losses when the bank does not profit. Deposit funds are of great importance since Islamic banks must maintain a sustainable level of money in order to finance the loans. As opposed to the fixed-interest incomes of conventional banks that is commonly between 0.5 to 1 percent, the *hiba* of Islamic banks is determined by each bank's policy (Hanudin 2013).

In an effort to ensure that Islamic principles are followed in all banking matters, a Sharia Committee is required to be set up in

Islamic banks and banking institutions that offer Islamic banking products and services. Although Islamic banking constitutes just 1.6 percent of the total assets of the 50 largest banks in the world, it is one of the fastest growth areas in financial services worldwide (15 to 20 percent annual growth), and as of 2013, there were over 600 Islamic financial institutions in over 75 countries (Botis 2013). Islamic banking has combined traditional Western banking with Islamic principles to create a completely new product that is spreading across the world.

Understanding Sensory Preferences

It is said that the best way to experience a culture is through its food. Thus, food and beverage companies have typically been at the forefront of cultural acceptability strategies, since food preferences are very deeply rooted in the tradition and culture of not just the country, but often the specific region of residence. The climate of a region influences the availability of food, which impacts food consumption preferences (Sheth 2007). For example, because Northern Europeans could not grow many spices, fruits, or vegetables, their food was typically not spicy and animal based. The reverse is true in Mediterranean or tropical climates where they have an abundance of fruits, vegetables, and spices, and hence a greater reliance on plant-based food. In fact, the common use of various spices has another benefit for those who live in hot climates—spicy foods increase sweating, which then results in evaporation because of the high temperature, and this automatically cools down the body.

Companies can leverage native conceptualizations of products by using local ingredients, design, and promotion to reduce resistance to changes in long held beliefs, traditions, and attitudes. Kraft's 100-year-old Oreo, one of America's favorite cookies, had been struggling in China since its launch in 1996 until a decade later, when research revealed that Chinese consumers prefer a mild sweet flavor for the cream and a less bitter flavor for the cookie. In 2006, Oreo relaunched with cookie creams in local flavors such as green tea, mango, and orange. Kraft also changed the shape and texture of the cookie so it became a rectangular wafer sandwich as well as a white-chocolate covered wafer stick—a cookie lined with cream that can be used as a straw—this new cookie design eventually also found popularity in countries such as Canada, South Korea, and Australia. The Oreo brand now has 19 cookie variants—9 of which are flavor based and 10 of which are based on basic form/texture (Smith 2012; Jou 2012). By fusing elements of its original Oreo product with local ones to create new flavors and formats, Oreo had captured 46 percent of the market share for the sandwich biscuit and 30 percent of the market share for the wafer market by 2012. Its 15-percent market share of the overall biscuit market in China is the highest market share for Oreo globally, including in the US and Canada (Beer 2012).

Another multinational's experience from China—Kentucky Fried Chicken's (KFC's)—demonstrates how transforming markets and consumers can often be an equally transformative experience for the company as well, helping it evolve in unexpected directions. These new skills and competencies often go beyond new product innovations and can be deployed in other parts of the world.

KFC in China

Contributor: Jun Yan

KFC, a subsidiary of Yum! Brands, is bigger than many other global fast food chains, including McDonald's, in China. KFC has over 5,000 restaurants—which is more than twice as many as McDonald's in China. Launched there in 1987, KFC opened its first restaurant five years before McDonald's. Long lines of curious Chinese queued up, eager to know about American fast food, standardized cooking, and the modern layout of the restaurant. But the initial curiosity and enthusiasm for items like fried chicken and burgers at high prices soon waned and KFC realized that it was difficult to incorporate such novelty items into the daily cuisine of Chinese consumers.

However, KFC's local managers, many of whom were educated in the West, were able to balance the need for local cultural adaptation with managerial best-practices from the West. They pushed for rapid expansion of stores across China, while adeptly managing the consumer adoption challenge. Their winning strategy was to rapidly develop and launch new menu items at the rate of one or two per month. Some items worked and were retained on the menu and others were removed.

Interestingly, KFC didn't just add on local items to their menu. Instead they created hybrids—Chinese in terms of taste and nutrition, but American in terms of quality and standardization. They selected their suppliers to ensure quality and maintained their standardized cooking process. For example, one of their star menu items is a Beijing-styled chicken roll, which mixes fried chicken with traditional Chinese sweet sauce and green Chinese onion and is wrapped in a steamed tortilla. To cater to the local preference for porridge as a breakfast item, KFC has added several kinds of innovative porridges, which are served with cheese, cooked egg, and even a crisp potato bar—a combination of Chinese and Western cuisine.

Taking their strategy a step further, in March 2008, following three years of research and preparation, KFC launched East Dawning, a purely Chinese fast food chain restaurant brand, which draws inspiration from traditional Chinese gourmet culture. This exemplifies how cultural fusion shapes not only consumers and consumption, but also companies. East Dawning now has over 30 restaurants in select cities, offering more than 60 items for breakfast, lunch, afternoon tea, and supper. Its R&D team develops 20–30 new menu items every year, adapting to different regional preferences and cuisines instead of treating China as a homogenous mass. East Dawning is currently targeting the business and office lunch segments; the price of most set meals is between 20–25 Yuan (CNY) (about 4 USD). These restaurants operate just like a KFC except their menus and decor are Chinese (Adamy 2006), balancing elements of the East and the West.

Color is another important sensory preference. People living in countries with warm, sunny climates prefer warm, bright colors, whereas those living in cooler climates prefer cool, less saturated colors, mirroring the color of the natural landscape and vegetation

(Sheth 2007). Color has also been known to reflect the mood of an era; preferences change with time and as society changes. Naturally then, cultural factors do play an important role in color preferences and association. In China, red and black convey happiness, whereas white is the color of mourning in both China and India. Colors also have religious associations, such as green for Muslims and red and white in Mexico for Christianity (De Bortoli and Maroto 2001). In the U.K, China, and United States purple is associated with royalty, in Japan it is associated with wealth, in France, with freedom or peace, but in India, it is associated with sorrow and unhappiness (Lee n.d.).

Keeping these nuances in mind, marketers choose their colors carefully. Red Bull cans in China are bright yellow with black font (Dudovskiy 2012); the colors on the McDonald's website are also different for some countries. In India, LG, the South Korean company, is the market leader in home appliances. They entered the market post-liberalization in the 1990s, but a relaxation in foreign-investment rules permitted them to establish a research and development (R&D) center in Bangalore. This is their largest center outside of Korea and it employs Indian designers and engineers to get both aesthetics and functionality right for its consumers. In terms of color, it offers brighter colors, for its appliances, including refrigerators, since vibrant colors are a large part of the Indian psyche (Guild 2009).

While all of these are adaptations to local traditions and preferences, exposure to Western cultures does bring about change. For example, traditionally, at Chinese weddings, brides wore a red *qipao*—a floor-length sheath dress with a high collar and short sleeves, with a red veil. The red color symbolized good luck, happiness, and prosperity. Now, with increasing Western influences, Chinese weddings have changed, especially in larger, more modern cities. Chinese brides are opting to wear white Western-style gowns and veils for the wedding and they wear the *qipao* only at the reception (Chirolla 2013).

References

Adamy, Janet. 2006. "One U.S. Chain's Unlikely Goal: Pitching Chinese Food in China." *Wall Street Journal*. October 20. Accessed on October 17, 2015. www.wsj.com/articles/SB116127912953397916.

Baker, Steven. 2015. "Will We All Be Speaking Hinglish One Day?" *British Council.* October 30. Accessed on March 5, 2016. www. britishcouncil.org/voices-magazine/will-we-all-be-speaking-hinglish-one-day.

BBC News. 2012. "McDonald's Opens Vegetarian-only Restaurant." September 4. Accessed on January 18, 2015. www.bbc.com/news/business-19479013.

Beer, Jeff. 2012. "Marketing to China: Oreo's Chinese Twist." *Marketing Magazine.* December 6. Accessed on July 24, 2014. www.marketingmag.ca/brands/marketing-to-china-oreos-chinese-twist-67561.

Botis, Sorina. 2013. "Sharia'ah Concepts in Islamic Banking." *Bulletin of the Transylvania University of Brasov* 6 (2): 139.

Burkitt, Laurie. 2012. "Starbucks Plays to Local Chinese Tastes." *The Wall Street Journal.* Accessed on May 5, 2016. http://www.wsj.com/articles/SB10001424127887324784404578142931427720970.

Business Wire. 2010. "The Future of Alcoholic Beverages in India: Changing Consumer Preferences and Emerging Opportunities," December 17. Accessed on October 20, 2015. www.businesswire .com/news/home/20101217005762/en/Research-Markets-Future-Alcoholic-Beverages-India-Changing.

Chirolla, Amberly, and Ellen Wang. 2013. "Chinese Weddings: The History Behind Them." *Cultural Awareness.* May 20. Accessed on March 5, 2016. http://culturalawareness.com/chinese-weddings-history-behind.

Crabtree, James. 2013. "US Studios Seek Inroads into Bollywood as Industry Turns 100." *Financial Times.* May 15. Accessed on March 6, 2016. www.ft.com/intl/cms/s/0/0556465e-b3fe-11e2-ace9-00144feabdc0.html#axzz423DKovoI.

De Bortoli, Mario, and Jesus Maroto. 2001. "Colours across Cultures: Translating Colours in Interactive Marketing Communications." Paper presented at the Proceedings of the European Languages and the Implementation of Communication and Information Technologies Conference. November 9–10. University of Paisley, Outwith, UK.

De Souza, Ricardo Vinicius Ferraz. 2012. "Video Game Localization: The Case of Brazil." Universidade de São Paulo. Accessed on August 1, 2014. www.revistas.usp.br/tradterm/article/view/47438.

D'Souza, Jacinta. 2010. "Indian Wine Market Warming Up to International Labels." *Live Mint*. September 2. Accessed on September 15, 2015. www.livemint.com/Companies/vSUPrClErqoPNcXz9PcKyL/Indian-wine-market-warming-up-to-international-labels.html.

Dudovskiy, John. 2012. "Red Bull GmbH." *Research Methodology*. August 1. Accessed on August 15, 2014. http://research-methodology.net/red-bull-gmbh.

Guild, Todd. 2009. "Think Regionally, Act Locally: Four Steps to Reaching the Asian Consumer." *McKinsey Quarterly*. September. Accessed on September 19, 2015. www.mckinsey.com/insights/marketing_sales/think_regionally_act_locally_four_steps_to_reaching_the_asian_consumer.

Hanudin, Amin. 2013. "Some Viewpoints of Islamic Banking Retail Deposit Products in Malaysia." *Journal of Internet Banking & Commerce* 18 (2) (August): 1–13.

Hofstede, Geert, Gert Jan Hofstede, and Michael Minkov. 1991. *Cultures and Organizations: Software of the Mind*. London: McGraw Hill.

Holstein, William J. 2011. "How Coca-Cola Manages 90 Emerging Markets." *Strategy + Business*. November 7. Accessed on August 15, 2014. www.strategy-business.com/article/00093?pg=all.

Joerres, Jeffrey A. 2011. "Beyond Expats: Better Managers for Emerging Markets." *McKinsey Quarterly*. May. Accessed on August 15, 2014, www.mckinsey.com/insights/organization/beyond_expats_better_managers_for_emerging_markets.

Jou, Eric. 2012. "The Wonderfully Weird World of Chinese Oreos." *Kotaku*. October 1. Accessed on July 2, 2014. http://kotaku.com/5947767/the-wonderfully-weird-world-of-chinese-oreos.

Lee, Aelee. n.d. "An International Guide to the Use of Color in Marketing and Advertising." Accessed on October 21, 2015. http://six-degrees.com/an-international-guide-on-the-use-of-color-in-marketing-advertising.

Press Trust of India. 2012. "Dabur Crosses $1 Billion Turnover." *Business Standard*. April 16. Accessed on April 16, 2016, www.business-standard.com/article/companies/dabur-crosses-1-billion-turnover-112041600115_1.html.

Quereshi, Bilal. 2008. "'Hinglish' Films: Translating India for U.S. Audiences." *NPR*. November 12. Accessed on March 5, 2016. www.npr.org/templates/story/story.php?storyId=96914703.

Seiple, Chris. 2015. "How Does Faith Impact Business in Emerging Markets?" *World Economic Forum*. January 22. Accessed on August 15, 2015. https://agenda.weforum.org/2015/01/how-does-faith-impact-business-in-emerging-markets.

Sheth, Jagdish. N. 2007. "Climate, Culture, and Consumption: Connecting the Dots." Presented at the 12th Distinguished Faculty Lecture. February 6. Emory University, Atlanta, GA.

Sheth, Jagdish N., and Rajendra S. Sisodia. 2012. *The 4 A's of Marketing: Creating Value for Customers, Companies, and Society*. New York: Routledge.

Smith, Robert. 2012. "Rethinking the Oreo for Chinese Consumers." NPR. January 27. Accessed on September 9, 2014. www.npr.org/blogs/money/2012/01/27/145918343/rethinking-the-oreo-for-chinese-consumers.

Starbucks. 2014. "10 Stunning Starbucks Store Designs of 2014." December 26. Accessed on April 20, 2016. https://news.starbucks.com/news/10-stunning-starbucks-store-designs-of-2014.

Tang, Phillip. 2012. "Different Disneylands around the World." BBC. December 18. Accessed on October 13, 2014. www.bbc.com/travel/story/20121213-different-disneylands-around-the-world.

Wentz, Laurel. 2012. "Starbucks Delves Deeply into Local Culture to Reach Chinese Consumers." *Ad Age*. September 7. Accessed on October 9, 2015. http://adage.com/article/global-news/starbucks-delves-local-culture-reach-chinese/237036.

Werkmeister, 2013. "Making Great Games Better for Emerging Markets." *Gamasutra*. November 25. Accessed on August 6, 2014. www.gamasutra.com/blogs/JanWerkmeister/20131125/205598/Making_great_games_better_for_emerging_markets.php.

Yohn, Denise Lee. 2015. "How IKEA Designs Its Brand Success." *Forbes*. June 10. Accessed on Oct 21, 2015. www.forbes.com/sites/deniselyohn/2015/06/10/how-ikea-designs-its-brand-success.

4

Democratizing the Offer

When multinationals enter emerging markets, they often target the middle and upper tiers of the income pyramid by slightly tweaking the business models they import from developed countries. For years, the model for successful growth through international expansion involved making small changes, such as lowering prices, reducing pack sizes, and leveraging the entry country's resources and advantages such as lower labor costs. However, Prahalad and Hammond (2002) cautioned that by solely focusing on upper echelon consumers, companies were ignoring the potential offered by the nearly four billion people at the bottom of the pyramid (BoP). By innovating in all aspects of marketing, companies could sell large volumes of low-priced or low-margin models or versions. Even though the number of middle-income consumers is increasing in these countries, they often have no awareness of or prior experience with many brands or product categories. To minimize consumers' economic risk of purchase, successful companies have innovated in many ways to make their products and services more affordable. Although several such strategies are already seen in advanced economies, in emerging markets, companies need to take numerous ground-level challenges into account.

In this chapter, we consider how price can be viewed strategically in emerging markets by using the concept of affordability, as outlined in Sheth and Sisodia's 4 A's framework (2012). Affordability is the extent to which customers in the target market are able and willing to pay the product's price, and it is characterized by two dimensions—economic affordability, or the ability to pay, and psychological affordability, or the willingness to pay. In most emerging markets, even if consumers have the economic ability to pay, they may not be willing to do so due to psychological or other barriers.

Not all BoP-targeted businesses are profitable because their success hinges on a very high penetration of consumers in a given market. Neither Procter & Gamble's Pur water purifying powder sachets (which cost .10 USD) nor DuPont's soy protein packets (which cost .30 USD) could achieve profitability, despite their low prices. Not surprisingly, cost structures and operational expenses, such as distribution, geographical spread, and the high cost of consumer education and awareness, push costs to very high levels. A more realistic route to profitability may be to push down costs and, combined with raising price points, see increases in margin (Simanis 2012). Further, companies need to be mindful that even with lower costs, they can face formidable competition from traditional, indigenous, cheaper products through an informal economy where tiny businesses pay no taxes and do not abide by labor laws (Kay and Lewenstein 2013).

Another aspect of affordability to consider is that emerging market consumers do not always purchase at the lowest shelf prices possible. A study of Latin American consumers found that they were actually sensible shoppers who tracked prices, demonstrated self-restraint, and used credit sparingly. Affordability for them included the "absolute" price of an item, including the cost of transportation, child care, time, and the burden of carrying heavy purchases home. Since their incomes tended to be small and unstable, they preferred to shop daily and make small purchases, but not necessarily for the cheapest products (D'Andrea, Stengel, and Goebel-Krstelj 2004). Thus, in the emerging markets context, affordability is much more nuanced than simply a drop in price accompanied by a predictably commensurate drop in quality. This is, of course, one option. However, pricing decisions need to account for the opportunity cost of time, the convenience of purchasing the product, and other potential barriers to purchase. Companies have to rethink the total offer to be able to provide "value" that consumers find affordable. In this chapter, we describe five strategies companies can use to democratize their offer by making their products and services affordable for the masses in emerging markets. These are 1) reducing economic barriers to purchase, 2) overcoming noneconomic obstacles to purchase, 3) achieving reverse innovation, 4) extending product value, and 5) developing creative financing.

Reducing Economic Barriers to Purchase

Reducing the per unit price to ensure smaller payments per transaction can be done by unbundling or repackaging single products such as single-use shampoo packets (sachets), loose tea or rice, individual cigarettes, and prepaid cards. Reduced margins or smaller pack sizes are some other options. For example, The Coca-Cola Company has seen success with this strategy by offering a reduced-size 200 ml bottle for a lower price in India because it realized that its 300 ml bottle of Coke meant an entire day's wages for many consumers. In addition, many affordability goals are achieved through product innovation, as realized by Gillette in India.

Gillette in India

Gillette's brand recognition, market share, and technological and manufacturing prowess have helped it grab and retain a leadership position in the world razor market. Gillette (a Procter & Gamble [P&G] company) has successfully used a razor-and-blades strategy—it has invested in an installed base by selling the razor handles at low or zero prices, and then it has sold the razor blades at high prices to justify the prior investment. Gillette's strategy has been emulated by many companies, especially for modern technological products such as DVD players, video game systems like Xbox, and e-book readers (Picker 2010). However, even though Gillette's strategy has a proven track record of holding 70 percent of the worldwide razor market share, the company was still lagging behind in emerging markets like India.

India's 400 million shavers offered a tremendous opportunity. The razor-and-blade segment was estimated at 16.25 billion Indian Rupees (INR) (or about 270 million USD) and it was growing at 5 percent annually. However, 70 percent of Indians lived in villages, and therefore the key to success lay in rural penetration. But rural customers needed an affordable solution that also addressed issues like hygiene. A limited water supply meant that just one cup of water would need to effectively rinse the blade and razor after use. Gillette's top-selling Mach3 and Fusion razors were too expensive for the majority of consumers in India and other emerging and developing markets. Although Gillette's feature-rich Mach3 was slowly gaining ground in urban India (Jaiswal 2011), the needs of consumers in rural India and at the bottom of the pyramid remained a lucrative, but unaddressed, opportunity.

Reducing cost and prices were top priorities for Gillette because winning over low-income consumers in developing markets was crucial to the growth strategy of P&G's chief executive, Robert McDonald (Byron 2010). In such markets, Gillette's strategy was to reduce the cost of razors by focusing on product development. In India, a brand called Super-Max held the lead in double-edged blades, which cost 1.5 to 2 INR (about 0.03 USD). Competitors had no choice but to cut their prices.

To meet this challenge, Gillette conducted a year of intensive research, observing Indian men's purchases and usage of razors. They worked in reverse by fixing a price tag for the product before they started product reengineering. The Gillette Guard, launched in 2010, had an affordable razor for 15 INR (about 0.34 USD) and blades for 5 INR (about 0.11 USD). This low-weight, plastic, disposable razor offered a close shave minus the frequent cuts from the quick-rusting, double-edged products offered by competitors. Gillette Guard rapidly captured 50 percent of the Indian shaving market (Atkins 2013), despite being higher priced than Super-Max, demonstrating that affordability balances low cost and product performance. The Gillette Guard has been the company's best option for penetrating India's large rural market.

At times, companies collaborate to develop affordable products for emerging markets. Ford Motor Company and Fiat codeveloped an affordable, subcompact automobile specifically for consumers in the U.K., Brazil, and Mexico called the Ford Ka. Launched in 1996, the Ford Ka became a bestseller in those countries since diesel fuel was less expensive than regular gasoline in Brazil and Mexico, and the Ka's 1.3-liter Fiat-designed diesel engine yielded a fuel economy of 67.3 miles per gallon (mpg) (Love 2009; Keegan 2008). Collaboration to achieve affordability can even extend to other partners. Sistema Ser/CEGIN in Argentina reduced prices by removing both middlemen and social obstacles to provide healthcare to poor, rural women in Argentina, while also working with individuals, healthcare providers, and the community.

Sistema Ser/CEGIN

Contributors: Jaqueline Pels and Tomás Andrés Kidd

Sistema Ser/CEGIN (hereafter, Ser-CEGIN) is a social enterprise in Argentina launched in 1988 by Dr. Jorge Gronda to reduce the rate of cervical cancer by providing quality gynecological services to rural indigenous women (*cholas*). Today, Ser-CEGIN has over 60 affiliated independent doctors providing a wide range of private, quality medical services at below average market fees to over 46,000 women. Ser-CEGIN bridges the gap between quality medical service and BoP health demand.

As in many countries, in Argentina, available healthcare options were either private or public. Private services were targeted at the top of the pyramid with high prices and state-of-the-art technology, and offered either a syndicate-run medical insurance or private practice. With syndicated medical insurance, trade unions paid the doctor fixed fees averaging around 60 Argentine Pesos (ARS) (about 11.10 USD) for each appointment. In private practice, patients paid the doctors directly at an average rate per appointment of 300 ARS (about 55.50 USD). In the public system, patients were entitled to free medical assistance provided by the government, but this system was inefficient. Gronda quickly understood that the *cholas* could not afford private services but that public services were poor quality. Patients had to wait for months for appointments and hospitals often lacked personnel and equipment. Although public services were universal, just 30 percent of the population could use them due to lack of quality and access.

Gronda set out to disrupt this status quo by eliminating medical intermediaries (syndicate-run medical insurances) so that *cholas* could get high quality medical services at low prices. *Cholas* would affiliate with Ser-CEGIN by paying a minimum annual fee (10 ARS per year), and then pay doctors cash amounts comparable to those paid by the intermediaries. Doctors benefitted from this set up by being paid immediately by patients rather than 60 to 90 days after the visit by intermediaries, and also Ser-CEGIN did not charge doctors a commission. Gronda explained why all parties found this arrangement rewarding, "There is a huge gap between intermediaries' fees and private practice fees that makes no sense. By making the private practice fees comparable to those of intermediaries, the system became affordable to the users and attractive to the doctors."

Ser-CEGIN discovered a second challenge. Doctors were happy to receive their fees on the spot, but many of them discriminated against the *cholas*. Compared with services given to urban white women, *cholas* were given appointments at inconvenient times and were treated with contempt. To address this, Ser-CEGIN hand-selected the doctors they incorporated into their system. Gronda explained the screening process, "I would take each doctor to the mountains to live for a period of time with the community they would serve in the near future. This ethnographic work of turning invisible patients into visible ones is crucial to the business as we need to understand whom we are serving."

Over Ser-CEGIN's 25 years of existence, Gronda also identified obstacles in BoP healthcare demand rooted in cultural and social factors, such as local indigenous traditions and rural environmental hardships for which Ser-CEGIN had to establish a bottom-up, trust-based relationship with local community leaders. Also, Ser-CEGIN realized that due to low income, remote locations, and lack of knowledge, most *cholas* did not know their human health rights. Taking doctors to spend time in the mountains was critical to giving the *cholas* a chance to get familiarized with the importance of medical care. The vetting process converted doctors into company evangelizers. For the *cholas*, buying membership cards that gave them access to medical services at prices significantly below market rates meant more than just an economic benefit. "By paying a price and having a card with their name, these women feel empowered that they can claim good service from us," says Gronda.

On the cultural side, preventive healthcare was not prevalent, re-sulting in *cholas*' vulnerability to diseases. Jorge explained, "Our job is to create awareness amongst our future patients and show them how preventive healthcare is much cheaper than addressing a crisis." Ser-CEGIN worked through local community leaders to in-crease awareness. Ser-CEGIN's success lay in understanding that price discrimination was just part of the story. To convert nonusers to users by reducing economic barriers to purchase, it was also nec-essary to invest time and energy in creating trust-based relation-ships and empowering the *cholas*.

Emerging markets also have a growing middle and affluent class, and so segmenting the market in a way that addresses the economic barriers for each segment of the market is important. In doing so, companies have to think of multitier, multisegment strategies by creating multiple levels of price/performance value for a market. An example of this would be to develop "good, better, and best" products under the same brand or different brands in order to span the market and target consumers from different socioeconomic backgrounds with suitable value propositions. Thus, companies opt to produce either a different product or to develop a whole new brand at a lower cost (Casadesus-Masanell and Tarziján 2012). Many multinationals estab-lish manufacturing plants in emerging economies to leverage lower production and raw material costs and make their products afford-able for users or, more importantly, for nonusers (Guillén and García-Canal 2010), but it should not lead to lowering of quality.

The health industry offers many examples of such multisegment targeting. To address health issues, such as tuberculosis, malaria, HIV/AIDS, and other diseases that plague many emerging markets, several multinational pharmaceutical companies are investing in the development of new medical technologies. Many local companies from countries like India, China, and Latin America began by produc-ing generics but eventually shored up their research and development (R&D) to develop breakthrough drugs. The growth of both the middle class as well as health insurance products, has motivated multinational pharmaceutical manufacturers to view R&D as an effective source of future revenue. Innovative marketing strategies, combined with participation in social development, are often centered on affordable pricing that is both commercially and socially credible (Colleti and Ravanas 2010; D'Andrea, Stengel, and Goebel-Krstelj 2004). However, multisegment pricing strategies have also ignited some debate, as in the case of GlaxoSmithKline's vaccine in Latin America.

GlaxoSmithKline in Latin America

In 2010, GlaxoSmithKline's (GSK's) price segmentation of its pneumococcal vaccines, for protection against pneumonia, created a controversy. The Pan American Health Organization (PAHO) had been procuring pneumonia vaccines at low prices by aggregating the demand across several small and middle-sized countries in Latin America. However, many Latin American countries fell in the lower-middle income category while others were in the middle-upper income category. This created a conflict because PAHO's aggregation model for receiving the lowest global prices clashed with GSK's segmented pricing that pegged higher prices for middle-income countries.

PAHO had negotiated a price of 21.75 USD/dose from Wyeth for a 7-valent dose, but GSK had developed a 10-valent vaccine that covered a large range of serotypes and was going to supply it to 72 developing countries for 7 USD /dose for 20 percent of the total quantity, and the balance at 3.50 USD/dose. PAHO did not receive these prices for its lower-income countries since its aggregation model included middle-income countries as well, hence its customers opted for Wyeth's products initially. Meanwhile, the Brazilian government had already negotiated an 8-year deal with GSK to purchase a 10-valent vaccine at an initial price of 16 USD/dose, followed by a decrease of 7 USD/dose, after which GSK would transfer the technology to a Brazilian manufacturer. As a result, PAHO finally negotiated a price of 14.85 USD/dose with GSK. To differentiate its offerings, GSK supplied the same medication in two-dose vials for developing countries, but a one-dose vial for PAHO (Moon et al. 2011). Thus, multisegment pricing addressed the challenge of providing poorer countries with lower prices, thereby removing economic barriers, but insufficient product differentiation can cause a host of issues related to rationale and methods for classification.

Luxury brands also follow a multisegment, multitiered approach in emerging markets where they not only find eager consumers among the wealthy and neo-rich but also find aspiring ones among the burgeoning middle class. LVMH, the French luxury goods conglomerate formed by the merger of Louis Vuitton with Moët Hennessy, has an enviable collection of brands in its portfolio, such as Fendi, Louis Vuitton, Christian Dior, and Bulgari. LVMH believes that the "aspirational" luxury segment is far outstripping that of "elitist luxury," and so its Luis Vuitton and Gucci brands have launched low entry-level products such as fabric-based handbags and mini handbags. LVMH balances its high-end portfolio by having both niche brands for sophisticated luxury consumers who have the "need-to-differentiate" and megabrands that satisfy emerging market consumers' "need-to-belong" (BernsteinResearch 2009). Its challenge is to balance both upscaling and downscaling without eroding the brand's luxury positioning.

Overcoming Noneconomic Obstacles to Purchase

The earlier Ser-CEGIN example illustrates how economic barriers exist along with noneconomic ones. Thus, affordability is not just a monetary concept, but one that also considers the time and effort expended to overcome barriers to purchase. Some of these barriers include being able to acquire proper documentation to buy/use a product/service or having the knowledge to evaluate the price. Companies in emerging markets can help consumers overcome noneconomic obstacles to purchase in creative ways, like Capitec Bank in South Africa.

Capitec Bank in South Africa

Contributor: Amaleya Goneos-Malka

Capitec Bank, established in 2001, has over 668 retail branches nationwide, 3,418 ATMs, and over 6.2 million customers (Capitec Bank Holdings Limited 2015). It differentiates itself from other banking institutions by focusing exclusively on providing unsecured credit to underprivileged South Africans who lack the assets and/or the requisite legal paperwork to apply for credit from the traditional banking sector that operates on a secured-lending model. This approach was especially transformative for many underprivileged homeowners from the pre-1994 apartheid era who were disadvantaged because they did not have title deeds to their houses and thus could not leverage their homes as assets for credit applications in the traditional banking framework. Until the mid-2000s, banking services were too expensive and inaccessible for over half of South Africa's population.

In an interview, Charles Nel (Head of Communications: Marketing and Corporate Affairs) described how Capitec changed the entry requirements for its credit products to drive small-scale entrepreneurship by enabling poor people to obtain small loans. Essentially the bank helped the country's financial inclusion goals by offering unsecured credit for economic wealth creation. The founders leveraged BaNCS, a banking platform technology from an Indian software giant, Tata Consultancy Services (TCS), to create a simple, paperless, personalized service that was affordable and accessible, and provided real-time results across every bank branch for speedy action (Tata Consultancy Services 2012).

Capitec benefitted from a hands-on approach by the founding directors and their recruitment strategy of hiring people that shared the no-nonsense, transparent, straight-talking, entrepreneurial spirit of the founding members. Nel believed that these qualities were their strength in reinventing systems, processes, and products, helping them consciously ignore the textbook approach. Highly experienced division heads were recruited from banks, such as the old Boland Bank (currently Nedbank) who, in turn, recruited young people, not from banks, but from the retail industry. Capitec understood that young employees would better understand and empathize with their key target audience of 16- to 30-year-old customers who were generally new entrants into the banking sector.

Nel believed, "Young employees have less tendency to apply discretionary thinking with respect to assessing or profiling customers. Their role is to focus more on client service engagement." This was a lucrative and future-oriented strategy since a large part of the population was young.

By targeting an audience that had not been targeted by the banking sector before, Capitec managed to grow under the radar of other banks. Nel noted, "None of the traditional banks saw us as a serious threat as our initial focus was on credit only. While we secured the longer term income stream through credit, we were building the banking platform, testing it extensively and launching it to our existing clients." Once Capitec's national branch network and world-class banking system was set up, they started aggressive marketing. While traditional banks focused on "client numbers," Capitec focused on "*active* client numbers," that is, those representing an account where they earned above a specific amount of fees per month. Nel said, "We currently open more than 100,000 active accounts per month. Our market share has grown from nil to 9 percent, or 13 percent, whichever data you use, in less than 12 years. I believe we have reason to believe our marketing strategy (and business approach) is superior to that of traditional banks."

Capitec believes the difference between a rich and a poor person is in the way they manage their money—not in their banking needs. Staying true to this market need, Capitec intends to steer away from secured lending, investment wealth, or corporate markets for future growth. Instead, they plan to expand into developing economies, such as Brazil, that possess a stable legal/police system, consistency in business law, and Internet and electricity availability in remote areas. By successfully providing banking access to the masses, based on their stable income rather on what they already own, Capitec has demonstrated that unsecured credit will be the way forward in most developing countries (Capitec Bank n.d.; Lefifi 2012).

Achieving Reverse Innovation

The needs of emerging market consumers make both product and price innovation critical for competing there. Thereafter, many such innovations find a market in the developed world. This strategy of successfully creating an inexpensive product for the needs of developing nations and then exporting that as a low-cost innovation to the developed world is called *reverse innovation* (Govindrajan 2012). Typically, companies start their globalization efforts by targeting the higher-income or most affluent segments of society in developing countries and then for the less affluent, they try defeaturing their established products—that is, removing expensive features in a bid to lower costs. Reverse innovation, on the other hand, leads to products that are created locally for developing countries, are tested and marketed in local markets, and, if successful, are then upgraded for sale and delivery in the developed world. This creates new markets and uses for these innovations. Reverse innovation requires that companies make changes in their old, institutionalized thinking and underlying assumptions to create new ones. The new learning and organizational skills then grow in the organization and can be extended to other markets, thanks to the interconnectedness of the global economy organizational structures (Govindrajan 2012).

GE has been the classic example for this. It used what is called "frugal innovation" to develop ultra–low-cost medical devices for emerging markets that also factor in the impact of conditions in local markets such as power outages, voltage fluctuations, dust, pollution, and the usage intensity of the equipment. Their 1,000 USD electrocardiogram developed by Indian software engineers for India is now being sold in the U.S. and elsewhere (Bellman 2009). Similarly, GE had launched a cradle warmer in 2009 that heats an open cradle to help newborns adjust to room temperature. In India it sold for 3,000 USD but in the U.S. it had added functionalities, such as weight and pulse monitoring, and was priced at 12,000 USD. It was eventually marketed in more than 60 countries worldwide, including in developed ones such as Belgium and Switzerland. (Arasaratnam and Humphrey 2013). Reverse innovation requires that companies make changes to their old, institutionalized thinking and underlying assumptions to create new ones. The new learning and organizational skills then grow in the organization and can be extended to other markets, thanks to the interconnectedness of the global economy's organizational structures (Govindrajan 2012). Reverse innovation extends beyond technology-centric products too, as illustrated by Levi Strauss & Co.'s Denizen brand.

Levi Strauss's Denizen Jeans from China

Levi Strauss, the maker of Levi's jeans, developed its Denizen brand of low-cost jeans for China. After eight months of experience selling this brand to Chinese and other Asian shoppers, they brought Denizen to its home market in the U.S. where it retailed for one-third to one-half the cost of a pair of Levi's. Having learned how to launch a value brand and nurture it in China, Levi's has become one among a handful of multinational firms to leverage the growing influence of emerging economies for reverse product innovation. "Launching in India and China, which are two very different cultures with consumers who have different body types, style, and customs, gave us a chance to learn about how to make a brand relevant for the market," said Lance Diaresco, vice president of marketing for Denizen. "We learned about fit and how to work with our franchise and wholesale customers to help them select the fits most relevant for their consumers" (Zmuda 2011).

Although China has been home to many global apparel manufacturing companies, consumers in China have had little influence on global design and marketing. Clothing has lagged behind sectors such as telecommunications and beverages, where multinationals have boosted their R&D in emerging markets and local rivals are producing a growing volume of innovations. According to Aaron Boey, president of Denizen, Levi's had learned to produce affordable jeans in emerging markets by working out which features consumers were most sensitive to—the stitching, the way the fabric feels, or the wash of the denim. "It's not about taking costs out, it's about deciding what costs to put in to deliver the value that consumers appreciate," he said. "We've gotten that validation in the markets we're currently operating in. So, we know we can nail it as well in the U.S.... If launching a 'value brand' for emerging markets forced Levi to really think about what matters to consumers in jeans, and they incorporate that into how they make, market and sell them, the principles are just as valid in the U.S. as they are in China," he said. Since August 2010, Levi Strauss has opened more than 150 stores that sell only Denizen jeans in China, India, Singapore, South Korea, and Pakistan. In the U.S., the jean sells through Target, a discount retailer, for between 20 and 30 USD (Jopson and Waldmeir 2011).

Extending Product Value

Affordability can also be achieved by extending the life of the product and thereby its value. Organizing the used/second-hand product market is one way of creating affordability. Instead of viewing this as a cannibalization threat, companies operating in emerging markets with product categories that are new for the market must consider that lower prices of used goods facilitate trial of the product category/brand, which may lead to the purchase of a new one in the future. This is especially true for durable products that often become obsolete as new technologies emerge. Examples of this include personal computers, tablets, cell phones, servers, trucks, automobiles, scooters, and motorcycles.

Indigenous markets have thriving secondary markets for sales of used or lower-priced, often unbranded (sometimes counterfeit) goods. Known as flea markets in the developed world, such markets are referred to as Tiangge in the Philippines and Juna (i.e., old) Bazaar in India. They are typically open for business on weekends and space is rented out to sellers (IBEF 2008). In Sharjah, in the United Arab Emirates, the second-hand market has a large number of shops clustered by categories, such as personal computers or home appliances imported from the European Union and the United States (Shinkuma and Managi 2011). In Africa, second-hand markets, such as those in Kampala, have scores of bargain-hunting shoppers rummaging through mounds of clothes at what are basically open-air thrift stores. Western cast-off products, that might otherwise end up in landfills, are bought by wholesalers who export them to such markets to be sold at affordable prices (Curnow and Kermeliotis 2013).

This strategy is particularly relevant in industrial markets where products such as machinery, factories, aircrafts, ships, and military weapons are constantly becoming obsolete. Second-hand auctions of used machinery, such as dumpers, mixers, dozers, excavators, crushers, screeners, dump trucks, and so on, are popular, especially for emerging market customers. As these countries invest in infrastructure, demand for such equipment rises and provides developed countries with a cost-effective way to replace their old equipment. Manheim's experience in the used-car segment illustrates that a pioneering advantage also brings with it the cost of setting up basic systems and processes to ensure affordability.

Manheim in China

The Chinese used-car market is expected to grow to 28 percent between 2017 and 2020 (Government Fleet 2014). Emerging markets typically lack a well-organized used-car sales market. Given few disposal options and limited transparency in remarketing, consumers tend to be uncertain about the value of the used car and the purchasing process. Franchise dealers prefer to focus solely on new cars due to poor wholesale mechanisms. Thus, succeeding in the used-car markets in these countries will depend on companies' ability to create a shift in organizing and empowering independent dealers.

Manheim, a global used-car auction company, is providing solutions to such challenges. In 2006, Manheim reached an agreement with a Chinese counterpart to extend its auto auction operations into Shanghai, China. Shanghai Manheim Guo Pai Used Vehicle Auction Company Ltd. (Manheim Guo Pai) is a joint venture between Manheim China Holdings, a wholly owned subsidiary of Manheim, and Shanghai International Commodity Auction Company (Shanghai Guo Pai).

Around the same time this agreement took place, China's remarketing industry gained some ground with new government regulations aimed at facilitating the creation of an open, yet dependable, used-vehicle sector. Manheim Guo Pai provided a reputable, secure medium to facilitate the buying and selling of vehicles in an open-bidding environment while also maintaining regulations at the auction level. They offered ancillary services such as rigorous inspections on vehicle ownership and condition, arbitration between buyers and sellers, fee collections and distribution, title transfers, reconditioning, marketing, and marshaling (Chaney 2006). Manheim also created a *remarketing management system*, a technology that helped provide transparency and functionalities such as currency, language, and taxation localization (Manheim 2014).

Developing Creative Financing

Providing affordable solutions for consumers often entails making creative financing options available. In the business-to-business (B2B) industry, this is very common—such as leasing (machinery, aircrafts, copiers, and cars), third-party payments, and providing credit facilities for commercial and capital goods. In the business-to-consumer (B2C) space, one of the several myths of emerging markets is that consumers are very credit dependent. In Latin America, consumers use credit to extend their purchasing power for major purchases such as appliances, but they tend to use cash for daily consumables as a way of controlling their expenditures. For consumers who may find themselves short of cash, several Latin American countries have virtual wallets offered by neighborhood retailers. This virtual wallet comprises informal, short-term, interest-free credit for very small amounts and is offered by local shopkeepers to their regular customers based on their personal relationship. The loan is recorded in a notebook and removed when the customer pays off the loan. Defaulters' names and dues are posted on a sign in the neighborhood, thus enabling this model to work entirely on social incentives. This is a simple, but powerful example of being creative to create affordability (D'Andrea, Stengel, and Goebel-Krstelj 2004).

Creative financing can also mean buying a product that is then shared by several people or even the community. For example, Grameen Telecom's village phones in Bangladesh are owned by a single entrepreneur but are used by the whole community, generating anywhere from 90 USD–1,000 USD per month. Customers using the village phone have been found to spend almost 7 percent of their income on this service, higher than consumers in traditional markets (Prahalad and Hammond 2002). Celtel, a telecom company founded by Mo Ibrahim in Africa, found pent up demand for their service, but very low affordability, so they started offering prepaid cards (scratch cards) for a few dollars of airtime each. The additional benefit for Celtel was constant cash flows and no unpaid bills (Ibrahim 2012). In all of these examples across continents, the common theme is how companies innovated to create affordable solutions that democratized products and services. Some developing markets have innovated with their own homegrown systems to provide access to funds. One such creative form of financing in India is called chit funds.

Chit Funds in India

Chit funds, sometimes called kitty parties, can be considered an alternative to banking because they provide access to credit in a unique manner that enables both savings and borrowing. Chit funds are typically an informal savings system that pools together the savings of poor people and works like a raffle to lend money. Investors pay a prespecified amount at select intervals (say, monthly) for a limited period, which goes into a common pool. A lucky draw is conducted and the entire amount collected from all contributors goes to the winner. An auction system, with bidding options, can also be used in which the winner is the person with the lowest bid. This "winner" is the one who agrees to claim the lowest amount among the bidders so that the difference between the full amount and the lowest amount is distributed back to the other members. Winners continue to contribute. The system is prone to risks, such as misuse of pooled funds by promoters or default by subscribers, and hence the Indian government has laws to regulate it (Oberoi 2013).

In India, nearly 15,000 kitty-party companies exist, and they manage billions of dollars of funds. savings and borrowing. Chit funds are typically an informal savings system that pools together the savings of poor people and works like a raffle to lend money. Investors pay a prespecified one has been operated by the government of a southern state, Kerala, since 1969 (Oberoi 2013). The largest formal chit fund, operated by a large conglomerate—the Shriram group—manages funds in four cities (Shriram Capital n.d.). They have 12,000 employees, 700 branches, and 80,000 agents (Shriram Chits n.d.).

Financing is not just relevant for BoP consumers. Thinking creatively about pricing has fueled the growth of many web-based products where the price to the consumer is effectively zero, such as with email. Being able to monetize such products has been a challenge and advertising-based revenue models face profitability challenges. It is possible, however, to offer a free basic model with upgradable services that are available for purchase. This "freemium" monetization model is used by Internet businesses such as Dropbox and LinkedIn who provide basic software, media, games, or web services that are free to consumers, but money is charged for premium, add-on, proprietary features, functionality, or even virtual goods. The premium may be a one-time charge or a subscription service. The freemium business model requires feature updates throughout the product lifecycle as well as a specialized marketing strategy (Kumar 2014). Attempts to offer free products may run into regulatory issues, however, as has Facebook's idea of offering free Internet in India and Egypt, which would have enabled access to select websites. This was perceived as a violation of net neutrality in those countries (Rivas 2015; Wagner 2016).

WeChat in China

The most common business model used in the Internet industry is advertising-based, where a free service is provided, enabling an audience to be created that then attracts advertisers who are looking for that target segment. Integrating advertisements into messaging applications has been a great challenge for companies in Asia. WeChat, an instant messaging application developed by Tencent in China, with over 300 million users, offers features like profile pages and photo sharing to consumers. Like Twitter, it also enables companies to set up free accounts for attracting followers.

Aiming to be a major advertising platform like Facebook and Google, WeChat has launched a new advertising service. However, instead of distributing ads as instant messages, WeChat has announced that companies with more than 100,000 followers could host advertisements at the bottom of their pages, splitting revenues with WeChat. They provide a powerful back-end system that can help companies target viewers based on gender, age, and location, as well as personal interests (Osawa 2014). Western brands like Starbucks and Buick signed on to WeChat early to reach out to Chinese consumers (Millward 2013).

Although the basic chat service on WeChat is free, the company has recently announced celebrity accounts as a paid subscription service at a 18 Renminbi (RMB, or Chinese Yuan; around 3 USD) per month for enabling fans to be close to their favorite celebrities and vice versa. Subscribers receive exclusive photos, songs/e-books, good night voice messages, or sometimes even videos or video chats from their idol. The launch of the new service was so successful that Chen Kun, a famous Chinese actor, received over 7 million RMB (about 1.14 million USD) in subscription fees the first day the service went live (van der Toom 2013). Hollywood celebrities like Selena Gomez, John Cusack, the Backstreet Boys, and even TV drama stars such as *Vampire Diaries* actress, Nina Dobrev, have been successfully engaging their Chinese consumers via WeChat too (Millward 2013).

References

Arasaratnam, Ajanthy, and Gary Humphrey. 2013. "Emerging Economies Drive Frugal Innovation." *Bulletin of the World Health Organization* 91 (1): 6–7.

Atkins, Ryan. 2013. "Gillette: The 11-Cent Razor, India, and Reverse Innovation." GlobaLens, a division of the William Davidson Institute (WDI). April 15. University of Michigan: Case #1-429-328.

Bellman, Eric. 2009. "Indian Firms Shift Focus to the Poor." *The Wall Street Journal.* October 21. Accessed on January 14, 2014. www.wsj.com/articles/SB125598988906795035.

BernsteinResearch. 2009. "LVMH: King of the Luxury Jungle." September. Accessed on March 4, 2016. www.luxesf.com/wp-content/uploads/2009/10/LVMH-King-of-the-luxury-jungle.pdf.

Byron, Ellen. 2010. "Gillette's Latest Innovation in Razors: The 11-Cent Blade." *The Wall Street Journal*. October 1. Accessed on August 9, 2014. http://online.wsj.com/articles/SB1000142405274 8704789404575524273890970954.

Capitec Bank. n.d. "About Us." Capitec Bank corporate website. Accessed on April 22, 2016. www.capitecbank.co.za/about-us.

Capitec Bank Holdings Limited. 2015. "Chief Financial Officer's Review 2015." Accessed on February 14, 2016. www.capitecbank. co.za/resources/2015_Chief_financial_officers_report.pdf.

Casadesus-Masanell, Ramon, and Jorge Tarziján. 2012. "When One Business Model Isn't Enough." *Harvard Business Review*. January-February. Accessed on December 25, 2015. http://hbr.org/2012/01/when-one-business-model-isnt-enough/ar/1.

Chaney, David. 2006. "Manheim Launches China Operations Joint Venture in Shanghai Key Step in Manheim's International Expansion." Cox Enterprises. May 10. Accessed on January 18, 2016. http://coxenterprises.mediaroom.com/index .php?s=26244&item=68034.

Chengalpattu, S.A. 2012. "Chit Funds in India: One for the Kitty." *The Economist*. November 2. Accessed on May 12, 2014. www .economist.com/blogs/banyan/2012/11/chit-funds-india.

Colletti, Paula, and Philippe Ravanas. 2010. "How to Implement a Tiered Pricing Strategy." *Culture Hive*. Columbia College Chicago. Accessed on January 18, 2016. http://culturehive.co.uk/ resources/how-to-implement-a-tiered-pricing-strategy.

Curnow, Robyn, and Teo Kermeliotis. 2013. "Is Your Old T-Shirt Hurting African Economies?" CNN. April 12. Accessed on May 9, 2015. http://edition.cnn.com/2013/04/12/business/second-hand-clothes-africa.

D'Andrea, Guillermo, E. Alejandro Stengel, and Anne Goebel-Krstelj. 2004. "6 Truths about Emerging-Market Consumers." *Strategy + Business*. Spring. Accessed on March 24, 2015. www.strategy-business.com/article/04106?pg=all.

Government Fleet. 2014. "Manheim's 2014 Used-Car Report Predicts Declining Margins." January 27. Accessed on January 14, 2015. www.government-fleet.com/channel/remarketing/news/story/2014/01/manheim-s-outlook-for-2014-used-car-market-report.aspx.

Govindrajan, Vijay. 2012. "A Reverse Innovation Playbook." *Harvard Business Review*. April. 120–124.

Guillén, Mauro F., and Esteban García-Canal. 2010. "The Globe: How to Conquer New Markets with Old Skills." *Harvard Business Review*. November. Accessed on March 24, 2015. http://hbr.org/2010/11/the-globe-how-to-conquer-new-markets-with-old-skills/ar/1.

Ibrahim, Mo. 2012. "Celtel's Founder on Building a Business on the World's Poorest Continent." *Harvard Business Review*. October 1. 41–44.

IBEF (Indian Brand Equity Foundation). 2008. "Business Opportunities in India." Accessed on May 6, 2012. www.ibef.org.

Jaiswal, Kamya. 2011. "Can Gillette Tap into Rural Markets and Yet Retain Its Value for Urban Consumers?" *Economic Times*. December 11. Accessed on December 12, 2014. http://articles.economictimes.indiatimes.com/2011-12-11/news/30502422_1_razor-and-blade-gillette-india-mach.

Jopson, Barney, and Patti Waldmeir. 2011. "Levi's Denizen Brand Poised for US Launch." *Financial Times*. April 12. Accessed on February 27, 2016. www.ft.com/cms/s/0/2345e5c2-648a-11e0-a69a-00144feab49a.html#axzz41UNLpAal.

Kay, Ethan, and Woody Lewenstein. 2013. "The Problem with the 'Poverty Premium.'" *Harvard Business Review* 91 (4): 21–23.

Keegan, Matt. 2008. "Ford Rolls Out Fiat Based New Ka." *Auto Trends Magazine*. September 29. Accessed on March 24, 2015. www.autotrends.org/2008/09/29/ford-rolls-out-fiat-based-new-ka.

Kumar, Vineet. 2014. "Making 'Freemium' Work." *Harvard Business Review* 92(5): 27–29.

Lefifi, Hekiso Anthony. 2012. "On Fast Track to Success." *Business Times*. November 18. Accessed on February 14, 2015. http://cdn.bdlive.co.za/images/pdf/Top100Comp_2012.pdf.

Love, Martin. 2009. "So Near, So Ka." *The Guardian*. May 9. Accessed on, May 9, 2014. www.theguardian.com/technology/2009/may/10/ford-ka-review.

Manheim, 2014. "2014 Used Car MarketReport." Manheim. Accessed on May 9, 2014. www.niada.com/uploads/dynamic_areas/wp6Q-IPSw6C83LYM1dGrU/33/UCMR_2014_Final.pdf.

Millward, Steven. 2013. "Hollywood Celebrities Get Chatty with Chinese Fans on WeChat." *TechInAsia*. February 11. Accessed on May 9, 2015. www.techinasia.com/hollywood-celebrities-wechat-chinese-fans.

Moon, Suerie, Elodie Jambert, Michelle Childs, and Tido von Schoen-Angerer. 2011. "A Win-Win Solution?: A Critical Analysis of Tiered Pricing to Improve Access to Medicines in Developing Countries." *Globalization and Health, BioMed Central*. October 12. Accessed on March 24, 2015. www.globalizationandhealth.com/content/7/1/39.

Oberoi, Rahul. 2013. "Pooling It Wisely." *Money Today*. June. Accessed on March 24, 2015. http://businesstoday.in/moneytoday/investment/tips-to-choose-best-chit-funds-and-get-good-returns/story/195260.html.

Osawa, Juro. 2014."Can WeChat Become a Major Advertising Platform?" *The Wall Street Journal*. July 9. Accessed on May 9, 2014. http://blogs.wsj.com/chinarealtime/2014/07/09/can-wechat-become-a-major-advertising-platform.

Picker, Randy. 2010. "Gillette's Strange History with the Razor and Blade Strategy." *Harvard Business Review*. September 23. Accessed on January 18, 2015. https://hbr.org/2010/09/gillettes-strange-history-with.

Prahalad, C. K., and Allen Hammond. 2002. "Serving the World's Poor Profitably." *Harvard Business Review*. September. Accessed on March 24, 2015. https://hbr.org/2002/09/serving-the-worlds-poor-profitably.

Rivas, Teresa. 2015. "Facebook's Free Internet in Egypt Shuts Down." *Barron's*. December 31. Accessed on February 3, 2016. http://blogs.barrons.com/emergingmarketsdaily/2015/12/31/facebooks-free-internet-in-egypt-shuts-down.

Sheth Jagdish N., and Rajendra S. Sisodia. 2012. *The 4 A's of Marketing: Creating Value for Customers, Companies, and Society*. New York: Routledge.

Shinkuma, Takayoshi, and Shunsuke Managi. 2011. *Waste and Recycling: Theory and Empirics*. New York: Routledge.

Shriram Capital. n.d. "Chit Funds." Accessed on June 9, 2015. http://www.shriramcapital.com/chit-funds.html.

Shriram Chits. n.d. Shiram Chits Tamilnadu Pvt Ltd. Accessed on June 9, 2015. www.shriramchits.com.

Simanis, Erik. 2012. "Reality Check at the Bottom of the Pyramid." *Harvard Business Review*. June. Accessed on May 9, 2014. https://hbr.org/2012/06/reality-check-at-the-bottom-of-the-pyramid.

Tata Consultancy Services. 2012. "TCS BaNCS Enables Banking for the Unbanked, and Drives Growth for Capitec Bank." December 15. Accessed on May 9, 2014. www.tcs.com/resources/case_studies/Pages/TCS-BaNCS-drives-growth-South-Africa-Capitec-Bank.aspx.

van der Toom, Thijs. 2013. "WeChat's Business Model Innovation: Monetizing via Celebrity Accounts." *Innovative China*. September 17. Accessed on May 11, 2015. www.innovativechina.com/2013/09/wechats-business-modelinnovation-monetizing-via-celebrity-accounts.

Wagner, Kurt. 2016. "Facebook's Regulatory Battle over Free Basics in India Is Getting Feisty." *Recode*. January 19. Accessed on February 3, 2016. http://recode.net/2016/01/19/facebooks-regulatory-battle-over-free-basics-in-india-is-getting-feisty.

Zmuda, Natalie. 2011. "P&G, Levi's, GE Innovate by Thinking in Reverse." *Ad Age*. June 13. Accessed on February 28, 2016. http://adage.com/article/global-news/p-g-levi-s-ge-innovate-thinking-reverse/228146.

5

Upscaling the Offer

In most emerging markets, local, unbranded goods proliferate. Most tend to be highly regional and do not have a national presence. A study across eight emerging markets revealed that emerging market consumers tend to stay with their local brands, possibly due to inertia or because those items do not have any status appeal (Credit Suisse 2013). If companies incorporate psychological appeal (social and emotional) into products, then as consumers' disposable income increases, they are more likely to explore "trading up" opportunities and move from unbranded to branded goods. This is not just applicable to lower-income consumers being introduced to brands but also to middle- or upper-income consumers who are moving to more expensive, or national, or even international brands.

The number of middle-class and affluent consumers is increasing rapidly in emerging markets. Indonesia, for example, has a middle-class and affluent consumer segment of 74 million people, which is expected to grow to 141 million by 2020 (Rastogi, Tamboto, and Tong 2013). This demographic and income change is not just happening in urban areas. In Brazil, interior cities are expected to contribute 130 billion USD in consumption (half of incremental household consumption) by 2020 and the affluent class is growing more rapidly there instead of in the cities. Yet, about 1,400 cities have no supermarket and 5,500 cities do not have bank branches to cater to the affluent and many have no luxury car dealership (Cunha et al. 2014). Thus, the opportunity to upgrade the consumption choices and experiences of emerging market consumers, across the income spectrum, is immense. We call this opportunity *upscaling*.

In this chapter, we once again apply the concept of affordability characterized by two dimensions: economic affordability, or the ability to pay, and psychological affordability, or the willingness to pay (Sheth and Sisodia 2012). Although, the concept of affordability has typically referred to lower prices, we urge a wider conceptualization so as to match the value of the offering to the consumer's situation. As incomes rise, both consumers' ability and willingness to pay higher prices increase. They're also more likely to be more discerning about quality and other non-price aspect of the offer. They're also more likely to be more discerning about quality and other non-price aspect of the offer. Consequently, brands can upscale to match what their consumers can afford. Adding value to a brand focuses consumers' choice evaluation on performance rather than on price. So in Chapter 4 we described reengineering the offer to lower prices, while here we describe how companies can add value or increase the existing value. Although the intuitive way of thinking about value addition is to increase the functionality of the product itself, as described in Chapter 2, other creative routes we offer in this chapter are 1) adding or changing packaging, 2) positioning, 3) enhancing services and benefits, 4) reversing the brand lifecycle, and 5) leveraging the country of origin.

Adding or Changing Packaging

One of the ways that companies can add value is by introducing packaging in ways that are either novel to a market or allow products to be sold differently because of the packaging. Interestingly, although packaging is the norm in developed markets, particularly for fast-moving consumer goods found in drug- and grocery stores, consumption of unpackaged goods is still quite high in developing and emerging markets. For example, China has the highest consumption of unpackaged foods and only 30 percent of foods consumed there are processed. Recently, however, urbanization, rising incomes, and an increase in the number of working women have spurred the need for convenience—hence the need for more prepared and prepackaged foods. Thus, multinationals, as well as large local companies, have the opportunity to use packaging as one way to transform large commodity markets (Seth, Saharia, Mukherjee 2013).

Packaging modifications entail big changes in the supply chain. Companies like McDonald's and PepsiCo in India integrate upstream with suppliers to stabilize and standardize their inputs supply, providing technical and other assistance in return. Others integrate downstream partnering with retailers. In doing so, these companies are seen as trailblazers, paving the way for small manufacturers to scale up, package, and position their own offering. Gradually they are weaning consumers off unpackaged, often undifferentiated commodities, thus allowing for a wider range of qualities and prices as the market slowly upscales. This is also true for industrial goods, raw materials, and agricultural commodities (Seth, Saharia, and Mukherjee 2013).

Packaging changes commodity markets to branded ones by evolving the consumption benefits from primarily just taste, to elements like quality and hygiene, thereby changing consumer behavior. Take for example, the market for sauces in Vietnam. With 88 million people, Vietnam boasts the third largest population in Southeast Asia and it has a rapidly growing consumer goods market. In particular, the foods segment is expected to grow rapidly due to changing demographics, rising disposable incomes, and urbanization. This has spurred the demand for good quality, healthy, and convenient foods and has been giving rise to brands, new products, and variants. Masan Group, the largest local diversified consumer goods company, has successfully leveraged this opportunity by packaging and marketing branded table sauces, moving consumers away from the traditional soy, fish, and chili sauces that were sold in plastic bags at wet market stalls (Masan Group n.d.; Seth, Saharia, and Mukherjee 2013; BBC 2013). The extent to which packaging requirements affect the supply chain function is evident in a closer examination of Moroccan dates.

Packaging of Moroccan Dates

The demand for dates in Morocco far outstrips supply due to lack of consistency in quantity and quality, and due to poor packaging. Moroccan dates are usually sold loose, rather than packaged, and then only during the harvest season. In an effort to increase and improve production, the Fruit Tree Productivity Project has taken steps to improve irrigation infrastructure, expand date palm plantations, and introduce new practices in water management, production, and harvesting. Planting disease-resistant plants, rehabilitating about 220,000 date trees, building links to higher-end markets, and providing technical assistance for farmer cooperative development are some of the necessary steps that must precede packaging initiatives (Agency of Partnership for Progress n.d.).

Such quality control initiatives for providing high-quality dates are important precursors to packaging. After the date harvest, the fruit is separated from the damaged dates by laboratory workers. These workers also sample the batches, cutting some of the fruit to inspect the internal cavity, and then they publish these results along with insect treatment results for consumers. The dates are then packaged and transported in the early morning to avoid heat and prevent infection by pests. Packaging preserves the moisture of the fruit and enables it to better withstand treacherous transport. Not only is packaging a marketing tool, but it also helps comply with legal labeling requirements (Glasner et al. n.d.). Labeling products as being of "protected origin designation" by the National Agency for Agricultural Development increases consumer awareness of and demand for local products, possibly reducing demand for imported ones. With these practices, the Moroccan government is increasing agricultural exports and thus increasing income in rural areas (Zawya 2014).

Thus, packaging does not always refer to obvious visible results such as adding an outer wrapping or container, or launching an advertising campaign for a brand that did not exist earlier. As with Moroccan dates, and in fact many such commodity products, adding packaging enhances quality and life, thereby adding value. However, packaging also adds costs, which then leads to higher prices. Both quality enhancements and higher prices contribute to upscaling a brand.

Positioning

Companies can also upscale their offer by positioning their brand in such a way that it becomes more valuable in a new, relatively more affluent market. Positioning is having a company's offer and image occupy a favored place in the mind of the consumer (Kotler and Keller 2016). Customizing the positioning of their product to what specific markets value can be financially rewarding because select segments will favor the brand over other alternatives. Companies can reap the positive financial outcomes of positioning without necessarily incurring the additional costs of changing their marketing mix. Ford Motor Company did exactly that in the Middle East by simply repositioning itself to focus on elements of its offer in other countries.

Ford Motor Company in the Middle East

Contributors: Jyothsna Appaiah Singh, Anudeep Raghuthman, and Balakrishna Grandhi

In the Middle East, Ford aligns its marketing strategy to the local market with the help of its regional full-time engineering services. Each car is test marketed in desert conditions, well before the launch date, to ensure high quality, durability, heat endurance, and appropriate cooling. Paul Anderson, marketing director at Ford Middle East says, "In our business, it is all about the product. It has to start with the product. We can't say that technology is our biggest differentiator if we don't have goods to back it up.... Smart technology is where we as a company have elected to make a real point of differentiation. We offer more technology, available at affordable prices for the masses than any other manufacturer."

Anderson concedes that for all brands, the external measure of quality has become too close to allow for any clear point of differentiation, and there are country variations as well. For example, in Europe, Ford positions itself on its green technologies that address CO_2 emissions, while in developing countries, it positions itself on fuel economy. He explains the rationale behind these different positioning platforms, "In the Middle East, we are less focused on the 'green' aspect given the prices of fuel here. We are more focused on the driving experience and safety technologies, such as voice activated sync, which obeys 10,000 voice commands and allows you to customize your experience.... Now, one would comment, every luxury car has one of those, or many of those, but what about non-luxury cars? Almost nobody does it in the non-luxury segment, especially all of that. Fiesta and Focus have active park system. We offer these technologies at affordable prices, to everyone, not just the ones who can afford luxury."

Enhancing Services and Benefits

Intangible benefits often help differentiate brands in competitive environments. So companies increasingly use superior service, financing, loyalty programs, warranties, and even customer-oriented business processes to win customer loyalty. Even though emerging markets are burdened with numerous challenges, such as inadequate infrastructure and complex business and regulatory environments, they still provide many opportunities for companies that are able to successfully navigate past these obstacles to upscale their brands with extra benefits that add value. The challenge lies in identifying unique benefits given the rapid pace of change and high levels of local competition in such markets. Companies that have been successful in emerging markets have to continually rethink their marketing strategy as the market evolves. Many benefits that can be offered in emerging markets may be fairly standard in developed countries but would be very valuable in emerging markets since they are likely to be fairly new experiences.

Safaricom in Kenya

Although emerging markets have most of the loyalty programs seen in the developed world, some are uniquely adapted to local needs. For example, Safaricom is a mobile service provider in Kenya owned by the Kenyan Government in partnership with Vodacom of the United Kingdom. Safaricom offers two loyalty programs called Bonga Points and Okoa Jahazi, that have kept customers using their services in Kenya despite stiff competition.

The Bonga Points programs give users redeemable points after they use a given amount of airtime. For every 5 Kenyan Shillings (KSh) used on the service, the user receives 1 Bonga Point. The user can then redeem these points to purchase other products and services the company offers, including more airtime, free online minutes, text messages, mobile phones, tablets, laptop computers, and Internet data. The Okoa Jahazi program offers subscribers the opportunity to access airtime on a credit basis at a reduced interest rate. These programs have endeared the company to many Kenyans because customers can get service even without a credit balance and they can get credit at reduced interest rates (Ngugi and Mutai 2014). Well-conceptualized and properly implemented loyalty programs like these that innovate beyond typical loyalty programs to meet the needs of local customers, provide an upscaled experience that goes beyond the core service that customers expect. This helps build relationships with new customers and retain them.

Upscaling of services and benefits is especially pertinent to the luxury market. In the last decade, air travel had downscaled from a luxury service to being a routine purchase for most consumers. The decline of in-flight service quality reflects this erosion. However, recently several airlines from the Middle East are coming full circle and embracing the epitome of luxury once more by upscaling their offer in multiple ways.

Airlines from the Middle East

Business travel is booming in emerging nations in Asia, Africa, the Middle East, and the Americas. The United Arab Emirates (UAE) and Qatar were promoted to emerging market status in 2013 by Morgan Stanley. UAE has become the financial hub of that region and Dubai is driving the rise of the service sector in industries ranging from airlines to finance. The per capita income of the UAE is higher than the United States at 66,000 USD per year and the region boasts a large middle class (Rapoza 2014).

Dubai's airport boasts a new terminal paved with white marble devoted to its growing fleet of double-decker Airbus 380s. UAE also owns two airlines—Dubai-based Emirates and Abu Dhabi–based Etihad Airways—both of which are vying to be leaders in luxury. Both Emirates and Etihad Airlines are launching fully enclosed, private in-flight bedrooms, starting what a Wall Street Journal article dubs a "luxury arms race." Emirates has 1,562 suites—private pod-like structures—on its fleet of 218 aircrafts. Each costs around $500,000 to produce and each is expected to retail at prices such as $26,000 for a round-trip ticket for a New York to Dubai flight (Jones 2014). Emirates President Tim Clark said in an interview, "It's all about privacy. Our new bedroom concept will take it to the next level." Emirates has an onboard bar, as well as shower facilities for which aircrafts need to carry 132 gallons of water weighing 1,100 pounds (which is equivalent of carrying five additional passengers).

Meanwhile, Etihad is launching "The Residence," which is a 125-square-foot apartment in the nose area of ten of its A380 superjumbo jets, an area notoriously difficult to use well. The apartment features a living room with a 32-inch television, a double bed, an en-suite bathroom, a lounge area, Vera Wang crystal, Wedgwood china, and a butler trained at the Savoy Hotel in London. Etihad's chefs for the first class create culinary masterpieces in the air, such as Arabic tiramisu. Before a flight, passengers are asked about their preferences like favorite drinks, colors, foods, magazines, newspapers, and luxury-brand toiletries. Priced at about 20,000 USD for a non-stop one-way trip between Abu Dhabi and London, ticket prices compare favorably with the cost of hiring a private jet for the same journey with one refueling stop—about 100,000 USD—according to Etihad Chief Executive James Hogan who says, "Most of the European carriers have retreated from first class. That gives us the opportunity to sell."

With amenities and services much like a hotel, yacht, or private jet, these airlines are betting on luxury to upscale their brand. Both Emirates and Etihad are gearing up to take on Qatar Airways, which considers itself the world's only five-star carrier. Qatar Airways is launching a business-class-only service from its Doha hub to London Heathrow on an Airbus A319 (Jones 2014; McCartney 2014).

Upscaling a product by using a luxury platform can extend to a variety of traditional consumer purchases as well. For instance, traditional Islamic women's wear—the black burqas and abayas (head scarves)—is being upscaled with embroidery and expensive embellishments like Austrian crystals (Rathore and Khan 2013).

Reversing the Brand Lifecycle

Many brands start off their brand lifecycle by being proprietary, patented, and priced at a premium. Over time, they typically evolve into a value-for-money brand and can even possibly become a low/competitively priced brand unless constant intervention prevents this from happening. Reversing the brand lifecycle means starting with a low price, moving up to becoming a value brand, and eventually becoming a premium brand. Japanese car makers like Toyota, Korean consumer electronics companies like Samsung, and Chinese telecom companies like Huawei have all successfully followed this path in the United States and other parts of the world. In other words, they entered these markets with a low price point and then upscaled their offer by offering added value. Often this strategy has to be adopted simply to remain competitive in a rapidly evolving and highly competitive marketplace.

Multinational, Nokia, once the world's leading cell phone marketer, transformed connectivity in emerging markets with its cheap, sturdy cell phones. Designed and priced to provide access to scores of first-time users, its cell phones weathered the rough and tumble usage, even in the deep interiors of Asia and Africa. With the rise of smart phones in emerging markets, however, consumers who were once happy to just be able to leapfrog the landline bottleneck now wanted more from their devices. Nokia struggled to remain competitive at the high end as well as at the low end, which witnessed an influx of cheaper phones from countries like China. Now Nokia is upscaling its products to offer smart phones (Jesdanun and Wilson 2014). Although such reverse innovation may be common for technology companies, it can be seen even in very traditional commodities market as well. Much like Nokia's experience, Sundrop, a leading cooking oil brand in India, found itself struggling in the very market it pioneered, and it had to upscale its brand to reverse its brand lifecycle.

Sundrop in India

Contributor: Piyush Sharma

Launched in 1989 by ITC Limited (a member of the British American Tobacco [BAT] group of the U.K.) as one of the first refined sunflower oil brands in India, Sundrop has become one of the largest premium brands in the Indian cooking oil market. Using its unique positioning as "the healthy oil for healthy people," Sundrop has led the movement for converting the cooking oil market from a commodity to a branded, packaged, consumer goods business.

Around the time of Sundrop's launch, the Indian cooking oil market was estimated at about 4.8 million tons (worth about 2.3 billion USD) per annum, out of which about 3.9 million tons (or 80 percent) came from unrefined oils; the packed, refined oil brands were mostly restricted to urban markets and only represented about 41,000 tons (i.e., less than 1 percent of the overall cooking oil market).

Hence, one of the key challenges for the brand was converting consumers from using unrefined, unpackaged, and unbranded cooking oil, sold in loose, unhygienic conditions, to a refined, packaged, branded (and, of course, substantially more expensive) version. Sundrop was launched in a small market for branded oils that was dominated by a refined groundnut/peanut oil brand, Postman, and several regional unrefined oil brands that were using mustard, peanut, and sesame oils. The company chose sunflower oil since it was perceived to be "healthy" and could be priced competitively against peanut oil, the key ingredient for Postman.

Since 1997, Sundrop has been owned and managed by Agro Tech Foods Ltd (ATFL), formerly ITC Agro-Tech Ltd, a public limited company affiliated with ConAgra Foods, Inc., one the world's largest food companies. ATFL markets food and food ingredients to consumers and institutional customers all over India, with almost 85 percent of its business coming from cooking oils. In the process of marketing its oil, Sundrop has created a huge franchise and an enviable portfolio of brands; the original Sunflower version is now available as Sundrop SuperLite, and many other blended avatars are also available such as Sundrop Nutrilite (Soya), Sundrop Heart (Rice Bran), and Sundrop GoldLite (Corn).

The Indian cooking oil market has grown to 18 million tons, of which nearly 50 percent is now branded (Kesireddy 2014). However, recently, most of this growth has been captured by lower-priced generic brands and the intense competition from these lower-priced players has squeezed the space at the top for premium brands, such as Sundrop and Saffola from Marico, forcing them to innovate. Therefore, ATFL's new vision for the Sundrop brand is to leverage its strong position in the Indian consumers' minds by extending it into new variants, as well as new product categories, such as snack foods, peanut butter, ready-to-cook meals, and other high-value, branded, packaged food items. This would move the brand up the value chain by extending its core proposition of health to higher-value products, thereby reversing its brand lifecycle (Parameswaran 2001).

Sundrop's market entry helped change a commodity market into a branded, packaged goods market, and its reason for upscaling was the entry of competitors vying to take advantage of the branded segment that Sundrop had pioneered. Rapoo's experience of reversing the brand lifecycle in China was different. This new, local entrant perceived a gap at the lower end of the market and grabbed its share from higher-end competitors that were just skimming the market. Later it upscaled its offerings to enter the high end of the market.

Rapoo in China

Contributor: Jun Yan

In 2007, after five years of success in original design manufacturing for mouse and keyboard dealers from America, Europe, and Asia, the founder and CEO of Hot Key Co., 36-year-old Hao Zeng, decided to create and launch his brand in China's market. In 2006, the 27 MHz (megahertz) chip was the dominant technology worldwide, but a Norwegian chip producer, Nordic, had just been the first to launch a new 2.4 GHz (gigahertz) chip that was hugely superior to the 27 MHz chip. Zeng realized that the steadily falling price of laptops was igniting demand, which would also boost the demand for wireless peripherals. He negotiated an agreement with Nordic and two other solution providers and, in May 2007, founded the Rapoo Corporation.

Two months later, the first 2.4 GHz Rapoo-branded wireless mouse model 7100 appeared on the market. Stylishly designed, multicolored, shaped to fit Asian hands, and priced at only 20 USD per unit, Rapoo's model 7100 sold 100,000 units in the first month and quickly became a bestseller. By 2008, Rapoo was designing more mice and keyboards. "The quality of Rapoo's mouse is equivalent to 80 percent of Logitech's, but the price is half," said Zeng. Logitech's top management in China had realized the threat from Rapoo, but their headquarters in America had not. Logitech finally began to partially cut prices by late 2009, but by late 2008, Rapoo's market share in China had skyrocketed to 42.7 percent while Logitech's had fallen to 27 percent.

Rapoo then expanded rapidly from the mouse business to wireless peripherals at the top end of the market. Gaming has a much higher performance requirement from a mouse, when compared to office usage, and to target this market, Rapoo launched the V8, its first luxury wireless gaming mouse, in March 2009. Three months later, Rapoo announced four mouse models that won Industrie Forum (IF) Design awards in Hannover, Germany. In April 2010, Rapoo's 2.4 GHz wireless headset, priced attractively at just 99 Yuan (about 15 USD) ignited a storm in the audio market.

In 2011, Rapoo was the first in the world to launch several products: the smallest NANO receiver in March, the dandelion technology in May (i.e., one receiver for all peripheral devices), and the Blade series (the thinnest keyboard—which won three IF design awards) and 5.8 GHz wireless technology in July. To support their upstream strategy, Rapoo hired over 1,000 people in their R&D department, accounting for one third of their total employees—a rare move in a developing country. By the end of 2011, Rapoo had grabbed a 56.3-percent market share, leaving Logitech with only 18.5 percent. This was how upscaling drove Rapoo's rise from an ODM to a high-tech-mid-priced market leader.

Leveraging the Country of Origin

The *country-of-origin effect* refers to how a country's reputation influences the perceived value of products originating from that country in overseas markets. Country of origin has proven effects on product attributes—both real and perceived—and can sometimes serve as an indicator of product quality (Elliott and Cameron 1994). It can have a negative or positive effect, depending on overall/general associations that consumers make about the country of origin or specific ones related to the product category. In emerging markets, the general perception is that items from the developed world have superior attributes. This works in favor of multinationals entering emerging markets because people are willing to spend more money on products from countries with favorable or superior country images. Examples include French wines, German cars, Italian designs, Korean and Japanese consumer electronics, American pop culture, and so on.

Foreign Brands in China

In China, products originating from developed countries like Western Europe, the United States, and Japan generate positive images and perception. The key attributes associated with luxury products from these countries are higher quality, durability, prestige, and better design. Due to the large availability of fake products in China, consumers trust brands not just based on the "Made in…" label, but also based on where the product was manufactured. To be on the safe side, those who can afford to simply shop abroad (Jap 2013).

Alibaba Group has recently tapped into this opportunity by launching Tmall Global, a website dedicated to foreign brands, which enables Chinese consumers to buy from abroad directly. Businesses opening stores on Tmall Global also sell brands from the developed world (Meng 2014). Products from the U.S. tend to generate a high level of confidence for Chinese consumers as far as quality is concerned. A Boston Consulting Group (BCG) study found that 61 percent of Chinese consumers would pay more for a product made in the United States, and when products are of similar price and quality, 47 percent would pick the "Made in USA" product, more than double the number who would pick the "Made in China" item. In fact, both in the United States and in China, more than 80 percent of respondents would pay more for U.S. goods.

Thus, American consumer brands can leverage their U.S. sourcing in countries like China, whereas they cannot in countries like France and Germany (Zieminski 2012).

With more than a million millionaires and more than 120 billionaires, China has a culture that celebrates flashy gift-giving and visible spending. Chinese consumers are more eager than others to embrace global wealth trends, and so China accounts for 29 percent of the world luxury market. Popular luxury items on the gifting list include handbags, perfumes, fine French red wine, and Swiss watches (Frizell 2014). The top 15 luxury brands include Louis Vuitton, Chanel, Apple, Hermes, Cartier, and Tiffany, but this list only boasts one Chinese brand—Maotai. In fact, Maotai is dropping in ranking because of alcohol regulation (Alice 2014). The crackdown on luxury gifting by the Chinese government, in addition to the slowdown in the number of Chinese who are joining the ranks of the super rich, has meant an overall decrease in spending on international brands, especially in the luxury segment. To bypass the crackdown, many Chinese are being discreet by buying luxury goods abroad instead of at home, but the Chinese market still remains a hot target for luxury marketers (Frizell 2014).

References

Agency of Partnership for Progress. n.d. "Invest in Morocco: Date Post-Harvest Handling and Packaging Activities."Accessed on May 21, 2014. www.mcc.gov/documents/investmentopps/bom-morocco-english-dates.pdf.

Alice. 2014. "Secrets to Luxury Life of Chinese Multimillionaires Revealed." *China Internet Watch*. February 18. Accessed on July 14, 2014. www.chinainternetwatch.com/6186/secrets-to-luxury-life-of-chinese-multimillioinaires-revealed.

BBC. 2013. "Vietnam's Masan Group in $200m KKR Deal." BBC News. January 9. Accessed on July 9, 2014. www.bbc.com/news/business-20954875.

Credit Suisse. 2013. "Emerging Consumer Survey 2013." Credit Suisse Research Institute. January. Accessed on February 8, 2016. http://online.wsj.com/public/resources/documents/Emerging ConsumerSurvey2013.pdf.

Cunha, Olavo, Masao Ukon, André Xavier, and Rim Abida. 2014. "Brazil's Next Consumer Frontier: Capturing Growth in the Rising Interior." BCG Perspectives. June 3. Accessed on February 8, 2016. www.bcgperspectives.com/content/articles/consumer_insight_globalization_brazil_next_consumer_frontier_capturing_growth_rising_interior.

Elliott, Gregory R., and Ross C. Cameron. 1994. "Consumer Perception of Product Quality and the Country-of-Origin Effect." *Journal of International Marketing* 2 (2): 49–62.

Frizell, Sam. 2014. "Despite Slowdown, the Cult of Luxury Grows in China." *Time*. February 13. Accessed on July 14, 2014. http://business.time.com/2014/02/13/despite-slowdown-the-cult-of-luxury-grows-in-china.

Glasner, Baruch, A. Botes, A. Zaid, and J. Emmens. n.d. "Chapter IX: Date Harvesting, Packinghouse Management and Marketing Aspects." *Date Palm Cultivation*. FAO Corporate Document Repository. Accessed on May 21, 2014. www.fao.org/docrep/006/y4360e/y4360e0d.htm.

Jap, Dr. Warveni. 2013. "Does 'Made in …' Matter to Chinese Consumers?" *The Journal of Global Business Management* 9 (1): 186–195.

Jesdanun, Anick, and Joseph Wilson. 2014. "Nokia Targets Emerging Markets with Android Phones." Associated Press on Yahoo! Finance. February 24. Accessed on July 2, 2014. http://finance.yahoo.com/news/nokia-targets-emerging-markets-android-093151309.html.

Jones, Rory. 2014. "Gulf Airlines Raise the Stake on Luxury." *The Wall Street Journal*. May 4. Accessed on June 10, 2014. http://on.wsj.com/1s6M84a.

Kesireddy, Raji Reddy. 2014. "Packaged Oil Offer 5–10% Margins, Making It Highly Attractive for the Edible Oil Producers." *The Economic Times*. May. Accessed on February 14, 2016. http://articles. economictimes.indiatimes.com/2014-05-09/news/49742808_ 1_oil-segment-sunrich-sunflower-oil-brand.

Kotler, Philip, and Kevin Lane Keller. 2016. *Marketing Management*, 15th ed. Upper Saddle River, NJ: Pearson Education, Inc.

Masan Group. n.d. Accessed on March 24, 2015. http:// masangroup.com.

McCartney, Scott. 2014. "Airlines Compete to Become First in First Class." *The Wall Street Journal*. December 17. Accessed on December 21 2014. www.wsj.com/articles/airlines-compete-to-become-first-in-first-class-1418852552.

Meng, Jing. 2014."Alibaba Site Offers Channel to Foreign Products." *ChinaDaily USA*. February 2. Accessed on July 14, 2014. http:// usa.chinadaily.com.cn/epaper/2014-02/20/content_17294571.htm.

Ngugi, Karanja, and Geoffrey Mutai. 2014. "Determinants Influencing Growth of Mobile Telephony in Kenya: A Case of Safaricom LTD." *International Journal of Social Sciences and Entrepreneurship* 1 (10): 218–230.

Parameswaran, M.G. 2001. "Sundrop: Positioning for Healthy Success." *FCB-ULKA Brand Building Advertising: Concepts and Cases*. Mumbai, India: Tata McGraw-Hill Education. 25–34.

Rapoza, Kenneth. 2014. "Meet Your New Emerging Market." *Forbes*. April 29. Accessed on July 9, 2014. www.forbes.com/sites/ kenrapoza/2014/04/29/meet-your-new-emerging-market.

Rastogi, Vaishali, Eddy Tamboto, and Dean Tong. 2013."Indonesia's Rising Middle-Class and Affluent Consumers." *BGG Perspectives*. March 5. Accessed on February 8, 2016. www.bcgperspectives .com/content/articles/center_consumer_customer_insight_ consumer_products_indonesias_rising_middle_class_affluent_ consumers.

Rathore, Vijaya, and Sobia Khan. 2013. "Burqa Reinvents Itself, Makes a Global Fashion Statement." *The Economic Times*. July 5. Accessed on July 15, 2014. http://epaper.timesofindia.com/Repository/ml.asp?Ref=RVRELzIwMTMvMDcvMDUjQXIwMTUwMA.

Seth, Akshat, Amit Saharia, and Debashish Mukherjee. 2013. "Winning in Food in Emerging Markets: One Size Does Not Fit All." AT Kearney. April. Accessed on May 20, 2014. www.atkearney.com/consumer-products-retail/ideas-insights/featured-article/-/asset_publisher/KQNW4F0xInID/content/winning-in-food-in-emerging-markets-one-size-does-not-fit-all/10192.

Sheth, Jagdish N. and Rajendra S.Sisodia. 2012. *The 4 A's of Marketing: Creating Value for Customers, Companies, and Society*. New York: Routledge.

Zawya, Oxford Business Group. 2014. "Moroccan Dates to Support Regional Development." Morocco on the Move. February 3. Accessed on May 21, 2014. http://moroccoonthemove.com/2014/02/03/moroccan-dates-support-regional-development-zawya-oxford-business-group/#sthash.BRhmaaeo.dpbs.

Zieminski, Nick. 2012. "'Made in USA' Label Popular in China, Too: Study," *The Huffington Post*. November 15. Accessed on May 10, 2014. www.huffingtonpost.com/2012/11/15/made-in-usa-label-popular_n_2137583.html.

6

Managing Reach

Multinationals are accustomed to technology-driven supply chains where products move quickly, logistics are generally error free, payments are automated, and inventory management is highly efficient. Even drone deliveries seem plausible. Moving from that to the reality of deliveries by dusty oxen carts is not easy. Marred by the lack or even nonexistence of basic infrastructure to support supply chains, emerging markets pose challenges ranging from roads, electricity, water, and storage to banking, payment, and point-of-sale. Roads are often blocked or in need of repair, transportation breaks down, slow moving vehicles traverse narrow lanes, and suppliers and retailers do business with cash and a handshake.

Moreover, emerging markets are large, informal, and typically controlled by sociopolitical institutions rather than businesses. Channels are highly fragmented with seven to nine different middle men (Sheth 2011). Lack of market research data impedes the understanding of distribution complexities, market and consumer heterogeneity, cultural and regional differences and needs, and sudden competitive or consumer entrants (de Uster et al. 2012). Poor communication infrastructure, including digital connectivity, impedes information flow, and this is compounded by governmental inefficiencies, regulatory hurdles, and the absence of logistics providers. Often this means businesses have to build and manage their infrastructure, eliminate middle men, improve supply chain efficiencies, and forge into rural areas.

Emerging markets are home to several of the 44 *megacities* in the world (urban areas of 10 million or more people such as Jakarta, Manila, Delhi, Mumbai, Shanghai, and Shenzen), and a host of lower-income countries from Asia and Africa are gearing up to join their ranks (Kotkin and Cox 2013). Most economic activities tend to take place in the 600 largest urban centers that are practically quasi-nations (Kotler and Kotler 2014). The high density—over 29,000 people per kilometer in Mumbai compared to fewer than 8,000 in New York—creates a logistical challenge (SupplyChainBrain 2011). Though people in megacities earn about 80 percent more than rural consumers, they still prefer to shop at local stores to avoid traffic congestion or because of poor local transport.

Thus, companies have to rethink ways of providing *accessibility*, which is the extent to which customers can easily acquire and use the product. This means ensuring the right amount of product availability as well as a convenient way for consumers to acquire such products (Sheth and Sisodia 2012). In this chapter we focus on the age-old retailing mantra that, "it's all about location, location, location" because companies need to be where the customers are. The strategies we offer in this chapter for providing accessibility by managing with what exists in these countries, means businesses must be creative in the following: 1) adapting to traditional channels, 2) navigating indigenous channels, 3) developing channel partnerships, 4) building for access, and 5) managing channel ownership.

Adapting to Traditional Channels

The perception of oxen carts in a rural landscape often undermines the thriving network of local distribution avenues in these markets. Traditional distributors and retailers exist in emerging markets, and multinationals often do have experience serving mom and pop stores, but neighborhood stores in emerging markets look markedly different and operate on a much smaller scale. Retail stores in emerging markets may be tiny homes with a front room or porch that serves as a store front, or they may be a corner store or kiosk crammed with a wide range of goods serviced by a retailer/owner who serves customers from behind a counter and therefore exercises an enormous influence on the brands displayed, offered, and recommended for purchase (Diaz, Lacayo, and Salcedo 2007).

Neighborhood Stores in Latin America

Brazil has more than a million neighborhood stores, Mexico has more than 800,000, and Colombia has more than 400,000. Neighborhood stores account for 25 to 50 percent of all grocery sales in Latin America, 95 percent of beer sales in Colombia, and 80 percent of carbonated beverage sales in Mexico. Such stores are located in neighborhoods where consumers may not have transportation options. Since they do not pay taxes and have low overhead, neighborhood stores are nimble and resilient enough to match the prices of large, modern retailers (Diaz, Lacayo, and Salcedo 2007).

Neighborhood stores typically have little or no technology, deal predominantly in cash, lack access to credit, and vary in their level of skills, resources, and reach. Often, large packaged goods companies sell directly to such stores in return for lucrative merchandising, access to coolers and shelves, or even exclusive distribution. Neighborhood stores typically offer fresh produce, local brands, convenient locations, and home delivery, and they can be specialized by product category, such as medicines and produce. Due to their low overhead and long-term relationships with customers, neighborhood stores are also able to offer credit.

Often, retailers find that these stores struggle with basic infrastructure such as electricity, water, or access to credit, and retailers have to help them address these challenges. Small store owners are appreciative even of companies painting their walls or roofs with their logos and advertising because it makes their stores attractive. Given limited shelf space, companies have to be creative in creating visibility for their products—for example, providing short, one or two meter racks, with a few shelves that can be lined horizontally against a wall or can flank a cooler. Sometimes racks can have wheels to serve as carts. Some companies provide coolers painted in their logo colors, which serves to advertise their brand, while also making the store attractive and the owner happier (Butler and Tischler 2015).

In Mexico, many companies, including multinationals, find it difficult to be accepted by these stores due to preexisting agreements that the stores have with other major brands. One option is for them to route their supply through wholesalers that supply to these stores. For example, Sam's Club has a *Mi Tienda* program that has a Walmart format offering credit and ready-made packages of assorted goods, like cleaning products and canned foods, for small shop owners (Bolio et al. 2014)

Navigating Indigenous Channels

Emerging markets offer numerous indigenous channels that multinationals may never have served in their home countries, such as hawkers or vendors carrying baskets of goods or pushing wooden handcarts or setting up a counter at a street market. These individual entrepreneurs change their place of operation and the wares they have for sale depending on convenience, demand, and resource availability. They wander through neighborhoods peddling their wares or congregate at central locations to create marketplaces.

Such markets have existed since medieval times and were historically associated with peasant economies, based on bilateral bargaining—an ancient informal trading practice. The markets are known by different names: *bazaars* or *mandis* in India, *jua kalis* in East Africa, and *souqs* or *bazaars* in the Middle East. They are large, multipurpose, bustling hubs of activity, usually in open-air marketplaces, that have a collection of shops, street vendors, roadside stalls, or farmers' markets. Often sellers are clustered category-wise and they operate late hours, well near midnight. They serve over half of the urban populations in their respective countries and provide income to poor rural and urban traders. Their informal structure and lack of formal regulation means that customers get fair price bargains and quality products. However, traders usually lack insurance coverage, the markets have poor hygiene, and sales pose taxation problems for authorities (Meier and Rauch 2008).

In Kenya, Safaricom, the largest telecommunications company, set up several M-Pesa stalls in *jua kalis*. *M-Pesa* is a mobile phone–based money transfer system that requires a simple, no-frills cell phone to which money is loaded in the form of transferable airtime. It can be used for retail purchases, bill payments, or even transfers to other people. Its huge success in Kenya was driven in part by Safaricom's adoption of such unusual distribution channels that helped them reach even the poorest sections of Kenyan society. Multinational companies like The Coca-Cola Company and PepsiCo also routinely have beverage vendors in street market stalls in India, the Middle East, and Kenya (McCormick and Pedersen 1996). Street markets can even specialize in commodities such as iron. The Zaveri Bazaar of Mumbai is known for its precious stones— diamond, for example. Some street markets like the Gold Souk of Dubai specializes in jewelry and manage to attract not just buyers, but also tourists.

Gold Souk in Dubai

The souks in the Middle East are self-contained, unified markets featuring narrow passageways. They serve as commercial centers for low-income earners, but interestingly enough, they also sell products to the wealthy (McCormick and Pedersen 1996). Dubai boasts a perfume souk, a textile souk, a spice souk, and a world-famous gold souk. The Gold Souk is located in the heart of Dubai's commercial business district and it has been attracting Indian and Iranian sellers since the 1940s, bolstered by Dubai's free-trade policies (Sherwood 2005). The most common item sold is gold, and daily transactions are approximately 10 tons, worth billions of dollars. India has been the chief source of the gold and it is also the major consumer, accounting for a total of 68 percent of the gold trade in Dubai (Struijk 2013).

The per capita consumption of gold jewelry in the Arab world and India is the highest in the world, but branded jewelry only accounts for around 5 percent of all jewelry sales. Lack of branding has resulted in nearly 80 percent of Middle East shoppers shopping online for jewelry from overseas vendors. Also, even though the government regulates the quality of jewelry sold, there is considerable bargaining and some street vendors do sell fakes (Puri 2014). Therefore, the government is taking steps to grow the branded jewelry market by providing infrastructure, transparency, competitive freight rates, and no value-added tax. They are also strictly controlling the quality of the gold sold (Mathur 2007). Although dominated by small family-owned businesses, a number of international brands like Damas have found that they can considerably widen their reach with their presence in the souks rather than by just being located in large malls or other modern-format retail stores (Struijk 2013). Other big brands at the Gold Souk include Dhamani jewelers for exclusive 99-facet diamond cuts, Marhaba Jewellery for European-styled jewelry, and Joyalukkas for Indian designs (Dubaisouks.net n.d.).

Despite a lack of even basic infrastructure, squatter communities such as those in Mumbai, Rio de Janeiro, and Kenya are home to 800 to 900 million people and are thriving centers of industry, enterprise, and innovation. Some street markets in Lagos have transformed into huge global operations. Alaba International Market has sophisticated networks for international trade with countries such as China to import mobile phones, consumer electronics, and car parts (Gilbert 2015). Street stands in cities like Hong Kong and Dubai sell Louis Vuitton bags, because in those countries these are perfectly acceptable methods of distribution for luxury goods (Dumitrescu and Vinerean 2010). However, such venues can also be a conduit for counterfeit trade selling to unsuspecting and even expectant consumers.

The Coca-Cola Company in India

Muhtar Kent (2013), chairman and CEO of The Coca Cola Company recounts Coca-Cola's experience in India when the company was forced to close its operations in 1977 due to regulatory restrictions. They returned in 1993 when India liberalized its economy and found that India's population was over 1.12 billion and that over 70 percent of them still lived in its villages. Both urban and rural Indians routinely shopped at small neighborhood stores instead of supermarkets, but at the same time organized retail was also growing rapidly. Faced with the multitude of nonretail access points, as well as new, modern retail options, Kent decided to "see the Indian market as it is, not as we wished it to be." This included being cognizant of the new generation of tech-savvy young Indians and the rise of mobile commerce.

Unlike other countries where Coca-Cola could simply negotiate display and supply, in India Coca-Cola had to think outside the box to keep their drinks cold by overcoming challenges like lack of regular electricity supply or maybe not even a connection to the power grid. When Atul Singh, their Indian CEO at the time, saw their beverages being stocked in conventional ice chests with very little ice, or sold by vendors using wooden pushcarts he partnered with Mumbai-based Western Refrigeration to develop the eKOCool, a solar-powered pushcart that cools the contents of the cart as well as generates electricity for recharging mobile phones or electric lanterns. The eKOCool became part of Coca-Cola's 5by20 initiative to empower 5 million women entrepreneurs across the world by 2020. It was then tested in other emerging markets such as South Africa and Turkey (Moye 2013). Coca-Cola launched several other similar initiatives, traditional and indigenous retailers get access to credit and provide water to their bottlers. They also became engaged in improving the lives of entire villages. By 2020, India is expected to be one of Coca-Cola's top five global markets.

Developing Channel Partnerships

New channels can be developed by collaborating with a variety of partners, such as nongovernmental organizations (NGOs), supply chain members, customers, communities, employees, or even other corporate entities. Partnering with NGOs is called establishing *cross-sector alliances*. A well-known example of this is Hindustan Unilever Limited's (HUL's) *Project Shakti* in India where partnerships with government-established women's self-help groups (SHGs) in rural villages empowered women through collective savings and helped them become micro-entrepreneurs. To increase its market share, HUL had to reach 500,000 villages with less than 2,000 inhabitants that were poorly connected and lacked a retail distribution network, advertising coverage, and even roads. HUL trained these women in sales and bookkeeping and delivered products to them that they would then sell door to door to consumers and small retailers in their local area. In this way, the women learned to save money and borrow from/

lend to each other rather than from usury moneylenders (Rangan and Rajan 2007). More recently, HUL reached out to the husbands of these women, financing the purchase of bicycles that the men use for extending reach and growing sales (Unilever website, n.d.). They also forge partnerships with existing distributor/retailer networks. In China, when SANY was entering a new market, it adopted a new-to-the-industry approach for managing distributors by taking into account industry and country level factors, including *guanxi*.

SANY Heavy Industry Co., Ltd.

Contributor: Yaping Chang

SANY, a heavy machinery company, was founded in 1994, in China. From concrete machinery, SANY expanded rapidly to excavators, truck cranes, crawler cranes, pile driving machinery, road construction machinery, and, more recently, into rotary drilling rigs. They invested in and built research and development (R&D) and manufacturing plants in India, the U.S., Germany, and Brazil, and established 169 sales centers and over 2,000 service stations, employing over 7,500 service engineers globally.

In 2004, SANY encountered a critical distribution challenge when they entered the excavator industry. They were no longer able to use their direct sales model because they had a large number of geographically dispersed buyers of excavators for whom they had to build a new dealer network and quickly segment the market, while also competing with established international brands like Caterpillar and Komatsu at the high end, and Korean and domestic brands at the low and middle end. An industry analysis helped them realize that (1) dealers in the excavator market demanded high after-sales service for free, but they were not used to paying for it; (2) *guanxi*, the practice of forming a network of mutually beneficial relationships, played an important role in the business-to-business (B2B) market in China; (3) local dealers were typically short-term, profit oriented; and (4) selling heavy machinery was mainly credit based and outstanding payments were a common problem.

Working with these new realizations, SANY devised a channel-management strategy that was unique for their industry in China.

They contracted one exclusive distributor for each province (or two for large provinces) and offered them a policy similar to that of a consignment agent where SANY collected its payments when the distributor received payment for the machinery and they also reimbursed the distributors for the cost of after-sales service. SANY set up a specialized information system to enable close monitoring. Thus, SANY built solid partnerships with a select set of loyal distributors who were rich in *guanxi*, but short of capital.

Partnering also extends to collaborating and training employees to help them set up and operate new work processes that improve an existing channel or build a new one. Such partnerships involve communicating the organization's vision while also helping employees understand their role in achieving that vision, their potential for effecting change, and the outcomes of their actions. This is even more important in service businesses where front-line employees are the key touch-point for customers and corporate reputations are strongly based on these interactions. In many emerging markets, access to banking is limited, and so process improvements such as the ones undertaken by Sberbank are crucial for expanding reach.

Sberbank of Russia

Contributor: Vera Rebiazina

Established in 1841, Sberbank is a commercial bank in Russia; it provides a broad range of banking services to individuals and corporate clients as well as state-owned, sub-federal units and municipalities. With over 100 million individual customers (more than 70 percent of the Russian population) and 1 million corporate clients (out of the 4.5 million legal entities in Russia), Sberbank is one of the largest and most prominent financial institutions in Central and Eastern Europe with a notable presence in the global financial market.

Historically customers had a negative attitude toward the bank because of its old-style service, long queues, and limited use of information technology. It used to be viewed as reliable, but not client-oriented. Poor customer relationships, service systems, and skills had resulted in inefficient utilization of its distribution networks, a low rate of cross-selling, and low profitability of product sales. Customers used to perceive Sberbank negatively compared to its competitors in terms of the time it took to make decisions, the complexity of its processes and procedures, its customer interaction and communication levels, and the general convenience and functionality of the branches. In addition, Sberbank's risk management systems were insufficiently formalized and, therefore, not only ineffective, but also expensive. These problems were systemic, resulting from weaknesses in the corporate culture due to excessive bureaucracy, insufficient responsibility for end results, and the quality of customer service.

In 2009, under the consulting firm McKinsey & Company's advice, Sberbank embarked on a major project, the Sberbank Production System (SPS), to streamline and rationalize all of its processes, to build a systemic capability for continuous improvement, and to shape the staff's mindset and attitudes. They first addressed their customer facing departments and followed it up with a detailed analysis of their back-end processes, optimizing 127 business processes by 2011. This resulted in an increase of 11.5 percent in workforce productivity and 25 percent in efficiency. They also improved their service quality for loan products, increased customers' financial literacy, reduced customer waiting time, created a complaint and claims management system, and increased customer feedback via social media. In addition, they partnered with their employees by changing work processes, improving working conditions, introducing flexible work schedules, and providing training for process optimization. By automating systems and moving away from paper bankbooks to card-based services, they helped free up employees' time, which was then directed toward improving engagement with customers. Sberbank's service quality and customer satisfaction have increased dramatically as a result of their distribution system transformation.

Increasingly, companies are being called upon to move beyond their customer and investor focus in order to pay attention to the entire community and the ecosystem in which they operate. We discuss the importance of partnering with the community and integrating into the ecosystem in greater detail in Chapter 9, but here we focus on how members of communities can help companies widen their reach.

E Health Point in India

HealthPoint Services India (HSI) was founded in 2009 in order to democratize healthcare in rural India. HSI set up eHealthPoint clinics (eHPs) in villages in the state of Punjab in north India to provide clean drinking water, medicines, comprehensive diagnostic tools, and a "doctor" via telemedicine. Each clinic was self-sufficient, with its own power, water, and Internet tower. Doctors based in the city of Bhatinda would appear on a large television screen and use web cameras to visually examine the patient with the assistance of an onsite nurse and modern equipment. Lab tests would be performed and good quality, genuine medicine would be dispensed on site.

The modern, Western medicine that HIS offered through eHPs was far removed from the local healers or medicine men that most villagers depended on for healthcare. eHPs were also much better equipped and better staffed than the government clinics where people often waited for hours only to receive poor-quality or inadequate care. However, simply providing a better facility and service was not sufficient for adoption.

HSI had to launch several initiatives to integrate eHPs into the community. To create awareness about medical issues and solutions HSI hired two local women as healthcare promoters to visit homes. It hired clinical staff from the same village and trained them for the job. It also conducted educational camps. By creating employment opportunities, HSI was not just integrating into the community but also leveraging the relationships that its staff had with key influencers and consumers in the villages to educate and spread awareness.

All eHP clinics had taps outside the clinic that provided clean drinking water and villagers could fill their containers for free. Slowly, as word spread about the supply of drinking water and awareness built up about the importance of clean water for health, people began congregating at the clinics to collect water. This gave them an opportunity to chat with the staff, be invited in to examine the clinic and its facilities, and to ask questions about the services offered. Thus, HSI's grass-roots-level partnerships with local communities for hiring and educating created access to healthcare solutions. Seventy percent of India's population lives in its 600,000 or more villages where healthcare is inadequate, providing HSI with a huge expansion opportunity (Hamermesh, Sinha, and Vrolyk 2012; eHealthpoint.com n.d.; CHMI n.d.).

Partnering with local companies is also a common market-entry strategy used by many multinationals. Apart from know-how and established management teams, local partners also have existing distribution networks. In China, for example, multinationals have been using joint ventures as a new market-entry strategy for over 30 years. Increasingly, however, companies know they need to partner with companies that share their strategic goals. For instance, in the recent past, GlaxoSmithKline has partnered with Shenzen Neptunus Interlong Bio-Tech Company and Novartis has partnered with Zhejiang Tianyuan Bio-Pharmaceutical Company because the Chinese partners have access to government vaccine-procurement programs, talent, R&D, and an entrepreneurial mindset. (Bosshart, Luedi, and Wang 2010).

Building for Access

In the absence of adequate systems for providing consumers with access, companies may have no choice but to build it themselves. Navigating large geographical areas with a complex network of cities and towns is challenging especially when it comes down to the last mile. Adding infrastructure or building a channel where it is inadequate or completely missing requires deep pockets, an appetite for taking on high risk, and the ability to cross regulatory hurdles and obtain multiple clearances. Many emerging and transitional economies, unable to build their own infrastructure, look to other countries and foreign investors. For example, China has signed an 8.5 billion USD deal for a rail link between Kenya's Indian Ocean port of Mombasa and Nairobi that will eventually link to neighboring countries—Uganda, Rwanda, Burundi, and South Sudan. Funded by the Export-Import Bank of China, this will replace the British colonial-era line, and it will likely have a huge economic impact on the trade between the countries (AFP News

Agency 2014). Manufacturers in emerging markets often have to build their own captive infrastructure, especially since they tend to be located in interior, less developed areas, away from major cities and towns. For Shark Design Studio, a a retail design service provider, the lack of infrastructure and poor quality of supplies spurred them to expand beyond design services to set up their own manufacturing.

Shark Design Studio Private Limited in India

Contributors: Meghna Rishi and Sanjaya S. Gaur

Shark Design Studio Private Limited (Shark Designs), established in India in 1999, is one of the largest design studios in India. It offers turnkey solutions to national and international retail brands that would otherwise source such retail fixtures and design services from outside of India at high cost. Their retail designing services include everything from design to execution, like designing the store layout, selecting materials, and synergizing the retail space with the brand personality and existing store design of their retail client. Shark Design custom manufactures each element of the design and sets up the entire retail store for the brand. Manish Jain, director of Shark Designs explains:

> We understood that retail is growing in India but organized retail is still nascent. Clients are not satisfied with the alignment between the design and manufacturing services. Architects used to offer design capabilities but the execution capabilities of the manufacturing vendor seldom translated the architect's design accurately into the real fixture or structure. Shark was initiated to bridge this gap by offering "Design-Build Strategy" expertise to the market.

Struggling with infrastructural issues, such as limited water supply, broken roads, and less than two hours of electricity a day, Shark Designs decided to build its own captive infrastructure, use their own trucks, and train their drivers extensively. They worked closely with their vendors and supply-chain partners to better control delivery and ensure timely access. This improved their overall functioning, increasing their retail store rollouts. As a result, they have added companies like Frito-Lay, Yamaha, Sony, Xerox, Microsoft, Puma, and Kenneth Cole to their list of satisfied clients.

Although the earlier examples focused on traditional ways of thinking about building up channels via infrastructure, another way to think about channels is building a completely separate and parallel distribution network, such as in Islamic banking, which we described in Chapter 3. Religion has the ability to influence many aspects of an individual's personal and professional life. The complex process involved in expanding access is important to know for companies that seek to provide *halaal*-compliant products to adherents of the Muslim faith.

Halaal Foods

Islam is the fastest growing and the second largest religion in the world. The Muslim population is expected to grow to 2.2 billion by 2030 according to the Pew Research Center (Rarick et al. 2012). *Halaal* refers to anything that is allowed under Sharia law. Adhering to the *halaal* code in foods means that meat must be prepared in ways that ensure certain hygiene standards and norms. A *halaal* committee monitors and regulates *halaal* suppliers for appropriate product groups, and a *halaal* purchasing team reviews contracts to meet the Islamic banking and financing principles as well as to replace animal-based ingredients with plant-based ingredients (Tieman and Ghazali 2013). Producers of *halaal* food (poultry, meat, and freshwater fish) must use feed that is in-line with *halaal* policy as well as use the slaughtering technique that is permissible under Sharia law. They must also ensure that the transportation, storage, and warehousing of *halaal* products are clearly separated to avoid cross-contamination (Zailani et al. 2010).

Getting *halaal* certification is the main way to widen access to products for adherents of the Muslim faith, but this is an expensive process. There is not one overarching globally-standardized *halaal* authority that can ensure and maintain that the production process meets the requirements set out by Sharia law. Instead, each country has its own *halaal*-certifying agency. Saudi Arabia has established complex standards known as the *Gulf Standard* and *Saudi Standard*. Under these standards, all imported products must be *halaal* certified by a recognized Islamic organization in the exporting country and the certificates have to be endorsed by the National U.S.-Arab Chamber of Commerce or consulate of the importing country (Riaz and Chaudry 2003). The process of establishing a recognized and acceptable certification is complicated since it involves buy-in from religious leaders, multiple agencies, and vendors/suppliers. It also relies on consumer education and awareness. Often, the certification process has to be repeated in multiple countries, many of which may differ in their interpretation and understanding of religious norms.

The Asia-Pacific region has the largest Muslim population in the world at one billion people. Major importers of *halaal* products are mostly Muslim-majority countries in the Middle East and North Africa. Saudi Arabia and the United Arab Emirates (UAE) are the major import markets in the region and Brazil is the largest exporter to these two countries. Other large exporters of *halaal* products include Indonesia, China, India, Malaysia, Thailand, the Gulf Cooperation Council members, Australia, New Zealand, Singapore, and South Africa. In Singapore, even though Muslims are a minority, non-Muslim consumers trust the quality and hygiene of *halaal* products, and so international food brands like McDonald's, Kentucky Fried Chicken, and Taco Bell have gone 100 percent *halaal* (Riaz and Chaudry 2003).

Channel development is a critical requirement for rural penetration because of geographical dispersion and lack of connectivity. Avon saleswomen are a classic rural marketing example; they travel by ferries, small boats, and canoes to reach isolated Brazilian towns in the Amazon to sell products in return for payments such as chickens, eggs, gold, fruit, vegetables, and services. This nontraditional channel has helped to push Avon to the head of the Brazilian cosmetics market (Brunke et al. 2013). A number of companies have successfully emulated Avon's approach, for example, Living Goods in Uganda.

Living Goods in Uganda

Living Goods sells affordable healthcare in Uganda by sending their salespeople to poor consumers in isolated villages to deliver healthcare products such as sanitary pads, soap, deworming pills, iodized salt, and so on. This microfranchise model is self-sustaining since the business has an "assured supply chain, low-cost inputs (due to bulk purchases by the franchiser), training for managers and a trusted brand" (Rosenberg 2012). Living Goods trains local village women in basic healthcare for two weeks, covering medical issues such as disease prevention, diagnostic methods, common cures for diseases like malaria, and knowing when to refer a patient to a health clinic. After they finish basic and field training for two weeks, the village women return to their villages and go door to door introducing themselves and the Living Goods brand; they also use the time to inquire about the health of the family members.

The work and progress Living Goods has accomplished in healthcare is remarkable and especially significant because local hospitals in the region are commonly out of supplies. Moreover, Living Goods has mixed the door-to-door model with mobile and enterprise technology to help empower women in the franchise. These microentrepreneurs can log their visits and sales on their mobile phones and remain in contact with their clients and with Living Goods. Overall the company aims to "save lives, empower entrepreneurs to earn a living, increase access to innovative devices, and at the same time, create a financially sustainable business" (Cisco n.d.). The microfranchisees of Living Goods serve as a valuable and successful alternative to traditional healthcare while promoting their goods and services through entrepreneurship and increasing accessibility through untapped/nontraditional channels.

Managing Channel Ownership

Increasingly, companies are adopting multiple channel strategies to expand in emerging markets and often these strategies vary across countries. If companies have full channel ownership, it enables them to have a distribution chain that grows at an organic rate in a controlled manner, giving them greater control over their customers' brand and shopping experience. On the other hand, using a franchise model enables rapid expansion with lower investment on the company's part. However, training becomes critical so that franchisees can understand what the repercussions are to the brand if they fail to comply with guidelines (Wehner 2008). Managing good relationships with franchisees allows both parties to have higher exchange of resources, competencies, and knowledge in order to reduce opportunism. Trust-based franchiser relationships ensure better governance, enforcement of agreements, and adherence to standards. In turn, franchisees gain greater autonomy and are motivated to introduce suggested changes in routines and adopt innovations (Dant and Gundlach 1999).

Because franchises are generally run by locals, they are better able to understand consumer expectations toward the product. The company's choice of channel structure depends on their overall marketing penetration strategy. Apart from the distribution realities of the market, as discussed earlier in this chapter, companies must also keep market conditions in mind—including factors such as geographical distance, cultural distance, uncertainty avoidance, individualism, political stability, corruption, gross domestic product, the efficiency of contract enforcement, and nascent entrepreneurship—when they consider channel ownership options (Baena 2012). Luxury brands have typically owned their own stores in order to maintain control over the customer experience. In emerging markets, they have also had to experiment with partnerships and the use of agents.

Luxury Brands in Emerging Markets

Consumers in emerging markets are warming up to luxury brands, and socially such consumption is now more likely to be admired rather than perceived as ostentatious. After establishing a presence in well-known emerging nations and their big cities, luxury brands are moving into second- and third-tier cities as well as eyeing what may be considered the "emerging markets of the future." Recently Louis Vuitton has ventured into Ulan Bator (Mongolia), and Almaty (Kazakhstan). Africa's most developed luxury sector is in South Africa, which has 60 percent of Africa's millionaires, but many luxury brands do not yet operate there, leaving great potential for new entrants (Moorad 2014).

Many brands are moving from stand-alone stores, for example, in luxury hotels to megastore spaces/venues. For example, the Dior Cosmetic boutique in Shanghai's Nanjing Road, which was set up in 2003, was considered the most luxurious at the time, and China was only the third country in the world to have such a Dior store (KPMG 2007). Such megastores can showcase an extended range of products, which helps luxury brands educate consumers as well as inspire consumption. France's LVMH, the world's largest luxury goods company, claims that 40 percent of its world sales come from Asia, so in 2013, they announced their goal of opening eight new stores over the next two years in India. Although most luxury brands maintain strict retail store formats in order to retain their global brand positioning, some, like Burberry and Zegna minimize/ reduce costs with no-frills stores or franchises in secondary cities in order to make higher returns (*The Economist* 2004).

No doubt full ownership enables luxury brands to tightly control the shopping experience in markets where brand knowledge has to be built from scratch, but the investments required for establishing a brand-congruent retail presence pose huge risks. Louis Vuitton was funded by the deep pockets of its parent company, LVMH, in order to retain full ownership of its stores. Some brands have to reduce risk by going the partnership route. For example, the U.S. watch retailer, Tourneau, established a joint venture with Hong Kong's Peace Mark Limited and International Watch Group to open luxury stores in mainland China, Hong Kong, Taiwan, and Macau. Brands like Polo Ralph Lauren and Brooks Brothers prefer to use agents instead of stepping in themselves. Home-grown luxury brands such as Ports International are also adopting the retail strategies of multinationals, which then enable their expansion outside their country (KPMG 2007).

Full ownership of the channel carries larger risk. So recent changes in the global economy as well as in emerging markets have compelled many luxury brands to rethink or even slow down their retail expansion. Bulgari closed its only mono-brand store in Mumbai, while Fendi, Botegga Veneta, and Chanel closed stores in the Russian city of Tekaterinburg (Minder 2013).

The previous example pertains to retail stores that are at the front end of the retail chain. However, channels in emerging markets are fairly complicated and must include consideration of the entire supply chain, especially the downstream components where modernization tends to lag. Grupo Los Grobo from Argentina developed a business platform for producing and commercializing agricultural commodities while also challenging traditional land ownership.

Grupo Los Grobo in Argentina

Contributors: Jaqueline Pels and Tomás Andrés Kidd

Grupo Los Grobo (Los Grobo) is a leading agribusiness and investment company in Latin America; it came up with an innovative business model that challenges the land-control paradigm of traditional agriculture. Established in 1910 by Gustavo Grobocopatel as an agricultural family business, Los Grobo is a B2B company that operates in agricultural production (soy, maize, and wheat) and provision of services (grains purchase, storage, financial assistance, etc.). Gustavo passed the business down to his two sons, Adolfo and Jorge, but in 1984, when Adolfo's son, also named Gustavo, entered the family business, he realized that to gain scale, lower fixed costs, and reduce risk, he needed to outsource as much as possible.

This was a bold move as it implied erasing land ownership from the equation. The challenge was to reconfigure and reconceptualize the traditional control-paradigm creating a new business model that would allow this shift without losing information of the overall agro-process. Traditionally, farmers retained control over the farm lands and ownership passed down through generations; even when multinationals entered the market, they would purchase the land and gain ownership. However, Gustavo proposed a model based on partnerships rather than ownerships.

Los Grobo positioned itself as a coordinator of the entire knowledge network, linking suppliers, shareholders, landowners, investors, and technicians as partners without any exclusivity agreements imposed on them. This changed the focus of the business from measuring success by the number of hectares you farmed to measuring success in the number of partners with whom you operated. Gustavo explained, "partnering guarantees a better identification of new business opportunities and a lower investment and financial risk.... The day my partners choose solely to work with Los Grobo is the day that the company fails as we need competitive drive to generate new innovative services and procedures."

Over 90 percent of the farms coordinated by Los Grobo do not belong to them; instead they belong to private landowners or group of investors that partner up with the company. Los Grobo's differentiation from its competitors is not by the actors, activities, and resources, but by the interactions between them. By sharing risks, information, and knowledge, trust and mutual commitment played a more important role in business development than formal agreements. To keep the network virtuous and create win-win solutions for all partners, they introduced GroboSoft, a GPS and Wi-Fi device that allows members of Los Grobo's network to input significant agricultural data on the spot and access crop reports and recommendations shared by other partners. Thus, land rental and an inclusive knowledge network allowed for flexible farming and made Los Grobo a nodal actor in the agricultural supply chain. "With our system, an agronomy student who doesn't come from a family that owns land can enter our network, become our partner, and invest money and knowledge in a joint operation," remarked Gustavo.

References

AFP News Agency. 2014. "China to Build Railway Linking East Africa." *AlJazeera*. May 12. Accessed on August 6, 2013. www.aljazeera.com/news/africa/2014/05/china-build-railway-linking-east-africa-201451263352242135.html.

Baena, Verónica. 2012. "Market Conditions Driving International Franchising in Emerging Markets." *International Journal of Emerging Markets* 7(1): 49–71.

Bolio, Eduardo, Jaana Remes, Tomás Lajous, James Manyika, Eugenia Ramirez, and Morten Rossé. 2014. "Bridging the Gap: Modern and Traditional Retail in Mexico." April. Accessed on April 27, 2016. www.mckinseyonmarketingandsales.com/ bridging-the-gap-modern-and-traditional-retail-in-mexico.

Bosshart, Stephan, Thomas Luedi, and Emma Wang. 2010. "Past Lessons for China's New Joint Ventures." *McKinsey Quarterly*. December. Accessed on February 13, 2016. www.mckinsey.com/ business-functions/strategy-and-corporate-finance/our-insights/ past-lessons-for-chinas-new-joint-ventures.

Brunke, Bernd, Christopher Angoulvant, Wilifried Aulbur, Andreas Bauer, Benno van Dongen, William Downey, Duce Gotora, et al. 2013. "Think: Act Study." Roland Berger Strategy Consultants. January. Accessed on June 7, 2014. www.rolandberger.at/media/ pdf/Roland_Berger_Studie_8_Billion_Strategies_20130128.pdf.

Butler, David, and Linda Tischler. 2015. *Design to Grow: How Coca-Cola Learned to Combine Scale & Agility (and How You Can Too)*. New York: Simon and Schuster.

CHMI (Center for Health Market Innovations). n.d. "E Health Point." Accessed on April 22, 2016. www.healthmarketinnovations.org/ program/e-health-point.

Cisco. n.d. "Impact Story: Living Goods Uganda." Cisco, Corporate Social Responsibility. Accessed on October 16, 2015. http://csr .cisco.com/casestudy/living-goods.

Dant, Rajiv P., and Gregory, T. Gundlach. 1999. "The Challenge of Autonomy and Dependence in Franchised Channels of Distribution." *Journal of Business Venturing* 14 (1): 35–67.

de Uster, Maria Valdeviesa, Jon Vander Ark, and Wesley Walden. 2012. "Act Like a Local: How to Sell in Emerging Markets." September. McKinsey&Company. Accessed on April 10, 2014.

www.mckinseyonmarketingandsales.com/act-like-a-local-how-to-sell-in-emerging-markets.

Diaz, Alejandro, Jorge A. Lacayo, and Luis Salcedo. 2007. "Selling to 'Mom-and-Pop' Stores in Emerging Markets." *McKinsey Quarterly*. 71–81.

Dubaisouks.net. n.d. "Dubai Souks."Accessed on June 15, 2015. www.dubaisouks.net/diamond-jewellery.html.

Dumitrescu, Luigi, and Simona Vinerean. 2010. "The Glocal Strategy of Global Brands." *Studies in Business and Economics*. 147–155.

The Economist. 2004. "Luxury's New Empire." June 17. Accessed on June 15, 2015. www.economist.com/node/2771531.

eHealthPoint.com. n.d. "Wellness via Water for All." Accessed on April 22, 2016. www.ehealthpoint.com.

Gilbert, Jonathan. 2015. "Can Argentina's 'Ragmen' Make It in the Mainstream?" *Fortune*. June 18. Accessed on February 14, 2016. http://fortune.com/2015/06/18/argentina-ragman-trapito.

Hamermesh, Richard, Mona Sinha, and Elizabeth Vrolyk. 2011. "eHealthpoint: Healthcare for Rural India." Harvard Business School. October. Accessed on December 15, 2012. www.hbs.edu/faculty/Pages/item.aspx?num=41060.

Kent, Muhtar. 2013. "Thinking Outside the Bottle." McKinsey& Company. December. Accessed on April 1, 2013. www.mckinsey.com/global-themes/asia-pacific/thinking-outside-the-bottle.

Kotkin, Joel, and Wendell Cox. 2013. "The World's Fastest-Growing Megacities."*Forbes*. April 8. Accessed on May 7, 2014. www.forbes.com/sites/joelkotkin/2013/04/08/the-worlds-fastest-growing-megacities.

Kotler, Philip, and Milton Kotler. 2014. *Winning Global Markets: How Businesses Invest and Proposer in the World's High-Growth Cities*. Hoboken, NJ: John Wiley & Sons.

KPMG. 2007. "Luxury Brands in China." Accessed on May 9, 2014. www.kpmg.com.cn/en/virtual_library/Consumer_markets/CM_ Luxury_brand.pdf.

Mathur, Piyush. 2007. "Building Jewelry Brands in the Middle East." *Idex Magazine*. March 1. Accessed on May 14, 2014. www.idex-online.com/portal_FullMazalUbracha.asp?id=27067.

McCormick, Dorothy, and Paul Ove Pedersen (eds.). 1996. *Small Enterprises: Flexibility and Networking in an African Context*. Nairobi: Longhorn Kenya.

Meier, Gerald M., and James Rauch. 2008. *Leading Issues in Economic Development*, 8th edition. London: Oxford University Press.

Minder, Raphael. 2013. "Watchmakers Find Gold Rush in China Is Slowing Down." *The New York Times*. April 26. Accessed on May 12, 2014. www.nytimes.com/2013/04/27/business/global/27iht-watch27.html?_r=0.

Moorad, Zeenat. 2014. "Purveyors of Luxury Goods Have One Eye Set on Africa." *Business Day: BDlive*. May 2. Accessed on May 12, 2014. www.bdlive.co.za/business/retail/2014/05/02/purveyors-of-luxury-goods-have-one-eye-set-on-africa.

Moye, Jay. 2013. "Coca-Cola India Develops Solar-Powered Coolers for Rural Areas." The Coca-Cola Company. April 22. Accessed on May 9, 2015. www.coca-colacompany.com/stories/coca-cola-india-develops-solar-powered-coolers-for-rural-areas.

Puri, Shamlal. 2014."Let's Saunter into the Gold Souk in Dubai's Deira Business District." *Standard Digital*. March 30. Accessed on October 16, 2015. www.standardmedia.co.ke/business/article/2000108134/let-s-saunter-into-the-gold-souk-in-dubai-s-deira-business-district?pageNo=2.

Rangan, V. Kasturi, and Rohithari Rajan. 2005. "Unilever in India: Hindustan Lever's Project Shakti—Marketing FMCG to Rural Consumers." Harvard Business School. February 23. Accessed

April 1, 2013. https://hbr.org/product/unilever-in-india-hindustan-lever-s-project-shakti-marketing-fmcg-to-the-rural-consumer/an/505056-PDF-ENG.

Rarick, Charles, Gideon Falk, Casimir Barczyk, and Lori Feldman. 2012. "Marketing to Muslims: The Growing Importance of Halaal Products." *Journal of the International Academy for Case Studies* 18 (1): 81. Accessed on May 7, 2014. http://connection.ebsco-host.com/c/articles/78049311/marketing-muslims-growing-importance-halal-products.

Riaz, Mian N., and Muhammad M. Chaudry. 2003. *Halaal Food Production.* CRC Press.

Rosenberg, Tina. 2012. "The 'Avon Ladies' of Africa." *The New York Times*. October 10. Accessed on June 7, 2014. http://opinionator.blogs.nytimes.com/2012/10/10/the-avon-ladies-of-africa/?_php=true&_type=blogs&_r=0.

Sherwood, Seth. 2005. "The Oz of the Middle East." *The New York Times*. May 8. Accessed on May 9, 2014. www.nytimes.com/2005/05/08/travel/08dubai.html?_r=0.

Sheth, Jagdish N. 2011. "Impact of Emerging Markets on Marketing: Rethinking Existing Perspectives and Practices." *Journal of Marketing* 75 (4): 166–182.

Sheth, Jagdish N. and Rajendra S.Sisodia. 2012. *The 4 A's of Marketing: Creating Value for Customers, Companies, and Society*. New York: Routledge.

Struijk, Adriaan. 2013. "Dubai: City of Gold." The Jurisdictions: Dubai. February. Accessed on May 14, 2014. www.freemontgroup.com/wp-content/uploads/2014/06/Dubai-City-of-Gold.pdf.

SupplyChainBrain. 2011. "Mega-Cities in Emerging Markets Pose Special Logistics Challenges." December 15. Accessed on May 6, 2014. www.supplychainbrain.com/content/logisticstransportation/transportation-distribution/single-article-page/article/mega-cities-in-emerging-markets-pose-special-logistics-challenges.

Tieman, Marco, and Maznah Che Ghazali. 2013. "Principles in *halal* Purchasing." *Journal of Islamic Marketing* 4 (3), 281–293.

Unilever website. n.d. Accessed on April 22, 2016. www.unilever.com.

Wehner, Sherry. 2008. "Protecting a Brand without Stifling Franchisees." *Franchising World* 40(12): 60.

Zailani, Suhaiza, Hanim Mohamad, Zainal Ariffin Ahmad, Nabsiah Abd Wahid, Rosly Othman, and Yudi Fernando. 2010. "Recommendations to Strengthen Halal Food Supply Chain for Food Industry in Malaysia." *Journal of Agribusiness Marketing*. January 1. Accessed on May 12, 2014. www.fama.gov.my/documents/10157/8e4b06bf-ac70-458e-a026-51726fb30568.

7

Reinventing Reach

Emerging markets are lands of great contrast. In the previous chapter, we emphasized the importance of companies being able to leverage existing distribution options in such countries. In this chapter we acknowledge the rapidly modernizing retailing landscape that is turning the distribution mantra from "location, location, location" to "procurement, possession, and convenience." Even as emerging-market customers continue to use traditional channels, new channels are also becoming integral to their lives and are leading to a change in shopping habits. Unlike in the West where modern retail has existed for decades, in emerging markets it is a very recent phenomenon. As a result, the brand-new construction there reflects more modern design and architectural elements than in the West. Globalization, economic volatility, and technological advances have led to a blurring of the borders between doing business in a physical and virtual space. This has transformed the retail industry and created radical rethinking of the purpose of a "store" and how companies can best reach their consumers (Deloitte 2011). With rapid advances in technology, a new generation of start-up e-commerce websites is springing up. Notably, upstarts like Flipkart and Snapdeal in India are giving Amazon India stiff competition. Reach is also widening due to new ways of financing and varied payment options; some of these involve technology, while others involve creativity.

Providing accessibility via game changing technologies and new retail concepts overcomes the distribution challenges in emerging markets and helps consumers to acquire, consume, and dispose of products (Seth and Sisodia 2012). In this chapter, we add to the strategies we offered in the previous chapter for providing accessibility. These strategies involve modern, new, and possibly technology-based options for helping widen companies' reach. Our breakthrough ideas for expanding access center on solving consumers' time and location constraints. Technology provides many options for solving consumers' time and location constraints, such as 24x7 online access, delivery tracking, information availability, and digitized billing/ticketing/payments. These are the five strategies we offer for reinventing reach: 1) modernizing retailing, 2) setting up e-commerce, 3) accessing self-service technologies, 4) enabling payments, and 5) providing financing.

Modernizing Retailing

In emerging markets, one-stop shopping convenience is still a novelty because traditional bazaars are typically specialized by product. Therefore, horizontal retailing chains such as Mustafa in Singapore and Big Bazaar in India are potential game changers. Modern retail already accounts for over 50 percent of sales in emerging markets like Brazil, Russia, China, Mexico, and South Africa, and 46 percent of sales in transitional markets like Turkey, but it accounts for less than 15 percent of sales in countries like India, Nigeria, and Indonesia (Diaz, Magni, and Poh 2012). Since both traditional and modern formats need to be managed, even within a given country, the same company often has to adopt different retail strategies depending on which segments of the market it wants to penetrate. Companies like Procter & Gamble (P&G) have separate teams in India and China to manage the different formats (Saluja et al. 2011). Even though modern retail may be a small slice of the pie, for now, in emerging markets, the sheer volume is huge. For example, a 5 percent share in India translates to over 300 million shoppers. However, shoppers in emerging markets typically shop more frequently, for smaller quantities and pack sizes, and they prefer fresh, unpacked foods. This reflects in the value of the shopping basket which ranges from a low of 7 to 10 U.S. dollars (USD) in India at a hypermarket, to 10 to 18 USD in China, compared to 40 to 45 USD in the U.S. Interestingly, shopping is often seen as a welcome family outing rather than a chore in many emerging markets.

Multinationals often prefer entering China or Russia before countries like India because modern retailing in India and similar countries is perceived as expensive, and as a result, first-time shoppers are difficult to attract (Roy 2008). In India, nearly 75 percent of the apparel and jewelry is unbranded and traditional, or modern with an ethnic look, whereas in China over 70 percent of apparel sales in urban areas are from modern format, retail-like department stores and the style is predominantly Western (Chan, Cheung, and Tse 2007). In fact, in neighboring Thailand, the big-box format has even drawn in monks! A big box megastore, Hang Sangkapan (translated as Monk Supply), in Bangkok (the capital of Thailand), has been successful because over 90 percent of the population is Buddhist and men are expected to live for a time like a monk at least once in their lives. At any given time, there are over 300,000 monks and 60,000 novice monks, which translates into a retail business of over 10 billion baht (THB) (320 million USD). Built on over 250 square feet of land, this air conditioned warehouse offers aisles stocked with supplies for monks (Watcharasakwet 2013; Kuo 2013).

Multinationals like Carrefour, Walmart, and Tesco are rapidly trying to grab market share in emerging markets. A variety of modern retail formats, such as convenience stores, discount stores, specialty stores, department stores, supermarkets, and hypermarkets, dot the landscape. Despite the expertise and experience of multinational retailers, several domestic retailers, such as China Resources (CR) Vanguard and Lianhua Supermarket Holdings Co., Ltd. also have a significant retail presence. This is largely due to their intrinsic knowledge of the market, access to the right people in government, and their ability to pivot in response to cultural and social changes that impact demand.

CR Vanguard in China

China's retail market, at 26.2 trillion CNY in 2014, is the second largest market after the United States (Lam et al. 2015). However, foreign retailers such as Tesco and Walmart have been losing money and closing stores in China, largely due to expensive, hard-to-secure real estate, high price points, and adaptation problems. They also no longer get preferential treatment from regional governments (Fung Business Intelligence Centre 2013). Modern-format retailing enables cost savings in distribution for retailers, and lower prices and the convenience of one-stop shopping for customers.

However, the nationwide infrastructure required to serve such outlets, such as trucks, highways, and cold storage warehouses, is not yet in place outside of urban areas. The three large cities—Shanghai, Guangzhou, and Beijing—have the best logistics and experienced distributors, and they serve as entry points for most imports, even for cities along the eastern coast that have fairly good infrastructure.

Many smaller cities have distribution limitations, such as the number of distributors, especially for high-value or temperature-sensitive products. Distribution varies widely throughout China based on product type, retail sector, store type, and even city. Large-format stores are a relatively new phenomenon in this highly fragmented market that is primarily dominated by small, traditional, independent retailers. Recognizing this gap, many retailers develop local partnerships to create modern cold chain and distribution systems that include multimodal refrigerated rail transportation to inland cities. Improved national highway systems are also contributing to easing this bottleneck. But the vast size of the country creates tremendous logistical challenges that have to be overcome by stores like CR Vanguard in creative ways (Askew 2013).

CR Vanguard belongs to China Resources Enterprise, a central, state-owned group enterprise, and was officially established in 1992 in Hong Kong. It operates over 4,800 stores across China with 252,000 employees. CR Vanguard's 2014 turnover was 21.78 billion USD. It was ranked 1200 on Forbes Global 2000 list (Forbes 2015; China Resources Enterprise Limited 2014).

CR Vanguard's main market segments include retail, distribution and food processing, beverages, property investment, and textiles (*The Guardian* 2013). It follows the self-operated model rather than the franchise model. Its two logistic centers in Suzhou and Shenzhen have a total combined space of 80,000 square meters, which helps them maintain zero inventory (Retail M&A 2013). CR Vanguard's collaboration with firms such as eFuture for supply chain management software (SCMS) to optimize store operations, marketing and sales, inventory management, and supply chain and stock turnover, has helped it streamline its loyalty card program and prepaid card systems (China Retail News 2014). CR Vanguard's expansion into lower-tier cities via a simultaneous acquisition and green field development route paid off with improved market share in county-level cities as well as in provincial capitals (Kantar World Panel 2011).

Modern retailing formats by multinationals and large domestic retailers are transforming rural areas, even those where infrastructural constraints lead to large delays in getting produce from the farms to consumers' homes. In India, a large conglomerate, ITC Limited, launched large-format rural shopping centers in 2000; these are called e-Choupals. Located alongside major rural roads, e-Choupals sell clothes, fertilizers, and motorbikes and also offer telemedicine. They double as information kiosks, provide agri-information to help farmers get a fair market price for their commodities by bypassing middlemen, and they also provide education (Farhoomand and Bhatnagar 2008). Given that the rural Indian population comprises 700 million people (1.3 million households) across 627,000 villages and a potential market of 28.6 billion USD, a number of large Indian conglomerates set up rural malls, such as Godrej Agrovet's Aadhaar, Tata Chemicals's Tata Kisan Sansar, and Shriram Group's Hariyali Bazaar (Pallavi 2007).

Setting Up E-Commerce

Asia is poised to surpass North America and become the world's largest e-commerce market. In India, Internet retailing in products such as apparel, footwear, electronics, beauty, and leisure is in serious competition with brick and mortar store retailing. India has the second highest number of Internet users (after China) despite limited availability of Internet infrastructure, high cost of access and usage (four times that of China), lack of awareness, and low digital literacy. By 2017, India is expected to have over 500 million Internet users (Shu 2015). In Latin America, a younger population base is boosting the adoption of mobile technology that, in turn, is driving online retail sales to a higher level than in many developed regions in the world.

Lead by Brazil, Latin America ranked second in terms of online retail sales, double that of the U.S. and just behind Asia-Pacific (O'Toole 2013). Surprisingly, rural regions are not far behind. MamaMikes is an online gifting website in Kenya. It was launched by Segeni Ngethe, a U.S.-educated Kenyan who realized the potential of an online gifting store where people could place orders for deliveries to be made in Kenya. The gifts available on this site go beyond the typical to include solar products, school/tuition fees, electricity bills, airtime, and even dowry payments such as live goats (Mulupi 2012).

Alibaba in China

China is the largest retail market in the world and is leading the e-tailing revolution. Because China has the world's largest online population e-tailing was a 314 -billion-USD industry in 2013 (Morgan Stanley 2015). One of the key players in this industry has been Alibaba Group. Alibaba operates several online and mobile marketplaces in retail and wholesale trade; the types of trade include business-to-business (B2B), business-to-consumer (B2C), and consumer-to-consumer (C2C) (i.e., Tmall, Taobao, and Alibaba Group). Despite its rapid growth Alibaba faces competition from the e-commerce platforms of brick and mortar companies, such as Haier Electronics Group Co., Ltd., Suning Commerce Group, and GOME Electrical Appliances Holding Ltd., many of which are attempting to dominate specific areas, such as electronics or appliances (Alibaba Group n.d.; Carsten 2013).

Other than competitive pressures, Alibaba has struggled with logistical issues such as an inadequate shipping infrastructure that hampered overnight delivery. In addition, an increasing transactions load made it difficult to rely on local partners to fulfill customers' deliveries and returns. As a result, Alibaba had to change its strategy and it partnered with or acquired major local logistics companies, such as its 4.5 million USD investment in Star Express and Best Logistics, and its 70 percent stake in HTO.

Also in 2011, Alibaba launched Fulfillment by AliExpress, a logistics and shipping service, an existing wholesale e-commerce platform. By combining multiple orders into one low-cost international shipment, fulfillment becomes more cost effective and order tracking and verification can also be done from a central warehouse. This new order fulfillment system was expected to reduce shipping costs of small and medium businesses by about 30 percent (*Business Wire* 2011). This is significant because last-mile delivery typically accounts for 53 percent of the shipping cost in China (Goh and Gan 2014).

Further, in 2011, Alibaba invested heavily in building a network of warehouses allocating 4.6 billion USD for the following five years (Goh and Gan 2014). By 2020, it aims to invest 16 billion USD in logistics and support to open up China's vast interior and expand access to scores of new customers; it is gearing up to overtake even Walmart as the world's biggest retail network. By providing access to rural areas, Alibaba will play a significant role in balancing the uneven distribution of wealth in China.

Many emerging market consumers have a thrifty mindset; we discussed the thriving market for used goods that caters to this trait in Chapter 4. In the modern world, online classified ads have been effectively using the Internet to connect buyers and sellers of both used and new goods. But unlike in the United States where Craigslist is the dominant player, OLX has made a bigger impact worldwide.

OLX Classifieds in Emerging Markets

Founded in March 2006 by Alec Oxenford and Fabrice Grinda as the "next generation" of advertising-based, free online classifieds, OLX has 240 million active users from 40 countries, with 34 million visits per day, and 54 percent of its traffic comes from mobile devices (Lourie 2015). OLX is the leader in Brazil, India, and Poland, which constitute 50 percent of its worldwide users. Inspired by Craigslist, the leader in North America, OLX's differentiating decision was to focus on international expansion for achieving reach. It has customized to 40 different local language preferences, and it has grown via acquisition and advertising.

Unlike most companies that start operations in their home country, OLX launched in India before entering its home market, Argentina, four and a half years later (Griffith 2014). For the security and comfort of its users, OLX has recently established public kiosks at select locations in Brazil; these are for exchanging goods, making contacts, and gathering information about OLX services (Giunta 2014). Amarjit Batra, CEO of OLX India explains: "We believe that every item can be used, but it is merely lying around with the wrong user. By connecting people who do not have the need for an item to ones who do, we encourage what is often called collaborative consumption, in which the same product is used by multiple users, not only enhancing its utility, but also lowering depletion of personal and national resources" (OLX n.d.).

Accessing Self-Service Technologies

Technological innovations have radically changed how people operate. Self-service technologies (SSTs) have reduced or even eliminated direct service employee involvement, which helps companies be more flexible, increase efficiency, and provide 24x7 service. Research on adoption of technology in developed countries has shown that, if companies deploy SSTs strategically, they can earn customer trust and loyalty. But the speed and manner of technology diffusion and adoption is likely to be different in emerging markets due to a host of socioeconomic and cultural factors. Although limited Internet penetration and low computer literacy have inhibited the adoption of some technologies, others, like the mobile phone, have transformed entire economies.

One such self-service technology that has cost-effectively transformed access to products has been vending machines, which were first introduced in the food and beverage industry. They dispense foods, cold and even hot beverages like soups, electronics, car rentals, gilded gold coins/bars (in the Middle East), socially taboo products like condoms (in India), and even live crabs (in China) (Haramis 2011; Bushey 2014; Kharif 2013; *The Times of India* 2014). A common use of vending machines is the automatic teller machines (ATM), which can be considerably different in emerging markets as compared to the ones in developed countries.

Automatic Teller Machines in Africa

Banks in Africa and Asia are using ATMs to make their services more accessible to their customers, especially in rural areas where branch setups are expensive and credit and debit card usage is low. Encouraged by governments aiming for financial inclusion, ATMs were forecasted to have growth rates of about 94 percent from 2009 to 2015 in Africa. But growth has not been even—nearly 80 percent of ATMs are concentrated in four countries—South Africa, Nigeria, Egypt, and Morocco (Cluckey 2012). Although ATMs are cash based, the rapid rise of mobile and new payment mechanisms, such as mobile money in Sub-Saharan Africa, has accelerated the expansion of ATMs to enable people to get their money (Kendall, Schiff, and Smadja 2013). Thus, although ATMs are meant for cash transactions, they enable other cashless transactions, so many governments, such as the one in Nigeria, encourage ATMs as a way of countering corruption (Thompson 2014).

ATMs in countries in West Africa, such as the Ivory Coast, have been customized and can be used for purchasing mobile airtime and bus tickets, paying traffic fines and electricity bills, and even registering for municipal elections (Cluckey 2012). In Bolivia, literacy levels and awareness of modern financial services are low. Plus, issues like unreliable telecommunication infrastructure also hamper access to financial services. ATMs that offer smart card and fingerprint recognition, are voice enabled, have multilingual capabilities, and even have color-coded touch screens are helping overcome adoption barriers. Moreover, ATMs store account balances locally, making this information available to clients even when there is no network availability (Hernandez and Mugica 2003).

Enabling Payments

Unreliable electricity access, weak regulation, and poor legal recourse in emerging markets, coupled with low penetration of credit and debit cards, increases reliance on cash transactions. In most emerging markets, payments are typically made in cash by relatively inefficient, expensive, and error- or fraud-prone mechanisms such as paper checks or drafts. Technology is a game-changer in the payments arena and enables dramatic expansion of reach for creating access.

LINE's M-Commerce in Thailand

Contributor: Piyush Sharma

Thailand is one of the fastest growing export-oriented emerging economies in Southeast Asia; it has a well-developed infrastructure, pro-foreign direct investment policies, a thriving tourism sector, and sizeable industrial and agriculture exports. Despite strong growth in industrial activity and urbanization, agriculture remains a vital component of Thailand's economy, employing about 60 percent of the total Thai population. About two-thirds of Thailand's population still lives in rural areas.

Rapid economic growth has led to a significant expansion in banking and retail finance sectors in Thailand during the last decade. Growth of prepaid cards is higher than debit cards, which is in turn higher than credit cards (Reportlinker 2014). With the growing market for e-commerce, and the adoption of mobile Internet and mobile shopping, e-commerce is expected to grow at much higher rates over the next several years in Southeast Asia, as compared to the United States and Europe (Westlake 2012). Unique capabilities of smart phone devices coupled with their declining prices and the exponential rise in mobile device applications are driving growth in m-commerce, which is resulting in the industry leapfrogging traditional channels such as retail branches and ATM networks. Thailand has a population of 68.3 million but has over 105 million mobile users; 90 million of these are prepaid subscribers (Wongcha-um 2015) and smart phone penetration is also growing rapidly.

Taking advantage of this trend, LINE, an instant messaging app, launched a mobile grocery service in Thailand. Its 33 million Thai users access LINE Shop's daily grocery deals by adding accounts such as LINE Hot Deal, LINE Hot Brand, and Hot Deal: Living to their mobile phone address book. This is a break-away from traditional e-commerce because instead of online product lists, users get a daily push message of deals. Innovative services such as these can build consumer adoption of m-commerce and push companies and the government to work toward overcoming the obstacles to m-commerce such as poor mobile payment options, unfriendly user interfaces, and lack of infrastructure and logistics for delivery.

LINE has partnered with aCommerce for managing its end-to-end m-commerce services, and since aCommerce has 70 to 80 percent of its customers in areas outside Bangkok, it provides LINE with a great opportunity to extend the reach of the brands it sells to a wider audience in Thailand (Loras 2015). About 42 percent of LINE's orders come from outside Bangkok and 37 percent are young—25–34 years old (Huang 2014).

Mobile phone sales growth is being driven largely by emerging markets like India, China, Indonesia, and Africa, and this is enabling the adoption of mobile payments that can boost financial access, especially at the bottom of the pyramid (BoP). Interestingly, a telecom operator in Africa found that higher gross domestic product (GDP) is not always indicative of the propensity to adopt mobile phones. Migrants in large towns were more likely to adopt cell phones for maintaining contact with their families and friends back home. In addition, people often used bartered goods and services when they were strapped for cash, which indicated great potential for prepaid cell phone minutes as a method of payment (de Uster, Vander Ark, and Walden 2012). The financial implications are enormous. For example, in developing markets, every 10 percent increase in mobile phone penetration results in a GDP growth of anywhere from 0.6 to 1.2 percent (GSM Association 2012). The most notable mobile-based payment system has been Kenya's M-Pesa, which is now spreading its reach beyond Africa. Other mobile-based payment options and digital wallets are also mushrooming—many of which supplement or compete with traditional banking.

Mobile Payments in India

Despite a population of over a billion and a rise in economic prosperity, India lags in terms of financial inclusion; a large part of the population either does not have or does not use bank accounts (Grossman 2010). Formal banking channels require a host of documents such as proof of address among others to open a bank account, so migrants prefer informal couriers (called *hawala*), friends, or relatives to carry cash home, despite the risk and high cost, or they wait until they can travel themselves. The cost per transaction of bank branching is higher than the cost of using ATMs or Internet banking, but Internet penetration is low and ATMs have not made sufficient inroads, despite banks providing multilingual, multipurpose, solar-powered machines to villages to increase access. Lately some banks have even been using mobile vans on a daily route to transport their ATMs to multiple villages (Saxena, Sinha, and Majra 2015).

Being watched with great interest is the performance of M-Paisa (M stands for mobile, and paisa, means money in India). This system originated in Kenya (as M-Pesa) and became the most successful money transfer system in the world for banking the unbanked population by simplifying the transfer and payments mechanism. M-Pesa is a mobile-phone–based money transfer and microfinancing service that was launched by Vodafone and Kenya's Safaricom. Money loaded onto phones as airtime is transferred by a text message (i.e., Short Message Service, SMS) to recipients who do not have to have a similar account. M-Pesa can be used to make retail purchases, pay utility bills, other bills, salaries, and even tuition (Ongoto 2013). Worldwide, over 150 payment systems are in use (EY n.d.), and this is opening up new business opportunities for small or even individual entrepreneurs.

In India, Vodafone launched M-Paisa and competes with other telecom companies as well as nonbanking players such as Eko India Financial Services. Eko is also a mobile-phone–enabled payment mechanism for small-value transactions sold at mini neighborhood shops, which later become their agents. It offers financial services such as peer-to-peer transfers, salary and wage remittances, withdrawals, and deposits of cash microcredit and microinsurance. Eko has also partnered with multiple banking and nonbanking organizations to develop products suited to regions and demographics in rural and remote parts of the country. Similarly, the Oxigen Wallet is a nonbank wallet used for bill payments and money transfer. It can be loaded with cash over the counter at authorized retailers/ Oxigen outlets or via bank fund transfer or by credit/debit card (Kalam and Singh 2011). Thus, in India, as in several other emerging markets, consumers are leapfrogging technologies like landlines, the Internet, and payment mechanisms like credit and debit cards, and instead are adopting mobile phones for such services.

Governments are also recognizing the impact of technology and the opportunities that technologies offer, not just for achieving financial inclusion goals, but also for helping connect with citizens for informing, educating, and, as in the following description from South Africa, even for collecting taxes.

South African Revenue Service

Contributor: Amaleya Goneos-Malka

The South African Revenue Service (SARS) is a state department that collects taxes and duties. Recently SARS has expanded its reach to convert nonpayers to payers by creating multiple access points (physical and virtual), simplifying its processes, increasing automation and self-service technologies, and adding value-added offerings. First, SARS initiated an internal cultural transformation that lasted almost 10 years; during this time changes included process automation, policy modernization, and technological change, which drove automation, developed and promoted self-service facilities, upskilled personnel, and redesigned employees to perform value-added activities. The current phase (2012–2017) is aimed at fiscal citizenship via a) increased customs compliance, b) increased tax compliance, c) increased ease and fairness of doing business with SARS, and d) increased cost effectiveness, internal efficiency, and institutional respectability. Group Executive for Strategy, Risk and Segmentation Peter Richer explained,

> *The grand prize for us is simplifying our systems— reducing the administrative burdens of systems to move to what we call fiscal citizenship. That is where all South Africans have a relationship with us; even if they do not have any tax or trade obligations... so that the moment they begin to have tax or trade obligations, we can develop a relationship with them, help them to begin to provide, say, book keeping, accounting, and record keeping services for them, so by the time they get to a point where they do have obligations to us, they have already got a relationship with us.*

SARS began involving school and college kids before they owed taxes to ensure future cooperative, rather than adversarial, compliance. They sped up processes through digitization, e-filing, and self-service, and they linked government systems together to avoid the need for multiple registrations. They segmented current and future taxpayers and provided customizable education and enforcement (SARS n.d.). To take their services to the people instead of having them visit a SARS office, they set up mobile teams staffing them with employees made redundant due to automation. The teams would visit informal business areas with mobile registration kits to make it easier for businesses to register. Thus SARS widened its reach in multiple ways to convert nonpayers as well as future payers.

Providing Financing

Typically, emerging markets are financed by international agencies like the International Monetary Fund (IMF), the World Bank, and the Asian Infrastructure Development Bank (AIIB), but these are for large-scale projects. For individual consumers, banks are increasingly offering financing options for the middle and upper class, which are much like what is offered in developed countries. We focus here on financing options for people at the BoP for whom traditional financing schemes may not be useful, affordable, or accessible. Microfinance has been a break-through idea in financing small businesses via micro loans. Launched jointly by Grameen Bank (GB) and Dr. Muhammad Yunus in Bangladesh, for which they received the Nobel Peace Prize in 2006, this model aims for economic and social development of the poor (Nobel Prize.org 2006). GB set up a decentralized, pyramidal banking structure including lending units, centers, branch offices, area offices, zonal offices, and a head office in Dhaka (the capital of Bangladesh) through which they attracted over 7 million clients (of which notably 97 percent were women) from 81,386 villages (Grameen Bank 2008). The most important part of this structure was the solidarity groups, the principle lending units at the village level, which had most decision-making authority. GB helped organize active, on-the-ground campaigns to collect savings from nonmembers to raise additional loan funds (Rahman 2011). They tapped into social capital by lending money to groups of five people, generally women, and made everybody in the group accountable for the obligations of the group. Also, the bank assigned an agent to the group to ensure appropriate money management (Hossain 2013). This model has spread through many emerging markets as described here.

Microfinance in Emerging Markets

The Grameen Bank's model has been replicated in more than 40 countries worldwide including India, Latin America, and Africa (Rahman 2011). Established in 1997, the Mann Deshi Mahila Sahakari Bank (Mann Deshi Bank from now on), the first rural cooperative bank for women in India, has become the largest cooperative for women, with over 185,000 customers. This was followed by the government of India recently creating a bank dedicated to women who fully or partially own around 3 million small enterprises across the country. The Mann Deshi Bank, the Mann Deshi Foundation, and the women's chamber of commerce train women in money management skills and also provide legal and administrative advice to women entrepreneurs via a toll-free line (Seervai 2014 a and b).

Latin America has followed the trend of using microfinance to fight against poverty, but penetrating remote, rural areas has been a challenge. First, microfinance in Latin America began as a social mechanism run by nongovernment organizations (NGOs) that gradually transformed into microfinance banks (Dacheva 2007). Money does not come just from the poor; savings are collected from the rich to give as loans, which increases the availability of money and reduces risks for the providers.

In Cameroon, the model has been deployed a little differently. Instead of just getting people together and giving them loans, the community creates a microbank to provide financial services (e.g., saving, credit, insurance) and generate income for the villages. Supported by an NGO, which provides training, capacity building, linkage with sponsors, and donors, this model ensures that villagers benefit from the right opportunities for growth. The microbank controls accounting of every unit and mentors the network, ensures an external audit, secures excess liquidity, and facilitates operations such as money transfers (Fotabong 2011, 2012). This model has been very successful; it has brought nearly a million Cameroonians out from poverty and competes with the top five banks in Cameroon (Investir au Cameroun, 2015).

Even though microfinance has provided considerable opportunity to enable people at the bottom of the pyramid to be drawn into a formal financing network, its reach is still limited, and recently mismanagement and other factors have raised questions about the model.

References

Alibaba Group. n.d. "Alibaba Defined." Accessed on January 4, 2016. http://news.alibaba.com/specials/aboutalibaba/aligroup/index.html.

Askew, Katy. 2013. "Comment: Tesco, China Resources JV Part of Growing Trend." *just-food*. August 9. Accessed on May 5, 2014. www.just-food.com/comment/tesco-china-resources-jv-part-of-growing-trend_id124114.aspx.

Bushey, Ryan. 2014. "China Made Renting an Electric Car as Easy as Buying Skittles from a Vending Machine." *Business Insider*. January 24. Accessed on May 15. 2014. www.businessinsider.com/chinas-electric-car-vending-machine-2014-1#ixzz30yjdqxjr.

Business Wire. 2011. "Alibaba.com Introduces Logistics Warehouse and Shipping and Logistics Management Services on AliExpress." January 18. *Business Wire*. Accessed on March 15, 2015. www.businesswire.com/news/home/20110118005889/en/Alibaba.com-Introduces-Logistics-Warehouse-Shipping-Logistics-Management#.U2cCLld-hhI.

Carsten, Paul. 2013. "Alibaba to Transform China's 'e-conomy' with $500 Billion Marketplace." *Reuters*. October 13. Accessed on May 15, 2014. www.reuters.com/article/2013/10/13/us-alibaba-retail-idUSBRE99C0BP20131013.

Chan, Wai-Chan, Richard C. Cheung, and Anne Tse. 2007. "How Half the World Shops: Apparel in Brazil, China, and India." McKinsey&Company. November. Accessed on March 15, 2015. www.mckinsey.com/industries/retail/our-insights/how-half-the-world-shops-apparel-in-brazil-china-and-india.

China Resources Enterprise Limited. 2014. "Annual Report 2014."Accessed April 22, 2016. www.crc.com.hk/IR/results/direct/cre_r/201509/P020150914529050624484.pdf.

China Retail News. 2014. "CR Vanguards Eyes 78 New Stores in East Asia." January 13. Accessed on May 5, 2014. www.chinaretailnews.com/2014/01/13/6927-cr-vanguard-eyes-78-new-stores-in-east-china.

Cluckey, Suzanne. 2012. "An IAD's-Eye View of Africa." *ATM Marketplace*. June 22. Accessed on March 4, 2016. www.atmmarketplace.com/articles/an-iads-eye-view-of-africa/.

Dacheva, Petra. 2007. "Commercialization in Microfinance—A Study of Profitability, Outreach and Success Factors within the Latin American Context." Sweet Briar College. Accessed on January 4, 2016. www.sbc.edu/sites/default/files/Honors/PDacheva.pdf.

Deloitte. 2011. "The Changing Face of Retail—The Store of the Future: The New Role of the Store in a Multichannel Environment."Accessed on April 28, 2016. rasci.in/downloads/2011/The_Store_Future.pdf.

de Uster, Maria Valdeviesa, Jon Vander Ark, and Wesley Walden. 2012. "Act Like a Local: How to Sell in Emerging Markets." McKinsey&Company. September. Accessed on January 11, 2014. www.mckinseyonmarketingandsales.com/act-like-a-local-how-to-sell-in-emerging-markets.

Diaz, Alejandro, Max Magni, and Felix Poh. 2012. From Oxcart to Walmart: Four Keys to Reaching Emerging Market Consumers. *McKinsey Quarterly*. October. Accessed on April 28, 2016. www.mckinsey.com/industries/retail/our-insights/from-oxcart-to-wal-mart-four-keys-to-reaching-emerging-market-consumers.

EY. n.d.. "The Mobile Money Revolution Is Here." EY. Accessed on January 18, 2016. www.ey.com/GL/en/Industries/Financial-Services/Banking---Capital-Markets/Financial-services-meet-the-electronic-wallet.

Farhoomand Ali, and Saurabh Bhatnagar. 2008. "ITC e-Choupal: Corporate Social Responsibility in Rural India." *Harvard Business Review*: June 30. Case #HKU765-PDF-ENG.

Forbes. 2015. "#1,200 China Resources Enterprise." The World's Biggest Public Companies. Accessed on April 22, 2016. www.forbes.com/companies/china-resources-enterprise/.

Fotabong, Leonard Ajonakoh. 2012. "The Microfinance Market of Cameroon: Analyzing Trends and Current Developments." Microfinance Gateway. March. Accessed on July 14, 2014. www.microfinancegateway.org/sites/default/files/mfg-en-paper-the-microfinance-market-of-cameroon-analyzing-trends-and-current-developments-mar-2012.pdf.

———. 2011. "Comparing Microfinance Models: MC2 Model versus Other Microfinance Models." Microfinance Gateway. December. Accessed on July 14, 2014. www.microfinancegateway.org/library/comparing-microfinance-models-mc2-model-versus-other-microfinance-models.

Fung Business Intelligence Centre. 2013. "Retail Market in China." September. Accessed on June 10, 2015. www.funggroup.com/eng/knowledge/research/china_dis_issue114.pdf.

Giunta, Kyle. 2014. "OLX Opens New Public Kiosks for Exchanging Goods in Brazil." Business Wire. February 12. Accessed on May 14, 2014. www.businesswire.com/news/home/20140212006159/en/OLX-Opens-Public-Kiosks-Exchanging-Goods-Brazil#.U3OgXSg8D9s.

Goh, Mui-Fong, and Chee Wee Gan. 2014. "China's E-commerce Market: The Logistics Challenges." ATKearney. November. Accessed on May 15, 2015. www.atkearney.com/consumer-products-retail/chinas-e-commerce-market-in-2014/full-report/-/asset_publisher/spbeTMyyaxTb/content/chinas-e-commerce-market-in-2014-the-logistics-challenges/10192.

Grameen Bank. 2008. "Grameen Bank at a Glance," March 12. Accessed on February 9, 2016. www.grameen-info.org/grameen-bank-at-a-glance.

Griffith, Erin. 2014. "Meet OLX, the Biggest Web Company You've Never Heard Of." Fortune. October, 29. Accessed on February 9, 2016. http://fortune.com/2014/10/29/olx-emerging-markets.

Grossman, Richard. 2010. *Unsettled Account: The Evolution of Banking in the Industrialized World since 1800.* Princeton, NJ: Princeton University Press.

GSM Association. 2012. "What Is the Impact of Mobile Telephony on Economic Growth—A Report for the GSM Association." November. Accessed on March 6, 2016. www.gsma.com/publicpolicy/wp-content/uploads/2012/11/gsma-deloitte-impact-mobile-telephony-economic-growth.pdf.

The Guardian. 2013. "Tesco's China Merger Talks Leave Question Mark Over Future of Brand." August 8. Accessed on May 4, 2014.   www.theguardian.com/business/2013/aug/09/tesco-china-merger-talks-brand.

Haramis, Nick. 2011. "Automatic for the People." *The Wall Street Journal.* Accessed on Feburuary 9, 2016. http://online.wsj.com/news/articles/SB10001424052748704132204576285052067381070.

Hernandez, Roberto, and Yerina Mugica. 2003. "What Works: PRO-DEM FFP's Multilingual Smart ATMs for Microfinance." World Resources Institute. August. Accessed on July 10, 2014. www.wri.org/sites/default/files/pdf/dd_prodem.pdf.

Hossain, Dewan Mahboob. 2013. "Social Capital and Microfinance: The Case of Grameen Bank, Bangladesh." *Middle East Journal of Business* 8(4): 13–21.

Huang, Elaine. 2014. "Is Thailand a Hotbed for M-commerce? LINE's Flash Sales Data Says Yes." e27. February 8. Accessed on April 22, 2016. https://e27.co/is-thailand-a-hotbed-for-m-commerce-lines-flash-sales-data-says-yes/.

Investir au Cameroun. 2015."MC2: A Microfinance Network Overseen by Afriland First Bank." *CameroonWeb*. July 7. Accessed on February 15, 2016. www.cameroonweb.com/CameroonHome Page/economy/MC2-Un-r-seau-de-microfinance-chapeaut-par-Afriland-First-Bank-327600?lang=.

Kalam, A. P. J. Avul, and Srijan Pal Singh. 2011. *Target 3 Billion: Innovative Solutions Towards Sustainable Development*. New York: Penguin Books.

Kantar World Panel. 2011. "China: CR Vanguard's Strategy Producing Strong Performance." October 20. Accessed on April 1, 2014. www.kantarworldpanel.com/global/News/China-CR-Vanguards-Rapid-Expansion-Strategy-Producing-Strong-Performance-while-Walmart-Expands-Its-Footprint-in-the-Lower-Tier-Cities.

Kendall, Jake, Robert Schiff, and Emmanuel Smadja. 2014. "Sub-Saharan Africa: A Major Potential Revenue Opportunity for Digital Payments." McKinsey&Company. February. Accessed on October 30, 2015. www.mckinsey.com/industries/financial-services/our-insights/sub-saharan-africa-a-major-potential-revenue-opportunity-for-digital-payments.

Kharif, Olga. 2013. "Vending Machines Get Smart to Accommodate the Cashless." Bloomberg. August 29. February 1, 2015. www.bloomberg.com/articles/2013-08-29/vending-machines-get-smart-to-accommodate-the-cashless.

Kuo, Lily. 2013. "Buddhist Monks Are Buying into Thailand's New Religion: Consumerism." Quartz. July 23. Accessed on May 9, 2014. http://qz.com/107169/buddhist-monks-are-buying-into-thailands-new-religion-consumerism.

Lam, Teresa, Christy Li, Echo Gong, Wendy Hong, and Winnie Lo. 2015. "Spotlight on China." Fung Business Intelligence Centre. April. Accessed on February 14, 2016. www.fbicgroup.com/sites/default/files/Spotlight%20on%20China%20Retail%20APR%2015.pdf.

Loras, Sophie. 2015. "Line Paves Way for M-Commerce in Southeast Asia with Mobile Grocery Service." ClickZ. February 15.

Accessed on April 22, 2016. www.clickz.com/clickz/news/2393357/line-paves-way-for-m-commerce-in-southeast-asia-with-mobile-grocery-service.

Lourie, Gugu. 2015. "OLX Reaches 240m Active Users." *Tech Financials.* June 29. Accessed on February 14, 2015. http://techfinancials.co.za/2015/06/29/olx-reaches-240m-active-users/#.VsFmM8cjnoo.

Morgan Stanley. 2015. "China's eCommerce Revolution." March 13. Accessed on April 22, 2016. www.morganstanley.com/ideas/china-e-commerce-revolution.

Mulupi, Dinfin. 2012. "Want to Send a Goat to Your Family Back in Africa? Mama Mikes Is the Place to Go." How We Made It in Africa. July 26. Accessed on March 24, 2014. www.howwemadeitinafrica.com/want-to-send-a-goat-to-your-family-back-in-africa-mama-mikes-is-the-place-to-go.

Nobel Prize.org. 2006. "The Nobel Peace Prize 2006." Accessed on May 19, 2014. www.nobelprize.org/nobel_prizes/peace/laureates/2006.

OLX. n.d. "We Are OLX." Accessed on March 15, 2014. www.olx.co.uk/about.php.

Ongoto, Mogaka F. 2013. "Kenya's M-PESA Overhauls African Mobile Money Transfers," *IDG Connect*. August 22. Accessed on February 26, 2014. www.idgconnect.com/abstract/3108/kenya-m-pesa-overhauls-african-mobile-money-transfers.

O'Toole, Gavin. 2013. "Young Latin Americans Embrace the Internet—and Start Shopping." *The Guardian*. November 13. Accessed on March 23, 2015. www.theguardian.com/media-network/media-network-blog/2013/nov/13/latin-america-internet-shopping-mobile-online.

Pallavi. 2007. "Harvesting Rural India for Retail Growth," Indian Retailer. September. Accessed on April 22, 2016. http://retail.franchiseindia.com/magazine/2007/september/Harvesting-rural-India-for-retail-growth.m10-2-7/.

Rahman, Rafiqur, and Qiang Nie. 2011. "The Synthesis of Grameen Bank Microfinance Approaches in Bangladesh." *International Journal of Economics and Finance* 3(6): 207–218.

Reportlinker. 2014. "Thailand's Cards and Payments Industry: Emerging Opportunities in Trends, Size, Drivers, Strategies, Products and Competitive Landscape." *PRNewswire*. August 12. Accessed on March 6, 2016. www.prnewswire.com/news-releases/ thailands-cards-and-payments-industry-emerging-opportunities- trends-size-drivers-strategies-products-and-competitive-land- scape-270899581.html.

Retail M&A. 2013. "Chinese Grocers Go on a Shopping Spree." *China Economic Review*. Retrieved on May 5, 2014. www.china economicreview.com/Tesco-CRE-CR-Vanguard-supermarkets- grocers-chains-retail.

Roy, Aurnob. 2008. "The Great Indian Bazaar: Organised Retail Comes of Age in India," McKinsey&Company. August. Accessed on November 2, 2015. www.researchgate.net/publica- tion/232743944_The_Great_Indian_Bazaar_Organised_Retail_ Comes_of_Age_in_India.

Saluja, Pankaj, Mike Booker, Bruno Lannes, and Satish Shankar. 2011. "Are You Ahead of the Curve in Emerging Markets?" Bain & Company. October 7. Accessed on March 9, 2015. www.bain .com/publications/articles/are-you-ahead-of-the-curve-in- emerging-markets.aspx.

SARS. n.d."South African Revenue Service Strategic Plan 2010/11– 2012/13." Accessed on April 15, 2013. www.sars.gov.za/AllDocs/ SARSEntDoclib/Ent/SARS-Strat-05%20-%20SARS%20 Strategic%20Plan%202010%202011%20to%202012%202013.pdf.

Saxena, Rajan, Mona Sinha, and Hufrish Majra. 2015. "Self-Service Technologies: Building Relationships with Indian Consumers." *Handbook of Research in Relationship Marketing*. Editors: Rob- ert M. Morgan, Janet T. Parish, and George Deitz. Northhamp- ton, MA: Elgar Publishing, Inc. 177.

Seervai, Shanoor. 2014a. "Bank Built for Women Blooms in India." *The Wall Street Journal*. March 3. Accessed on March 24, 2014. http://blogs.wsj.com/indiarealtime/2014/03/03/bank-built-for-women-blooms-in-india/?KEYWORDS=microfinance.

————.2014b. "How to Run a Business in Rural India," *The Wall Street Journal,* February 25. Accessed on April 5, 2015. http://blogs.wsj.com/indiarealtime/2014/02/25/how-to-run-a-business-in-rural-india/?KEYWORDS=microfinance.

Sheth, Jagdish N., and Rajendra S. Sisodia. 2012 *The 4 A's of Marketing: Creating Value for Customers, Companies, and Society*. New York: Routledge.

Shu, Catherine. 2015. "India Will Have 500 Million Internet Users by 2017, Says New Report." TechCrunch. July 21. Accessed on February 29, 2016. http://techcrunch.com/2015/07/21/india-internet-growth/.

Thompson, Christopher. 2014. "Reforms Prompted by Nigeria's Central Bank Boost Professionalism." *Financial Times*. May 4. Accessed on March 15, 2015, www.ft.com/intl/cms/s/0/fa3e2578-bb15-11e3-948c-00144feabdc0.html#axzz420953quO.

The Times of India. 2014. "DMRC to Have Condom Vending Machines." May 29. Accessed March 15, 2015. http://timesofindia.indiatimes.com/Life-Style/Health-Fitness/Health/DMRC-to-have-condom-vending-machines/articleshow/34525600.cms.

Watcharasakwet, Wilawan. 2013. "Megastore for Thai Monks Brings One-Stop Retail to Buddhism." *The Wall Street Journal*. July 23. Accessed on April 4, 2014. http://online.wsj.com/article/SB10001424127887324783204578619950520621128.html.

Westlake, Adam. 2012. "Rakuten Looking to Enter Thailand's Credit Card Market." *Japan Daily Press*. November 19. Accessed on March 15, 2015. http://japandailypress.com/rakuten-looking-to-enter-thailandscredit-card-market-1918601.

Wongcha-um, Panu. 2015. "Millions of Prepaid Phone Numbers to Be Cut Off in Thailand with New SIM Card Rule." Channel News Asia. July 31. Accessed on February 14, 2016. http://www.channelnewsasia.com/news/asiapacific/millions-of-prepaid-phone/2021062.html.

8

Building Brand Identity

The ability to develop and establish brands is a key strategic advantage for companies that enter emerging markets because it insulates them from price competition. A dominant thought for marketers has been that brand essence, or the meaning placed on a brand, and branding techniques must remain consistent across countries. However, due to a host of varying cultural and social factors in different markets, how consumers in a given market experience a brand, the branding techniques companies use, and the elements they use often need to vary. Well-established branding research has focused on conceptualizations from developed countries which are usually culturally close to each other. The impact of culture on brands and vice-versa has not yet been examined in other parts of the world. For companies to successfully enter emerging markets with existing brands, they must understand what it takes to manage their brand while retaining their brand's essence and, at the same time, building upon this essence in a way that resonates with the consumers in the markets they enter. The width of this gap between brand essence (as intended by marketers) and brand identity (what is experienced by consumers) separates the successful companies from less successful ones.

The fourth A in the 4 A's framework is awareness, which is a prerequisite for establishing a brand identity. *Awareness* is the extent to which consumers are informed regarding product characteristics, are persuaded to try a new product or service, and, if applicable, are reminded to repurchase it. There are two dimensions of awareness— product knowledge and brand awareness (Sheth and Sisodia 2012). What makes building awareness in emerging markets more challenging than building it in developed markets is that consumers in emerging markets are generally more heterogeneous in terms of their experiences and their preferences. Moreover, in several emerging markets, products that are considered ubiquitous in developed markets, such as dryers for drying clothes, or one-cup coffee makers, are still rarely adopted by the minority, let alone even known about by the majority. In such cases, companies find that they must educate consumers about the product category first and then try to create brand awareness, as has been the experience of companies like Kimberly Clark and Unilever. Emerging markets have become intensely competitive due to the entry of multinational corporations (MNCs), the rise of local brand powerhouses, and increasingly discerning consumers. Thus, companies have to get smarter about their target audiences and sometimes even consider practicing niche marketing to avoid competition. Such a laser-focused approach to segmentation and targeting has proven successful for companies like Xiaomi, Lenovo, Samsung, and Haier. For MNCs as well as local companies, a one-size-fits-all mentality to market segmentation is no longer a viable option.

Brands are created through a wide range of touch points and so every time a customer interacts with a brand, the customer forms associations. In this way, a brand is much like a reputation or the promise of a specific customer experience. In order for customers to form consistent and coherent brand images, companies must manage the elements that go into communications as effectively as possible. In emerging markets, companies must often create product awareness first and then consider three important communication elements—source, message, and channels—for building a brand identity. Based on this, our five strategies for creating awareness are 1) establishing product knowledge, 2) identifying sources of communication, 3) developing appropriate messaging, 4) using traditional channels of communication, and 5) leveraging new and unconventional media.

Establishing Product Knowledge

In emerging markets the reality is that for many product categories, most customers are severely lacking in basic product knowledge and/or knowledge of the product category as a whole. For example, few customers understand the basics of various financial service offerings, such as variable life insurance or defined pension plans (Sheth and Sisodia 2012). Moreover, products that are commonplace in developed markets may be entirely new to consumers in emerging markets. Many marketing setbacks can be blamed on companies failing to properly educate customers about their product. Unilever found that its detergent Ala was successful in most of Brazil but failed in northwest Brazil where women were unfamiliar with detergents and were accustomed to washing clothes in streams with bar soap. Consumers who are only recently moving into a consumer society can be confused about what a product can do, how it works, how it fits into their lives, and why they should use it. This is a significant barrier to converting nonusers to users. Moreover, even retailers or customer contact employees may suffer from a similar lack of product knowledge (D'Andrea, Marcotte, and Morrison 2010). Thus, the first step in a brand's journey in an emerging market is likely to be creating product knowledge. This is applicable in a number of industries ranging from something considered fairly simple, such as a toothbrush, to something very complex, such as financial services. The powerful opportunity that imparting product knowledge provides is illustrated in the example below from Uganda.

Financial Education Program in Uganda

In Sub-Saharan Africa, particularly in the country of Uganda, nearly 20 percent of the population lives at or below the national poverty line (The World Bank 2016). Literacy levels of about 25 percent meant that less than 2 percent of Ugandans knew about savings and investment products. They were making poor financial decisions including how best to spend the money they earned, how to invest the money they saved, and how to borrow for future spending. According to Patrick Bitature, chair of the Uganda Investment Authority, too many Ugandans lacked financial literacy skills and the ability to manage personal finances, which was leading to low levels of wealth creation. Financial education was urgently required so that people could select the best products and services to meet their needs (The MasterCard Foundation 2011).

The MasterCard Foundation commissioned Microfinance Opportunities and Genesis Analytics to review the experiences of 12 organizations worldwide and to determine what assistance could be provided. They selected Uganda and its Association of Microfi-nance Institutions of Uganda (AMFIU) organization as having one of the most pressing needs for assistance. The AMFIU was estab-lished in November 1996 as an umbrella organization of microfi-nance institutions in Uganda. AMFIU's goals were to establish a market-driven microfinance industry with informed and financially literate customers.

In 2004, AMFIU initiated its Consumer Education Program, a large financial education program it planned to use to educate consum-ers on their rights and responsibilities and to ensure that con-sumers could make educated choices about products and financial institutions. Its primary target audience was the economically ac-tive poor, who were over 18 years old, and had low literacy and income levels. AMFIU focused on this group primarily because it had the minimum age requirements to access financial services, including savings accounts, in Uganda. What was apparent was that although people were capable of earning, they were unclear about how to manage the money they earned, and they considered all financial institutions to be banks.

Based on these findings, AMFIU realized that most of these key issues revealed a lack of general product knowledge about finances and entrenched attitudes toward financial institutions, rather than a lack of specific skills. This meant that financial education would not necessarily need to involve significant personal interaction or training sessions with the target audience. Rather, a successful in-tervention could entail an awareness campaign, primarily targeting public perceptions of microfinance institutions and the financial industry.

Armed with this understanding, AMFIU partnered with Commu-nication for Development Foundation Uganda and the Straight Talk Foundation to design suitable materials and identify appropri-ate delivery channels. The group decided to adopt a multipronged approach to financial education using different media outlets, pub-lic events, and printed handouts to deliver their financial educa-tion material. Although AMFIU's program relied predominantly on mass media, AMFIU also used other outlets including music, dance, drama, posters, flyers, picture cards, flip charts, consumer handbooks, *Money World* (a newspaper specific to the campaign),TV talk shows, publications, and workshops. The results of the campaign showed an increase in awareness of financial institutions, an increase in the number of newly opened savings accounts and loans, and a positive shift in the attitude of the target audience toward savings (REEV Consult International 2007). Further, AMFIU also trained field officers and financial education trainers in financial management to better serve their clients (The MasterCard Foundation 2011). Only after such product knowledge is created, can companies, including MasterCard in this case, hope to successfully introduce their brands.

Identifying Sources of Communication

When working on branding strategies, companies must take into account between-country and also within-country differences. Emerging markets are characterized by what is termed as the *demographic dividend*—a country that has a larger population of young people compared to the population of old people. Young consumers around the world are responsible for developing a hybrid culture where, instead of abandoning their traditional culture or opposing the global culture, they allow brands to become an integral part of their identity (Arnett 2002). An interesting paradox observed in many countries is that as globalization increases, it leads to more localization, rather than standardization (Hung 2014). Although this adds to the challenge faced by multinationals in emerging markets, one upside they can benefit from is that despite the dominance of unbranded products in these markets, younger consumers do see the value in brands. Thus, MNCs must aim to be relevant in the local context instead of assuming that their foreign name tag will attract a loyal following.

Also, who or what delivers a brand message can be as important, if not more important, than the message itself. A direct source is a spokesperson for the brand and can be a celebrity, a sports figure, a CEO, or just an ordinary consumer. An indirect source can be an object or an image like a brand logo that does not deliver a message explicitly; instead, it draws attention to or enhances a brand's communications. In general, sources must be credible and attractive and they must possess the power to influence. Using experts, such as doctors for health products or celebrities for beauty products, is an effective method for product and brand communication. Using local celebrities is a great way to infuse a product or its communication with local culture while also being able to retain an existing global positioning, if required. Since they are generally well known and well liked in society, celebrities add credibility to a brand. Many brands, such as Lux, have established their communication on a celebrity platform.

Celebrity Advertising for Lux

Using celebrities as aspirational icons, style/fashion trendsetters, and conceptualizations of "ideal" beauty to localize brand perceptions is a strategy followed by many product categories. Cosmetics companies, such as Unilever, have used celebrity endorsement and advertising successfully to market their beauty-related products. Unilever's quality and price positioning is further shored up by localizing its global strategy as it competes in countries across the Asia Pacific, Europe, Latin America, the Middle East, and North America. Its global soap brand, Lux, is promoted as "the beauty soap of film stars" and local or even global stars feature prominently on its packaging. The choice of celebrity is based on the standard of beauty for each local market.

JWT's (J. Walter Thompson's) Sam Williams, global business director for Lux, noted in an interview how Lux is popular in 50 or 60 countries, but the top 10 markets for Lux include several emerging markets like India and China. In 2008, Lux launched its Diva campaign in 50 countries focusing on obtaining soft skin and increasing desirability. In India, Lux advertising has been featuring leading Bollywood stars since 1909. Its recent campaign featured Bollywood actress Priyanka Chopra (who most recently starred in the American show *Quantico*), and it was about helping women stand out and be unique. Williams said that Lux has a global identity, and in each country, Unilever uses Lux beauty (soap) bars to target women with a modest background by localizing its packaging and advertising. As affluence increases in those countries, Lux paves the way for Unilever to introduce products like shampoos, conditioners, and lipsticks, and eventually specialized products like moisturizers, fragrances, and whitening and skin tone products (Madden 2010). For China and Taiwan, Unilever created a seven-minute movie, called *Alchemist*, with Hollywood actress Catherine Zeta-Jones. Filmed as a spy thriller, it had a high-tech lab in Europe developing a secret formula to make hair rich and shiny (Madden 2009). So using a local or global celebrity is a choice to be made depending on the product and the target audience.

Using celebrities who fit with the brand promise is also important, like Unilever's connection between beauty and movie stars. When such celebrities also have corporate social responsibility (CSR) connections it can imbue brands with a higher purpose. This can be especially meaningful in emerging markets that have a compelling need for CSR activities. For example, Samuel Eto'o is a Cameroonian soccer (football) player with impressive wins such as an Olympics title, the UEFA cup, and the Spanish La Liga. He has also been a two-time winner of the African Footballer of the Year title. He endorses brands like Puma and Ford cars, which has been immensely helpful to both brands in communicating elegance and speed. Notably, Eto'o also has an impressive record as a humanitarian through his foundation, which is named after him. Cameroon, as well as most of the Sub-Saharan Africa, is plagued by the Acquired Immune Deficiency Syndrome (AIDS), poverty, communicable diseases, and illiteracy (Nkwi 2012). Eto'o uses his foundation to inspire hope for the youth in these countries in partnership with UNICEF's program for developmental assistance and humanitarian aid to mothers and children for long-term sustainability. The program uses celebrities as ambassadors to push its projects and enhance its image among the communities it works with (World Health Organization 2014).

A brand can stand out not only based on its spokesperson but also based on its distinctive looks. Packaging options and other packaging design elements are powerful source tools that address both aesthetics and functionality. One area of opportunity in emerging economies involves organizing the market by promoting packaging and branding of products that were earlier sold either as commodities, or as small, local brands with little or no visibility. Although in Chapter 5 we discussed packaging as a way to upscale the offer, here, with the example of Haldiram in India, we demonstrate how packaging can be an effective branding strategy for converting non-users to users.

Haldiram's in India

In the Indian snack food market, valued at 111 billion U.S. dollars (USD) in 2014 (P&S Market Research 2015), Haldiram is an iconic brand with revenues of about 538 million USD, surpassing the combined sales of McDonald's and Domino's (Malviya 2015). In 1937, Haldiram was just a small, corner snack store located in the town of Bikaner, Rajasthan, in western India. The company was trademarked in 1972 and set up manufacturing units in the 1990s. They established a national presence and then began exporting traditional Indian sweet and salty snacks, frozen foods, cookies, juices, *papad* (crispy lentil wafers), and chips to the U.S., U.K., Australia, Germany, Philippines, Nepal, New Zealand, and the Middle East. Their success in retailing impelled them to set up restaurants in select cities in India and abroad.

Despite inadequate infrastructure and no integrated common food law in the country, the snacks segment in India is growing rapidly. The growth is driven primarily by fast-changing consumer lifestyles, rising exports, and fiscal incentives. But this was not always the case. Up until the 1990s, the segment consisted of unbranded, loosely sold items. Haldiram took on the pioneering role of changing packaging and branding industry norms in the local snack food segment in India.

Not only did Haldiram's address the marketing mix (The 4 P's—product, pricing, place, and promotion), but they also took charge of the fifth P—packaging. Since price competition with the unorganized players was not feasible, Haldiram's decided to compete with packaging and promotion. They created attractive packaging for their wide range of products, which increased the shelf life of their products from one week to nearly six months. Then they leveraged their packaging by depicting the entire range of products with their attractive packages on posters and billboards that were strategically placed, including at railway stations and bus stops. They also sent out brochures to corporate and regular customers and used magazines and newspapers to widen their reach. Also, their premium gift packs became popular for festivals and corporate gifting. Their positioning statement, "six months on the shelf and six seconds in your mouth," creatively leveraged the fact that packaging extended their shelf life while maintaining the freshness of their product. Packaging also ensured high standards of quality and hygiene and won them many awards and accolades (Balakrishna 2011).

Developing Appropriate Messaging

A second critical element in effective brand building is to identify what message a company wants to send out to the market about its products and brands. Both the content and the structure of the message are important. Some communications are designed to appeal to the rational, logical aspects of the consumer decision-making process, whereas others appeal to feelings in an attempt to evoke some emotional reaction. Appeals that talk about competitors, specific brand attributes, price, or some kind of news are considered to be more informational in nature. Appeals that focus on feelings and psychological needs for purchasing a particular product or brand are more emotional in nature. When a company selects the type of appeal it plans to use in its communications, it determines the way it wants to be seen in the marketplace and this defines its positioning. Some ways we discuss in the following pages are illustrative rather than exhaustive, and marketers can determine how best to develop their unique selling proposition based on their product and target audience. The mobile phone company, Micromax, positions itself on functionality with speedy innovation and cutting-edge technology, aiming its products toward young Indians.

Micromax in India

Contributor: Rahul Singh

Established in 2000, Micromax is the tenth largest mobile phone company in the world and the second largest smart phone company. Micromax has positioned itself on a platform of speedy, innovative launches targeted at the youth (Micromax 2015), and has moved rapidly from low-end devices to the smart phone market. Its cofounders often worked at the retail counters of stores to understand consumer needs. Deepak Mehrotra, Micromax's CEO, said, "At Micromax, we constantly strive to innovate and develop technologically advanced devices."

Micromax entered the mobile phone handset market in India during a time when global players such as Nokia and Samsung were dominating the market. Vikas Jain, a cofounder, said, "You need to embrace the technology completely and not in a piecemeal manner. Be innovative in hardware and software, learn by being close to consumers, and appreciate competition." Accordingly, Micromax's first phone had a one-month battery backup (compared to the typical 2 to 3 days) and was aimed at rural consumers who had limited and unreliable access to electricity as well as urban consumers who also faced power outages. Micromax then launched a dual SIM phone with a single baseband and kept adding more features to their phones (such as an over 20-language capability, social media access, etc.); finally they introduced smart phones.

By taking off-the-shelf hardware from China and adjusting it based on trends to launch smart-phone models, they were able to launch nearly three products per month. Soon Micromax came to be known as the smart-phone equivalent of "fast fashion" chains (Bellman and Krishna 2015). Rahul Sharma, another cofounder, said, "Whatever we do has to be something unique….and so we keep finding components that will give a fantastic user experience, and simultaneously we also keep the cost down. Our thinking starts from the consumer and we optimize the market price and the device."

Targeted at the youth on the platform of speedy innovation, Micromax's promotion mix focused on music, movies, and cricket, the three entertainment pillars that resonate most with young Indian consumers. They partnered with some of the biggest entertainment events and personalities in India such as Sunburn, an electronic dance music festival, MTV's Video Music Awards India, and entertainers like DJ Tiësto and Snoop Dogg.

Brands can also position themselves based on emotions by appealing to consumers' aspirations. Although it is used in the developed world as well, this strategy is especially pertinent for emerging markets because typically, almost the whole nation, not just individual consumers, is raising its socioeconomic status fairly rapidly. Aspirational marketing techniques are generally more effective than low pricing for many lifestyle product categories such as automobiles, cosmetics, athletic wear, electronics, fashion, and luxury products. Brands from developed countries have been using aspirational marketing to influence less-developed nations and, as a result, their fashion and food brands have spread to emerging and developing countries as positive, image-enhancing products. On the flip side, often emerging market brands try to modernize their strategy and marketing mix by disassociating themselves with their cultural and traditional roots either by association, aspiration, or assurance.

When McDonald's and other fast food chains entered emerging markets, their level of cleanliness, standardization, and high pricing (relative to local foods and snacks) helped them create a premium positioning in those markets that was starkly different from their low-end, fast food positioning in their home markets. Although luxury brands do target an affluent population, surprising products and brands can earn the luxury tag in emerging markets. After all, luxury can mean a BMW for an affluent consumer, a home appliance like a refrigerator for a middle-income consumer, or even a sachet of shampoo for a bottom of the pyramid (BoP) consumer. In all of these cases, the consumption fulfills the aspiration for status and luxury.

Starbucks, which began in the U.S. as a premium brand, has become more mainstream now, but in China it maintains a premium positioning because its American origin appeals to the social status–conscious population. The design and layout of the modern store, the well-trained baristas, and the high quality of the drinks all symbolize its Western roots. Unsurprisingly, it is able to price its coffee a dollar more expensive than in the U.S. (DeVault 2015). Since China is the world's largest tea-drinking market, Starbucks invested heavily in training its baristas to improve the quality of customer service and to educate consumers about coffee, such as the different varieties of coffee, and the meaning of the word "latte" (Italian word for milk) as compared to American-style coffee, which is black (Beattie 2012). Because Starbucks is symbolic of affluence in China, the wealthy lounge in its cafés for hours. Not surprisingly Starbucks already had over 2,000 stores across 100 Chinese cities and China is poised to be Starbucks' largest market (Burkitt 2016). Though Starbucks may have started off as a premium brand in its country of origin, other brands that acquire the luxury tag in emerging markets may never really have been associated with luxury originally; take Buick, for example.

Buick in China

China's automobile market has become the largest vehicle market in the world. Given the 23 million affluent urban households in the country, McKinsey estimates that by 2020, the sales of premium cars in China will surpass those in the United States (*The Wall Street Journal* 2016). A surprising contender for the luxury tag has been GM's Buick line. Buick is considered an upscale car in China as compared to a car for the elderly in the U.S. Tradition is highly respected in the Chinese culture and the aspiration to emulate elites is also very high. So when the Buick brand was seen as the car of choice for elites, such as the country's last emperor, Pu Yi (the founding father of the Republic of China), and Sun Yat-sen (China's premier until 1976), Buick became associated with the elite, such as government officials, entrepreneurs, and CEOs. The Buick GL8 minivan, known as Daqui, or harmonious, or even "cool," is often used by business executives to carry out meetings in its spacious backseat while they are being chauffeured around (Wernle 2013). At a Buick display show in Beijing, a woman who worked in an online media company stated, "I think it's a business people's car. It's stylish, fashionable and dynamic." Buick offers its GL8 minivan in models costing between 45,200 and 64,000 USD but this is not a deterrent for the aspirational, luxury-loving Chinese consumers. It is no wonder that 80 percent of all Buicks are sold in China these days; in 2015, that amounted to nearly 990,000 vehicles—4½ times as many as sold in the United States (VanSickle 2014; Ramsey 2015; Frankel 2016).

Aspirations for love and romance stem from the basic need for social affiliation and belonging, both of which have been studied in various fields like psychology, sociology, and marketing, but only in the context of the developed world. Certain aspects of love and romance may be inherently universal and some commonalities may develop due to globalization of media and entertainment. However, in other aspects, tradition and culture may differ greatly between countries or even social classes. At its showroom in China, IKEA inadvertently realized how the aspiration for love and romance imbued its practical, contemporary furniture brand with the emotional allure of romance.

IKEA in China

IKEA's innovative marketing strategy in China is driving the demand for modern European-style furniture. In August of 2015, IKEA's revenue from China was up 20 percent, helping the Swedish retailer post sales of 35.8 billion USD in the 12 months through August (Magnusson 2015).

In the U.S. and Europe, IKEA stands for low-priced, practical, yet trendy furniture (Ad Age Staff 2013). However, in China, IKEA's key differentiator has been its experiential, in-store strategy that leverages the culturally acceptable practice of displaying romantic and personal feelings in the furniture store. IKEA realized that in China this was simply a different social construction of space (Wade 2014).

Deliberately staying away from low pricing and Chinese-themed designs, IKEA has managed to create an aspirational European-themed lifestyle experience in its stores. At its stores, Chinese families enjoy the comfort of the living room, friends socialize, and children play with the toys for hours. Consumers get so close to the product that they even curl up and take naps on the beds and sofas, even as a couple or a family. IKEA has even managed to tap into the warmest, fuzziest of feelings— romance. Its showrooms have become a place where couples date, snuggle up, and it is where many even first start talking about getting married. It is no surprise that one IKEA store in China has hosted several weddings, including a completely Swedish-themed one. Camilla Hammar, IKEA China's marketing director asserts, "IKEA is proof that in China luxury labels aren't the only aspirational brands.... If you compare [Chinese consumers] with Europeans, people here still believe that tomorrow is going to be better than today" (Ad Age Staff 2013; Wade 2014).

Tapping into aspirations for beauty is another route to successful positioning. What constitutes beauty has historically differed across countries; it depends on social norms, culture, genetics, and even climate. In a global study, nearly 83 percent of women believed that standards of beauty are higher today than before. With increased travel between countries, and the vast reach of media and entertainment, there has been a democratization of beauty. In China, 63 percent of women change their beauty routines once every few months, in Brazil 55 percent of women do this, but in France it is just 25 percent. The study on beauty aspirations also found that Brazilians admire Northern Europeans; Germans admire Brazilians; and the Chinese admire the French. This shows that there may be common global archetypes of beauty, but there are also local variations (McCann.com 2012). Understanding these similarities and differences in positioning beauty brands can be a huge opportunity, one that companies like L'Oréal have successfully leveraged.

L'Oréal in India

By 2020, L'Oréal aims to be a billion-dollar company in India, which is expected to be one of the top four beauty markets in about a decade (Trefis Team 2015). L'Oréal's aspirational marketing strategy is based on a deep understanding of consumers' needs. The managing director of L'Oréal India, Pieree-Yves Arzel, spent time getting to know the Indian consumer market by going door-to-door and asking women about their perceptions of beauty products, their beauty routine, the products they use, and why. One among his many discoveries was that Indian consumers are concerned about water shortages. Consequently, L'Oréal developed fast-rinse and fast-foaming shampoos. It also developed and introduced products to India such as the Garnier Fructis Shampoo plus Oil and Maybelline the Colossal Kajal (eyeliner), which are a combination of traditional beauty routines and modern technology. Arzel also found that fair skin, big expressive eyes, and long, shiny dark hair are key aspirations of Indian consumers (Arzel 2013). Because of this, L'Oréal signed on superstar brand ambassadors from Bollywood like Aishwarya Rai Bachchan and Katrina Kaif to promote its products. Although it is attempting to change consumer behavior by promoting Western products such as mascara and eyeliner instead of traditional products such as kohl, and hair colorants instead of henna, L'Oréal remains embedded in the social ethos and aspirations of the country. As a result of this strategy, sales have doubled every two years in India (Warc 2011; L'Oréal 2013).

Health and wellness are key universal needs that people all over the world are aspiring toward. Physical, emotional, mental, and even spiritual health are being widely perceived as basic human rights instead of luxuries. Brands that position themselves around this platform by offering benefits that contribute to these goals have the opportunity to provide tremendous value to consumers. Again, there are cross-cultural differences—for example, in United Kingdom, United States, and South Africa, people feel it is easier to have wellness without having children, whereas in China and Japan the opposite is true (McCann, 2013). Thus conceptualizations of what constitutes health and wellness differs across countries.

In Chapter 5, we shared the story of Sundrop cooking oil from India, owned by Agro Tech Foods Ltd. (Agro Tech). An interesting aspect of this story is how Sundrop is positioned on a platform of aspiring for health and wellness. The brand name Sundrop is associated with "goodness" and "purity" relating to the traditional belief that the sun's rays have purifying properties. Sundrop's packaging was designed accordingly. A team of packaging engineers designed an attractive and durable packaging that would not only look good on supermarket shelves but was also tamper proof and sturdy enough to be transported across the country without leaking, thus ensuring quality, which reinforced Sundrop's purity positioning. Agro Tech also decided not to position Sundrop against another existing brand, Marico's Saffola, which was seen as the "oil for the unhealthy," that is, for those who had already suffered some cardiac issue. Thus, many different elements of the marketing mix must synchronize in order to effectively communicate the brand promise.

Ultimately, the greatest manifestation of a brand's ability to inspire trust is in the form of customer loyalty to the brand, which manifests as repeated purchases. Positioning on platforms such as health and wellness or associating with spokespeople who are contributing to society and communities meaningfully are great ways of inspiring trust in brands and companies. The contemporary business environment is very competitive in emerging markets, and this calls for businesses to pursue aggressive strategies to ensure a loyal customer base in order to maintain their competitiveness. However, as more companies join the loyalty bandwagon, simply duplicating the loyalty programs from other countries and competitors may not be enough. Safaricom, a mobile service provider in Kenya, has devised one such innovative program as described earlier in Chapter 5.

Using Traditional Channels of Communication

The third major element in the communications process is the channel that companies use to disseminate messages. Channels can be personal and include sales presentations, events, demonstrations, and trade shows, or they can be impersonal and consist of elements such as advertising, direct mail, the Internet, or sales promotions.

Although these tools are widely accepted in developed countries, their use may be restricted to select audiences in emerging markets. For the vast majority of the population who may not be accustomed to such media or may not have access to them, companies must use other means of communication.

Television, radio, and print media may have limitations in reaching rural audiences for a variety of reasons—geographical distance, and income and education level, for instance. This is, of course, changing rapidly since technologies such as mobile phones and the Internet are transforming communication; for now, however, companies that need to target such audiences will have to adopt the traditional forms of communication that are used in rural areas. These might include wall paintings, street signage, cinema ads, or posters at high traffic areas like railway stations. Other effective ways of reaching rural audiences are by using village/opinion leaders, conducting product demonstrations, and being present at social gatherings such as community events or religious celebrations.

Rural Advertising in India

A good first step to advertise in rural areas is to influence opinion leaders who will then influence the rural masses. Opinion leaders are ideal targets as they tend to be literate and can understand conventional mass media in the same way as urban populations. Although they can be easily identified, there are very few such opinion leaders in rural areas, and the best way to target them is through direct one-on-one contact programs or direct mailers.

Rural retailers are also excellent opinion leaders. They provide information about product features, prices, and promotional offers to their customers and, due to the lack of other sources of information, retailers become pivotal in the rural population's purchase decisions. Given the tiny sizes of their stores, point-of-purchase materials and other product displays are dependent on retailer relationships. Lack of market research information also makes retailers a valuable source of customer feedback, including complaints. Thus, both companies and distributors are well served by investing in retailer relationships (Prialatha and Mathi 2012).

Arvind Limited, one of the world's largest denim cloth manufacturers and leading denim brand, identified local tailors as opinion leaders for entering the rural market. They came up with a new concept of ready-to-stitch jeans called Ruf & Tuf Jeans that cost 195 INR (about 3 USD). They then marketed the jeans by providing local tailors with the necessary equipment and training to stitch them. The tailors then became opinion leaders for the clothing promoting Ruf & Tuf as an affordable, yet national, brand of jeans that were available to rural consumers. A word-of-mouth promotional strategy is the most effective in rural areas since more than half of those who live there listen to the advice of opinion leaders on products prior to buying anything (Dogra and Ghuman 2007).

Another effective method for advertising in rural areas is wall paintings since they are long-lasting, highly visible, reach a large audience, and can be designed to match local needs, aesthetics, and environment. Not only are they economical, but they are also welcomed by retailers because they enhance the appearance of their tiny shanty-like stores.

In India, as in other emerging markets, a word-of-mouth strategy for building brand awareness is also often used at community events such as *melas* (fairs) and *haats* (village markets). Mobile vans, street theater, and puppet shows are other ways of communicating with a rural community. Cholayil, a personal care company, used a mobile van to promote its herbal soap called Medimix. The mobile van traveled to rural villages and stopped at select locations to allow a crowd of locals to watch videos and receive samples (Pidshetti 2007). Similarly, Brooke Bond Lipton India Ltd. employed a magician to promote its tea brand, Kadak Chhap (meaning "strong impact"). The local magician performed a skit as the promotional message by interacting with a local boy who played the role of the underdog who kills the evil guys after drinking a cup of Kadak Chaap. After the skit, the locals were given a free sample of the tea (Krishnamacharyulu and Ramakrishnan 2010).

Leveraging New and Unconventional Media

For the most part, new media includes a variety of digital media as well as several forms of social media. In addition to websites for branding and e-commerce, companies are also creating both print and video digital content for their own and other websites; they use paid search, blogs, rich media, and a host of social media platforms to get the word out about their brands. Perhaps the biggest change in marketing communication over the past decade has been the wide adoption of branded entertainment, which is a form of brand communication that blends advertising and entertainment through TV, film, music talent, and technology. Product placement and content sponsorship are among the largest areas of nontraditional communications growth. In addition to branded entertainment, another nontraditional way that advertisers are now able to reach consumers is called guerrilla or viral marketing, and technology often plays a large part in this. Depending upon the type of outreach, some marketers call this form of communication stealth marketing, ambush marketing, or buzz marketing. This type of marketing is very relevant in emerging markets because, although a vast majority of the population lives in its villages, the sheer numbers of those who live in urban areas or who have relatively large disposable incomes is attractive to marketers. However, standard communications tools may be unfamiliar or inappropriate, even for this urban audience. For example, to reinforce the consumption script that chicken nuggets taste best when dunked into ketchup, McDonald's put images of chicken nuggets on elevators in one of China's busiest shopping malls and images of bowls full of ketchup at the bottom to give the illusion of chicken nuggets being dipped into the sauce (Cruz 2014).

The Coca-Cola Company also uses many unconventional ways of associating itself with positive emotions. As part of its "happiness" campaign, it used novel methods like having a Coke truck with a big red button drive around the streets of Rio de Janeiro in Brazil. Local bystanders were enticed to push the red button for rewards, which varied from a bottle of Coke, to beach toys, Frisbees, and surfboards. In Bogotá, Colombia, Coca-Cola found a bustling street that was consistently packed with traffic; they sought to relieve tensions by setting up a large projector with entertainment and then they delivered a bottle of Coke and popcorn to those stuck in traffic (Lum 2011). In South Korea, Coca-Cola's Interactive Happiness Machine gave out free bottles of Coke if people danced along with the dance moves on the screen (Hall 2012). By involving customers in campaigns instead of using traditional advertising, companies not only leave a lasting impression, but also reach a larger population because the videos of the campaigns often go viral via social media.

The social media explosion has provided companies with many opportunities to reach out to their consumers directly. Managing this interaction well is an essential challenge for marketers. With the rapid adoption of technology in many parts of emerging nations, social media has found a young and eager audience, who is open to new ways of consumption and purchase. Facebook's second-largest market is India with 125 million users (*The Times of India* 2015). In Brazil, 75 percent of Brazilian social media users follow brands on Facebook and 60 percent follow them on Twitter and local social media platforms (Rowles 2014). China has the world's biggest Internet population. However, the big names in the social media—like Facebook, Twitter, and YouTube—are banned, and companies have to rely on local alternatives to reach the Chinese netizens. Sina Weibo is similar to Twitter. Tencent is the leading Internet portal in China and biggest Internet company by revenue. Tencent's wide range of products includes the QQ messenger service, which plays a big role in Chinese social media. Thus, emerging markets are witnessing the emergence of home-grown social media as well.

WeChat in China

In China, Tencent's subsidiaries provide media, entertainment, and services such as social networks, web portals, and online games for mobile devices. One of its subsidiaries, WeChat, is a mobile text and voice messaging service; this service is also a multisided platform that allows mobile game developers to sell their games on the platform and share the revenues with WeChat in the same way as stores that open up a virtual branch on WeChat do. WeChat has blended elements of Facebook and Instagram to attract many marketers.

We discussed WeChat's freemium model in Chapter 4, but here we talk about how this local social media innovates to provide advertisers the opportunity to offer their customers a uniquely local experience. For example, PepsiCo partnered with WeChat to promote a twist on the traditional celebrations for the Chinese New Year. People could record their greetings on WeChat, and the messages would then get mixed with a well-known soundtrack, "Bring Happiness Home." Customers could add effects like train sounds or a galloping horse to represent the feeling of being on the way home. People were especially fond of galloping horses since it was the Year of the Horse in China. The subtlety of the message via the theme song, combined with the overt expression of caring for the Chinese tradition, led to the perception that Pepsi was spreading happiness rather than advertising its product, and thus they won over many hearts.

WeChat has also been used by other international brands in China. In a runway show, Burberry, the British luxury brand, took WeChat fans behind the scenes where they were offered audio commentary by Chinese celebrities and the team behind the project. Fans received virtual plaques engraved with their names whenever they sent Burberry a text message. These one-on-one conversations with consumers have helped companies such as Burberry get wider recognition in China.

References

Ad Age Staff. 2013. "A Wedding in Aisle 3? Why Ikea Encourages Chinese to Make Its Stores Their Own." *Advertising Age*. December 10. Accessed on January 11, 2015. http://adage.com/article/cmo-strategy/ikea-encourages-chinese-make-stores/245573.

Arnett, Jeffery J. 2002. "The Psychology of Globalization." *American Psychologist* 57(10): 774–783.

Arzel, Pierrre-Yves. 2013. "L'Oréal's Lessons from Indian Homes." *Forbes India*. March 1. Accessed on June 25, 2014. http://forbesindia.com/printcontent/34795.

Balakrishna, Sidharth. 2011. *Case Studies in Marketing*. Pearson Education. 164.

Beattie, Anita C. 2012. "Can Starbucks Make China Love Joe?" *Advertising Age*. November 5. Accessed on June 25, 2014. http://adage .com/china/article/china-news/can-starbucks-make-china-love-coffee/238101.

Bellman, Eric and R. Jai Krishna. 2015. "India's Micromax Churns Out Phones Like Fast Fashion." *The Wall Street Journal*. June 4. Accessed on March 1, 2016. www.wsj.com/articles/indias-micro-max-churns-out-phones-like-fast-fashion-1433456543.

Burkitt, Laurie. 2016. "Starbucks to Add Thousands of Stores in China." *The Wall Street Journal*. January 12. Accessed on April 28, 2016. www.wsj.com/articles/starbucks-plans-thousands-of-new-stores-in-china-1452580905.

Cruz, Xath. 2014. "McDonald's Make Adults Feel Like a Kid Again." *Creative Guerrilla Marketing*. January 29. Accessed on June 5, 2014. www.creativeguerrillamarketing.com/guerrilla-marketing/mcdonalds-make-adults-feel-like-kid.

D'Andrea, Guillermo, David Marcotte, and Gwen Dixon Morrison. 2010. "The Globe: Let Emerging Market Customers Be Your Teachers." *Harvard Business Review*. Accessed on April 25, 2016. https://hbr.org/2010/12/the-globe-let-emerging-market-customers-be-your-teachers.

DeVault, Gigi. 2015. "Market Research Case Study—Starbucks' Entry into China." *About Money*. December 31. Accessed on January 4, 2016. http://marketresearch.about.com/od/market .research.competitive/a/Market-Research-Case-Study-Starbucks-Entry-Into-China.htm.

Dogra, Balram, and Karminder Ghuman. 2007. "Rural Marketing of Consumer Durables." *Rural Marketing: Concepts and Practices*. Delhi, India: McGraw-Hill Education.

Frankel, Todd C. 2016. "'That's a Buick?' In China, Unlike the U.S., There's No Doubt." *The Washington Post*. January 20. Accessed on February 26, 2016. www.washingtonpost.com/news/business/wp/2016/01/20thats-a-buick-in-china-unlike-the-u-s-theres-no-doubt.

Hall, Christopher. 2012. "Coke Launches Dance Dance Revolution in S. Korea with Digital Signage Kiosk" (Video). *Digital Signage Today*. October 18. Accessed on April 28, 2016. www.digital-signagetoday.com/articles/coke-launches-dance-dance-revolution-in-s-korea-with-digital-signage-kiosk-video/.

Hung, Kineta. 2014. "Why Celebrity Sells: A Dual Entertainment Path Model of Brand Endorsement." *Journal of Advertising* 43(2): 155–166.

Krishnamacharyulu, C. S. G., and Lalitha Ramakrishnan. 2010. *Rural Marketing: Text and Cases*. Delhi, India: Pearson Education. 608.

L'Oréal. 2013. "L'Oréal Unveils New Research & Innovation Center in India." Accessed on June 25, 2014. www.lorealusa.com/press-releases/loreal-unveils-new-research-innovation-center-in-india.aspx.

Lum, Ryan. 2011. "Follow Coca-Cola's Amazing Unconventional Marketing Efforts!" *Creative Guerrilla Marketing*. May 12. Accessed on June 4, 2014. www.creativeguerrillamarketing.com/guerrilla-marketing/cocacola-returns-outdoor-theatre-marketing-effort.

Madden, Normandy. 2010. "Unilever's Lux Grows Sales in Asia and Latin America." *Advertising Age*. July 22. Accessed on October 19, 2015. http://adage.com/article/global-news/marketing-unilever-s-lux-grows-sales-emerging-markets/145049.

Madden, Normandy. 2009. "Unilever Creates Short Firm to Launch Latest Lux Hair-Care Line." *Advertising Age*. March 18. Accessed on May 7, 2016. http://adage.com/article/global-news/unilever-creates-short-film-starring-catherine-zeta-jones/135333/.

Magnusson, Niklas. 2015. "Ikea to Keep Investing in Emerging Markets as China Fuels Growth." *Bloomberg*. September 10. Accessed on February 25, 2016. www.bloomberg.com/news/articles/2015-09-10/ikea-full-year-sales-advance-led-by-chinese-russian-growth.

Malviya, Sagar. 2015. "Haldiram's Leads Indian Snack Market; Surpasses Combined Sales of McDonald's and Domino's." *The Economic Times*. February 3. Accessed February 14, 2016. http://articles.economictimes.indiatimes.com/2015-02-03/news/58751638_1_east-india-crore-agarwals.

The MasterCard Foundation. 2011. "Taking Stock: Financial Education Initiatives for the Poor, a Report." *Global Study on Financial Education: Report*. The MasterCard Foundation, Microfinance Opportunities, and Genesis Analytics. Accessed on May 1, 2016. www.microfinanceopportunities.org.

McCann.com. 2012. "The Truth about Beauty." McCann Truth Central. Accessed on February 14, 2016. http://mccann.com/wp-content/uploads/2012/06/McCann_Truth_About_Beauty.pdf.

———. 2013. "The Truth about Wellness." McCann Truth Central. Accessed on February 14, 2016. http://mccann.com/wp-content/uploads/2013/01/wellness_Truth-Central_book-layout_individualpages.pdf.

Micromax. 2015. "About Us." Micromax Informatics Ltd. Accessed on March 5, 2016. www.micromaxinfo.com/about-us.

Nkwi, Paul N. 2012. "Football in Cameroon: Its Origins, Politics and Sorcery." *Fractures and Reconnections: Civic Action and the Redefinition of African Political and Economic Spaces*. Edited by J. Abbink. The Netherlands: LIT Verlag, 5.

P&S Market Research. 2015. "Global Savory Snacks Market (Size of $111 Billion in 2014) to Witness 7% CAGR During 2015–2020." *PRNewswire*. July 21. Accessed February 14, 2015. www.prnewswire.com/news-releases/global-savory-snacks-market-size-of-111-billion-in-2014-to-witness-7-cagr-during-2015--2020-520262011.html.

Piddshetti, Mahesh M. 2007. "Building Brands in Rural India." *Hyper Passionate Entrepreneurs: Word Press.* October 8. Accessed on June 14, 2014. https://hitechstartups.wordpress.com/2007/10/08/building-brands-in-rural-india.

Prialatha, P., and K. Malar Mathi. 2012. "Word of Mouth: The Key to Unlock Hinterland." *Journal of Management and Science* 2 (2): 81.

Ramsey, Jay. 2015. "Poll: Would You Buy a Buick GL8?" *Autoweek.* August 27. Accessed January 14, 2015. http://autoweek.com/article/car-news/poll-would-you-buy-buickgl8#ixzz40GT5DKGE.

REEV Consult International. 2007. "Uganda Microfinance Consumer Education Programme Learning Exercise: Final Report." London: DFID. September. Accessed on May 1, 2016. www.fsdu.or.ug/pdfs/CEP%20Learning%20Exercise%20Final%20report.pdf.

Rowles, Daniel. 2014. *Digital Branding: A Complete Step-by-Step Guide to Strategy, Tactics and Measurement.* Philadelphia, Kogan Page.

Sheth, Jagdish N. and Rajendra S.Sisodia. 2012. *The 4 A's of Marketing: Creating Value for Customers, Companies, and Society.* New York: Routledge.

The Times of India. 2015. "Facebook's User Base Touches 125 Million in India." June 29. Accessed on February 24, 2016. http://timesofindia.indiatimes.com/tech/tech-news/Facebooks-user-base-touches-125-million-in-India/articleshow/47866523.cms.

Trefis Team. 2015. "Some of the Key Regions Expected to Fuel L'Oreal's Future Growth." *Forbes.* December 21. Accessed on February 14, 2016. www.forbes.com/sites/greatspeculations/2015/12/21/some-of-the-key-regions-expected-to-fuel-loreals-futuregrowth/#19d6a7dc10cc.

VanSickle, Abbie. 2014. "Not Just Your Grandma's Car, Buicks Shine in Chinese Luxury Market." *The Seattle Globalist.* May 19. Accessed on June 29, 2014. www.seattleglobalist.com/2014/05/19/not-just-your-grandmas-car-buicks-shine-in-chinese-luxury-market/25116.

Wade, Lisa. 2014. "Sleep, Snuggle, Socialize: In China, People Do Just About Everything in Ikea." *Pacific Standard*. February 12. Accessed on January 11, 2015. www.psmag.com/books-and-culture/sleep-snuggle-socialize-china-people-just-everything-ikea-74521.

The Wall Street Journal. 2016. "China Car Sales Growth Slows Further." January 12. Accessed on February 14, 2016. www.wsj.com/articles/china-car-sales-growth-slows-further-1452587244?cb=logged0.4299596193241628.

Warc. 2011. "L'Oréal Gets 'Aspirational' in India." July 27. Accessed on June 24, 2014. www.warc.com/LatestNews/News/LOréal_gets_%22aspirational%22_in_India.news?ID=28598.

Wernle, Bradford. 2013. "In the Land of Many Buicks, One in Particular Stood Out." *Automotive News*. May 17. Accessed on May 9, 2014. www.autonews.com/article/20130517/BLOG06/130519893/in-the-land-of-many-buicks-one-in-particular-stood-out.

The World Bank. n.d. "Data by Country: Uganda." Accessed on May 1, 2016. http://data.worldbank.org/country/uganda.

World Health Organization. 2014. "Trends in Maternal Mortality: 1990 to 2013: Estimates by WHO, UNICEF, UNFPA, The World Bank and the United Nations Population Division." May. Accessed on September 9, 2015. www.who.int/reproductivehealth/publications/monitoring/maternal-mortality-2013/en.

9

Engaging Stakeholders

Typically, companies think of awareness-building as it relates to their brand or, at most, their products. But the opportunities and challenges that companies face in emerging markets provides an impetus for them to think beyond product sales and even customers or investors. Adopting a complete stakeholder orientation, and not just a customer orientation, has been a fairly recent idea for the discipline of marketing (Bhattacharya 2010). Sisodia, Wolfe, and Sheth (2007) describe the idea that companies can do well by doing good in their book *Firms of Endearment*. This is philosophically aligned with a stakeholder orientation that urges companies to address the needs of all entities (including the environment) that are affected by the company and its activities. Companies have been transcending from a purely philanthropic mindset to include corporate social responsibility (CSR) into their strategies. However, more recently, the acknowledgment that the environment is also a critical consideration is paving the way for what is referred to as sustainability initiatives that aim to achieve the triple bottom line— social, economic, and environmental. This is especially important at a time when companies are increasingly being vilified for profiting at the expense of society and the environment (Porter and Kramer 2006, 2011).

Stakeholder marketing is needed even more in developing and emerging markets, as compared to developed markets, because these countries tend to be economically disadvantaged and have fragile social and environmental ecosystems. Despite being rich in natural resources and labor, they are lower in income than developed countries. Some are socially and politically unstable and lack basic infrastructure whereas others struggle to build strong institutions and regulatory frameworks. Thus, for companies in emerging markets, engaging in sustainability initiatives is not just a feel-good thing to do but an operational imperative that can reap rich dividends in terms of building and enhancing corporate/brand reputation, and hence profitability (Sheth and Sinha 2015).

In this chapter, we extend the brand- and product-focused conceptualization of *awareness* as described in Sheth and Sisodia's 4 A's framework. The needs of emerging markets compel managers to think about numerous stakeholders and ways in which companies can mindfully make a positive impact on society. For this, we offer five strategies for engaging stakeholders: 1) educating consumers and markets, 2) involving communities and leaders, 3) engaging employees, 4) co-opting suppliers, and 5) developing partnerships with public, private, and nonprofit companies.

Educating Consumers and Markets

Introducing new products in the marketplace and getting consumers to like and adopt them can be challenging. As we discussed in Chapter 8, firms may have to provide education about the product category in emerging markets before any brand awareness can be created. Educating consumers and creating a positive environment for the initial product experience requires investment and commitment on the part of companies that enter those markets. However, these are critical for consumer decision-making because they enable consumers to derive their own conclusions about a product's efficacy and its relevance to their lives. In the developed world the consumption of many products is taken for granted, such as soft drinks, but in emerging markets some amount of education may still be necessary, not just about the product itself, but also the outcome from consuming it, as the Coca Cola example illustrates.

Coca Cola in China

The Coca-Cola Company's largest potential market is China where the annual average per capita consumption of soft drinks is just 39 8-ounce servings, compared to 401 8-ounce servings in the U.S. (Statista n.d). China is also one of the few places where Coca-Cola trails Pepsi in market share (Fowler and McKay 2008). One key challenge that Coca-Cola faces is that traditionally the Chinese prefer hot, rather than cold, beverages. Thus, category expansion must precede brand awareness, which makes education essential. One of the opportunities that Coca-Cola used for educating consumers was during the Beijing Olympics.

Coca-Cola has been a longtime sponsor of the Olympic Games. For the 2008 Beijing Olympics, Coca-Cola created a new logo with "lucky" Chinese symbols, like a red kite and clouds. It launched an innovative, new, *Sui Wo Ku* bottle designed to reflect the ambition, individualism, and adventure-seeking spirit of young Chinese consumers (Olympic.org 2007). More importantly, it created a giant pavilion where people could watch the games on large screens and get a free Coke. Part of Coca-Cola's goal was to reach a point where the consumer would say "I like it cold." This is, in fact, a significant goal to achieve, because traditions and habits are hard to change.

In addition to educating consumers about how to consume its products, Coca-Cola must also address the concern that its product is associated with health problems such as obesity. Accordingly, Coca-Cola actively engages in CSR programs in China to promote health-conscious consumption. In 2009, through a partnership with China's Ministry of Health, Coca-Cola launched a program called Balanced Diet—Active Living. The program delivers science-based health information to the public, promotes a "walking day" on the 11th of every month, sponsors awards at universities to encourage students to practice healthy living, and uses social media to facilitate an exchange of ideas for living a balanced and healthy lifestyle (The Coca-Cola Company 2012).

Governments can also engage with their citizens through a process of education in order to meet the goals of a nation. South Africa's Revenue Service (SARS) is a case in point. In Chapter 7, we shared SARS' initiative in providing access to its services across the country. However, just providing access would not have been effective in drawing in larger numbers of people if SARS had not also educated these potential taxpayers about their tax obligations, and informed them about how tax contributions make a positive impact on their society.

SARS ran thousands of workshops each year for small businesses to explain their tax obligations and the requirements and processes for meeting them. They launched a multimedia campaign, featuring actual taxpayers, to thank the businesses and tell them how their contributions had been put to use for the benefit of society—for instance, they told of the number of houses and clinics that were built and the water sources that were established. At the same time, they trained their customer-service front-level staff to improve their sensitivity to taxpayer's needs and to help older customers who struggled with technology. SARS considered this an educative-consultative process.

Apart from end customers and consumer markets, we must also consider capital markets. Although emerging markets have significantly increased their economic influence in terms of share of global output, they remain underdeveloped in many significant ways, such as the state of their capital markets. As political structures in these countries evolve, structural reform takes place, and markets liberalize, the number of companies coming to market will increase. This will fuel a rise in both debt and equity, which will lead to active capital markets. At the same time, rising income is expected to spur the savings rate of households as well as governments. This will likely lead to the rise of pension and mutual funds and insurance markets. Another factor that can trigger development is government pushing through liberalization for local as well as international investors, which, in turn, will provide more funding options for companies. Estimates indicate that China, which already has more than 1 million high-net-worth individuals, could potentially become the second largest equity market by 2030 if it continues to liberalize (Langridge 2015). Global firms are increasingly listed in the stock exchanges in emerging markets such as in Asia. The presence of global players in emerging markets provides experience and training for the local managers they hire and also educates local companies in the financial systems of the developed world. Another impetus for the strengthening of financial systems is cross-border investments. Developed countries can facilitate the development of capital markets in emerging economies by serving as advisors to policy makers and regulators, thus helping to propagate good practices and work with the government and local companies to identify policies that foster local capital market liquidity and development. They can also conduct training, provide experts, or fund such educational initiatives (Lipsky 2007).

Involving Communities and Leaders

The process of educating people in order to create awareness is not an easy one, especially for consumers at the bottom of the pyramid (BoP). Involving community leaders is an effective way to reach out to various target audiences, and doing so also helps managers identify issues pertinent to the people they wish to target. Often, this entails education that goes beyond product/brand information and includes social issues. For instance, pharmaceutical companies operating in developing countries often have to engage communities in order to create awareness about health issues and product category before they attempt to build their brand. This education has been beneficial both to the pharmaceutical companies and to the community (Hoene 2013). Many companies use teachers and government-assigned educators for instruction pertaining to products, brands, or CSR-related social initiatives. We now describe initiatives by GlaxoSmithKline (GSK) and DuPont, which depict different ways of partnering with members of the community.

GlaxoSmithKline in Africa and Latin America

GSK's mission for personal hygiene and sanitation is to improve the quality of human life by enabling people to do more, feel better, and live longer. For this, GSK partners with underserved communities to help reach the United Nations' millennium development goals. In West Africa, they trained over 500 teachers, school management committee members, community health workers, and district officials (GlaxoSmithKline 2013). They also constructed 52 gender-segregated latrines and hand-washing stations in 14 schools. In Kenya and Zambia in Africa, and in Nicaragua and Peru in Latin America, GSK teaches children about the importance of good sanitation and hand washing. They have created culturally appropriate education materials and trained teachers and community leaders to implement the program in schools for children between the ages of 6 and 13 in order to inculcate good life-long habits. Further, they encourage the children to take this knowledge back to their homes so they can educate their family and community members. GSK has reached 83,000 children in 247 schools in Kenya, and 47,000 children in Peru (Hoffman PR n.d.).

Using educators or trainers can be challenging, as DuPont discovered when promoting soy protein in rural India. Although soy protein is a healthy source of a much needed nutrient, its incompatibility with traditional Indian food and eating habits was a significant barrier, and DuPont had to think creatively to overcome this challenge.

DuPont's Solae in India

In India, DuPont's subsidiary, Solae, produces soy protein. DuPont had to use a multi-step creative approach to incorporate soy into traditional cuisine in India since soy protein was not part of traditional cooking. Solae first had to show homemakers various ways in which they could use soy in their cooking without compromising on taste. Additionally, they also needed buy-in from other members of the family who ate those meals.

To gain acceptance for this product, Solae recruited 20 women who were interested in being entrepreneurs from the slums in Hyderabad and from a village in the state of Andhra Pradesh. The business idea was to get these women to develop a service that would help housewives incorporate soy into their home-cooked meals. The entrepreneurs spent the first month experimenting with soy-based recipes and then they started hosting neighborhood cookery days, to which they invited their friends, family, and community leaders. This was followed by cooking outreach programs where several women would meet at one person's home and would jointly cook a soy-based dish. Friends, family and community leaders would get to taste the food cooked at the party. Eventually a recipe booklet was created containing community-inspired soy-based dishes. Within six months, this entrepreneur-led cooking outreach program was formally launched and was moving toward profitability (Simanis 2009).

Multinationals also have to overcome the significant mistrust of foreigners, some of which stems from the countries' colonial pasts. Being sensitive to the local culture, milieu, and traditions is an imperative. Successful companies often display their sensitivities to the land and its people by becoming societally relevant and contributing to broader objectives, like inclusive development and poverty alleviation, thus addressing the important issues that hinder development of any kind in emerging markets. All of these initiatives involve some level of education that then creates empowerment. For example, Vodafone tries to maximize the benefits of cellular communication by serving disadvantaged communities and societies many of which are in emerging markets. In 1994, they began a community service program to increase telecommunication services and employment opportunities in South Africa through phone shop franchises with five cellular lines in poor communities (Zhang 2008). The phone shops, made of old shipping containers, were open to the community at rates considerably less expensive than the commercial rate for prepaid phone calls, providing the franchisees with a livelihood while helping bring people and communities together via communication (Reck and Wood 2003).

Engaging Employees

Hal Rosenbluth and Diane Peters appropriately said in their book by the same name that the customer comes second (2002). Hiring, motivating, and managing employees are critical tasks because employees are a company's greatest assets. The role of employees is even more critical in emerging markets where challenges abound and opportunities are hard to grab. Local employees can bring in expertise, experience, and access to networks which, when combined with cultural insights, familiarity with traditions, norms, and even regulatory restrictions, become invaluable. Even when employees are brought in from other countries, their knowledge of the home country, headquarters, global policies, and procedures can bring value. Although all of these can contribute to the bottom line, we would like to note that emerging markets offer the opportunity to engage employees beyond what the job demands, as illustrated in Avon and Nestlé's example of rural marketing, where a simple sales function is not so simple and employees need to go the extra mile to reach consumers. In addition, the employees themselves may have no sales and business experience, and for many, this may be a first experience with attempting to earn a livelihood. Thus, companies need to invest in education for the employees, who then in turn will reach out to educate consumers about product categories, brands, or even social and health issues.

Door-to-Door Selling in Brazil

Avon is famous for successfully breaking into the large, untapped market in the Brazilian Amazon by training their door-to-door saleswomen. It built an enviable distribution model where the iconic Avon ladies would undertake tremendous hardship to travel by ferries, small boats, and canoes to reach isolated Brazilian towns in order to sell cosmetics to what companies once considered unlikely and unreachable consumers. Apart from Avon's skills in hiring and training its sales team, its flexibility in terms of acceptable payment methods also went a long way toward its success. The Avon saleswomen were permitted to receive payments in chickens, eggs, gold, fruit, vegetables, and services, as well. Just one year of sales from the Amazon basin in Brazil accounted for 70 million USD of the company's total 465 million USD in sales nationally (Harris 1994), which understandably propelled Avon to a leadership position in the Brazilian cosmetics market (Brunke 2013).

Nestlé is a similar example of how a company can build product awareness in rural markets. Nestlé did this by educating door-to-door saleswomen on nutrition and health; these women in turn educate BoP consumers. In addition to using this door-to-door model in Brazil, Nestlé reaches the rural markets through local distributors and wholesalers as well as by targeting consumers at social events, street markets, and community centers. It has a range of products in developing countries it calls Popularly Positioned Products (PPP). It has developed a new distribution model for which it hires women in rural communities as micro-distributors of its products at affordable prices. With 200 micro-distributors and 7,000 women going door-to-door in rural communities of Brazil, Nestlé's massive outreach program was reaching 700,000 people every month (Nestlé n.d.(a)). Since every woman worked as an independent sales representative in her neighborhood, she was able to work as little or as much as she needed. "On average these sellers make 40 percent more than the minimum wage and many make up to four times more than their previous income levels" (World Health Organization n.d.). The success experienced in Brazil has provided an impetus to Nestlé for rolling out the program in other Latin American countries.

Companies motivate employees and earn their loyalty in a variety of ways. However, taking this further, one of the greatest strengths a company can develop is galvanizing its employees in a way that spurs them to achieve a higher purpose—not just for the organization, but also for themselves. Engaging employees in sustainability initiatives is one such approach taken by the Dow Chemical Company.

Dow Chemical Company in Ghana

Dow is a diversified company and one of its interests is in agriculture. Through Dow AgroSciences, it offers a variety of products/solutions for crop yield improvement, development of better varieties of crops, and pest management (Dow AgroSciences n.d.). Dow collaborates with PYXERA Global, which specializes in creating partnerships between companies, governments, educational institutions, and even individuals to solve complex problems across the world (PYXERA Global n.d.). Although Dow has several projects with PYXERA Global, here we share their Leadership in Action initiative in Ghana from May to September 2013. As part of this program, 36 employees were selected to work in teams to solve challenges that six organizations in Ghana faced. They partnered with the local government, a non-profit agency, a social enterprise, and two universities—one of their projects was sustainable farming.

Medicinal plants are routinely used for healthcare in Ghana, but most of these plants are undomesticated and grow wild. Dow employees worked with the Department of Crop Science at The University of Ghana College of Agriculture and Consumer Sciences (CACS) to develop marketing protocols and optimum management practices for domesticating two types of medicinal plants that effectively treat malaria. In May 2013, the Dow team began consulting sessions with CACS to understand the problem and come up with solutions. During the initial months of such virtual consultations, they decided to expand the scope of their work to include stakeholders from the entire value chain, such as farmers, middle men, pill makers, and even drug/medicine clinics. Thereafter, the team went to Ghana for a week to work with CACS and all of the stakeholders. The outcome was a set of protocols that medicinal plan collectors can use for growing cash crops and improving their livelihood, while also being able to grow the medicinal plants in a sustainable way. At the end of this project Dow's Vice President of Human Resources—Center of Expertise Johanna Soderstrom said, "We are thrilled that Dow employees are being exposed to this kind of leadership development opportunity and pleased to be able to demonstrate Dow's commitment to the global community by putting some of our brightest minds to work on some of the country's most important challenges. Most importantly, we look forward to the potential impact on the Ghanaian community" (PYXERA Global n.d).

Co-opting Suppliers

Apart from employees, stakeholders are increasingly holding companies responsible for the actions of their supply-chain members as well. In response, companies are rethinking their entire supply-chain strategy, starting with education and awareness. In 2011, adidas Group persuaded 25 of its suppliers across 8 countries—the Philippines, Indonesia, Mexico, Brazil, Vietnam, China, El Salvador, and Thailand—to agree to a self-assessment of their policies and practices. adidas then used this to improve their process of monitoring compensation and pay issues at suppliers' factories and incorporated the fair wage idea into their supplier training in their human resources management system (Hower 2013). Similarly, Nike had its supply chain managers identify opportunities for improving sustainability and then implement and track them. These managers identified the highest polluters from Nike's 150 contract factories in China; Nike then worked with the factories to improve their operational, environmental, and social performance (Lee 2010).

Taking this a step further is the process of co-opting—when companies collaborate intensively with suppliers and make them a part of their team to achieve mutually beneficial goals. In turn, suppliers develop a deep understanding of the needs of not just the company, but also the end customers that their client serves. However, achieving this synchronization is challenging due to conflicting interests. For example, companies want to get the lowest possible price from suppliers while suppliers want to attain the highest possible margins from the companies they sell to. The example of Esquel Group illustrates how this can be achieved.

Esquel in China

In the early 2000s, Esquel, a world-wide leading producer of cotton shirts, found that its customers, like Nike and Marks & Spencer, required it to improve its environmental and social performance and also to use organically grown cotton. However, Esquel was growing its cotton in poor countries—for example, Xiniang province in China where the cotton crop required a lot of water and pesticides. Traditional farming methods were inefficient—for example, when farmers flooded the fields for irrigation, it resulted in an increasing number of insects and disease, which then required more pesticides. Growing organic cotton would result in a drop in yield per hectare by almost half, and the fibers were also of weaker quality. These challenges made it difficult for Esquel to ask its farmers to pursue organic farming.

Instead of imposing new norms on the farmers, Esquel took a holistic approach by helping its farmers adopt sustainable farming techniques such as drip irrigation and alternate harvesting techniques (e.g., handpicking instead of using chemical defoliants). They partnered with banks to get microfinancing for the farmers who adopted these new techniques. Esquel also guaranteed the farmers payment of either the company set price or the market rate for their cotton, whichever was higher, and agreed to pay and place orders when the cotton was planted. As a result, the farm yield of organic cotton doubled and Esquel's supply increased (Lee 2010).

Although companies helping their supply chain members seems logical from a profitability perspective, often such transformations can have far-reaching impacts on society and indeed the country. An example of this type of expanded social benefit is evident in the case of Nestlé, which found itself addressing not just training and clean water challenges, but also the much larger social and economic problem of child labor in Africa.

Nestlé in Ghana and Ivory Coast

Contributors: Kwaku Appiah Adu and George Amoako

Nestlé Ghana's marketing strategy is predominantly guided by Nestlé's global marketing strategy, but it has been adapted to local conditions based on consumer preferences, the availability of raw materials, and the state of distribution channels. Senior managers, consultants, and daily category teams work toward adapting global strategies for regional or local context. Apart from ensuring the quality and taste of its "Popularly Positioned Products (PPP)," as Nestlé terms its bestsellers, it has to be especially mindful of its competitors and also has to be creative in addressing constraints, such as long lead times on the supply side, because it needs to import almost 80 percent of its raw materials. One of the ways that Nestlé Ghana works to overcome demand-side challenges is by ingraining itself into the social and economic fabric of the country by undertaking a number of sustainability initiatives aimed at its supply chain.

Nestlé Ghana, has partnered with Source Trust, Armajaro (ECOMS), and Noble Resource to launch the Nestlé Cocoa Plan to support the lives of cocoa farmers and improve their crop quality. They trained 9,000 farmers, distributed higher yielding cocoa plants, and provided incentives for producing good quality cocoa. They built three schools and constructed eight borewells for water that have benefitted 14,000 people. They also set up Village Resource Centers that trained local students in farming techniques, often via videos (Nestlé n.d.(b)).

On the Ivory Coast, Nestlé created a team of 20 local and international experts to evaluate its supply chain. It mapped the stakeholders in its cocoa supply chain and assessed labor risks specifically with respect to child labor. Nestlé tried to understand the root causes of child labor and identify ways of developing a robust monitoring and remediation system so that it could plug the gaps in its internal management systems. For this, the company partnered with a number of government agencies, civil society organizations, and local associations, and visited seven of its largest suppliers, gathering data from 466 men, women, and children from 87 farms. The teams concluded that Nestlé faced several risks in terms of labor standards especially for child labor, forced labor, health and safety, discrimination, and compensation. Since one company cannot solve the extensive problem of child labor, Nestlé worked with other industry actors who also shared the same supply chain and created the Fair Labor Assessment report, which made several recommendations (Fair Labor Association 2012). Thus, improving its supply chain meant that Nestlé also had to be mindful of the needs of various direct and indirect stakeholders.

Developing Partnerships with Public, Private, and Nonprofit Companies

Companies find partnerships to be an invaluable route to engaging with multiple stakeholders in emerging markets. A public-private partnership (PPP) brings together private and public or government entities to collaborate for mutual benefit, as well as to benefit the intended targets of their effort. The parties typically sign a long-term contract and engage in providing a public asset or service. Typically, the private party takes on the risk and management responsibility with remuneration linked to performance (World Bank 2015). By leveraging the strengths of the different parties involved, the large challenges that emerging markets face can be more effectively addressed. Microsoft used PPPs in Latin America for overcoming the digital divide.

Microsoft in Latin America

Microsoft launched a Partnerships for Technology Access (PTA) initiative to develop a model for strategic technology alliances between public and private stakeholders in five key areas: education, public safety and national security, government, health, and city improvement (Microsoft n.d.). The PTA model targeted the second wave of technology adopters to help them cross the digital divide to connect more effectively with the government and become a productive part of the economy (Bennett and Howard 2007).

In Chile, PTA created a PPP called Mipyme Avanza (which translates to "my small business grows") to enable small businesses to buy their first computers with 36-month financing options and to help them register and bid for government projects. Partners such as Microsoft, Intel, and Olidata provided links to the e-government portal, the Internet, and business software (McKinsey&Company 2009).

In Brazil, in 2009, the São Paulo State Department of Rights of the Physically Disabled, the medical department at the University of São Paolo (USP), and Microsoft joined forces to improve computer accessibility by providing health notebooks to 400,000 patients. The notebooks were used to deliver telemedicine applications and enable online interactions between the patients and caretakers (Microsoft 2010).

In Argentina, Microsoft partnered with the city of San Luis to help create jobs through entrepreneurship in order to boost the economy. Indeed, this partnership had the intended result since unemployment dropped to 2.7 percent. The governor launched a transferable tax credit and a free Wi-Fi program called "I choose my PC" to accelerate adoption of personal computers (PC) by citizens and small businesses. PC retailers and local manufacturers reported a 1,000-percent sales increase over 2008. Retailers recorded hundreds of computer sales each day after the program started compared to hardly any before it began (Microsoft 2010).

PPPs are most critical when they address health-related education in poor and rural areas. For example, water purification systems are aligned with the United Nations' seventh millennium development goals to ensure environmental sustainability by improving the source of drinking water. Much work has to be done on this front in emerging markets, especially in Africa where despite advances made, 65 million people still do not have access to an improved drinking water source

(African Ministers' Council on Water 2012). Companies engage in PPPs to work toward helping countries achieve such goals, as illustrated by Unilever's initiatives in Africa.

Unilever in Africa

In 2012, Unilever launched its Sustainable Living Plan for improving the lives of 1 billion people in Sub-Saharan Africa, South Asia, and Latin America via three areas of action: promoting hand washing through its soap Lifebuoy; providing safe drinking water through its range of Pureit water purifiers; and ensuring clean, safe toilets through its Domestos household cleaners. Unilever partnered with governments and local organizations for its initiatives to scale up its programs in these three areas, thus improving the quality of implementation and making such hygiene and sanitation interventions sustainable in the long term. In Kenya, they partnered with PSI Kenya and the Kenyan Ministry of Health to train and monitor Lifebuoy's "The School of 5" hand-washing program, introduced through the school health plan for the country (Every Woman Every Child n.d.).

In Ghana, water sources are typically contaminated lakes, ponds, streams, and wells, and since less than 8 percent of the population purifies their water, the incidence of diseases such as cholera and diarrhea are high (Tonaton.com 2014). Unilever's Indian subsidiary, Hindustan Unilever (HUL), invested several years of research and development in India to create its Pureit water purifiers, which work without electricity and can filter germs, bacteria, and viruses in a multistep process that has been endorsed by agencies such as the U.S. Environmental Protection Agency (EPA) (Rangan and Sinha 2011). Pureit was taken to several other markets, including Ghana, where Unilever Ghana is the largest retailer of consumer goods in the country. There, Unilever donated 120 units to the Ministry of Health, valued at 50,000 Ghana Cedis (GHS), as part of its commitment to children's health and providing access to safe drinking water for Ghanaians (Ghana News Agency 2014).

Partnering with nongovernment organizations (NGOs) is another way of reaching poor and/or rural people. Typically, NGOs engage in relief, rehabilitation, and community development, focusing on grass-roots actions. Their deep relationships, networks, and expertise come from working closely with people and being a trusted part of the communities they serve.

Procter & Gamble in Africa

For over two decades, Procter & Gamble's (P&G's) brands Always and Tampax have been addressing the problem of nearly 2 million schoolgirls missing nearly 20 percent of their school days due to menstruation. Many schoolgirls even drop out of school completely when they reach puberty because of the lack of clean and private sanitation facilities in their schools. P&G has partnered with HERO, an awareness-building and fundraising initiative of the United Nations Association. Under the Protecting Futures program, P&G not only provides access to its products but also educates the schoolgirls on their use and their impact on health. For example, in 2007–2008 they had a traveling health educator who provided health, hygiene, and puberty education classes at nine regional schools in Namibia. The brands also sponsored a Youth Ambassador program where 24 teens from the United States flew to Namibia and South Africa to work in this program. P&G created a website targeted at teens called Beinggirl.com on which the experiences of the youth ambassadors were shown as webisodes to encourage teenagers to become global citizens. P&G has also partnered with The Ministry of Education, the Health Education Africa Resource Team (HEART), and the Girl Child Network, to provide over 6 million pads to nearly 100,000 girls. The girls receive the free supply of pads for at least two full school years to help keep them in school (P&G 2012).

Companies also collaborate with each other, and the term *collaborative marketing* has been proposed as the process of companies coming together with a common purpose, goal, or target audience to share resources in order to increase leads, customer value, and influence; retain customers; and increase brand recognition (Williams 2013). For example, in order to bring mobile banking and/or payments to emerging markets, banks have been partnering with mobile network operators because although 7 billion people in emerging markets have phones, only 2 billion have bank accounts (Gupta 2013). Companies like Nokia have developed programs to impart education, which has also served to encourage the use of their devices. In 2008 Nokia partnered with Microsoft to create a Windows phone application for learning mathematics called MoMaths, which makes learning personal, engaging, and exciting. Students can learn from examples, take tests, and also collaborate and compete with other students. Teachers can monitor their students' performance and even provide them with individual feedback (Microsoft n.d.). MoMaths is free for students and has a wide range of math problems with games and graphics that allows students to compare their scores to their peers in their class. The program has been tremendously successful because students who use the program increase their math scores by 14 percent on average (Balch 2012).

References

African Ministers' Council on Water. 2012. "A Snapshot of Drinking Water and Sanitation in Africa—2012 Update." 14–15 May. Accessed on May 1, 2016. www.wssinfo.org/fileadmin/user_upload/resources/Africa-AMCOW-Snapshot-2012-English-Final.pdf

Balch, Oliver. 2012. "Nokia Uses Mobile e-Learning to Align Social and Business Objectives." *The Guardian*. December 5. Accessed on August 15, 2015. www.theguardian.com/sustainable-business/nokia-mobile-social-investment-business-africa.

Bennett, W. Lance and Philip N. Howard. 2007. "Evolving Public-Private Partnerships: A New Model for e-Government and e-Citizens," Microsoft Corporation. Accessed on May 9, 2015. http://download.microsoft.com/download/0/2/2/0222c02b-ea6f-4d53-a6c2-0587d096a121/evolving_public-private_partnerships_lores.pdf.

Bhattacharya, C.B. 2010. "Introduction to the Special Section on Stakeholder Marketing." *Journal of Public Policy and Marketing* 29 (1): 1–3.

Brunke, Bernd. 2013. "Think: Act Study: In-Depth Knowledge for Decision Makers." Roland Berger Strategy Consultants. January. Accessed on June 7, 2014. www.rolandberger.at/media/pdf/ Roland_Berger_Studie_8_Billion_Strategies_20130128.pdf.

The Coca-Cola Company. 2012. "Coca-Cola 2011–2012 Sustainability Report." Accessed on December 25, 2015. www.coca-colacompany.com/sustainabilityreport/me/nutrition.html# section-nutrition-labeling-and-information.

Dow AgroSciences. n.d. "About Dow AgroSciences." Accessed on September 15, 2014. www.dowagro.com/en-US.

Every Woman Every Child. n.d. "Business Impact Stories." Unilever. Accessed on September 9, 2015. www.everywomaneverychild .org/images/EWEC_Unilever.pdf.

Fair Labor Association. 2012. "Improving Workers' Lives Worldwide: Sustainable Management of Nestlé's Cocoa Supply Chain in the Ivory Coast—Focus on Labor Standards." June. Accessed on September 9, 2015. www.fairlabor.org/sites/default/files/documents/ reports/cocoa-report-final_0.pdf.

Fowler, Geoffrey A. and Betsy McKay. 2008. "Coke Pins China Hopes on Blitz in Beijing." *The Wall Street Journal.* August 19. Accessed on August 15, 2014. http://online.wsj.com/news/articles/ SB121910643955651579.

Ghana News Agency. 2014. "Unilever Supports Government to Eliminate Water-Bourne Diseases." November 23. Accessed on September 15, 2015. www.ghananewsagency.org/health/unilever-supports-government-to-eliminate-water-bourne-diseases-82597.

GlaxoSmithKline. 2013. "A Review of GlaxoSmithKline's PHASE (Personal Hygiene and Sanitation Education) Programme." Accessed on March 6, 2016. www.gsk.com/media/378507/Personal-Hygiene-And-Sanitation-Education-Report-2013.pdf.

Gupta, Sunil. 2013. "The Mobile Banking and Payment Revolution." *The European Financial Review*. February-March. Accessed on January 4, 2015. www.hbs.edu/faculty/Publication%20Files/The%20Mobile%20Banking%20and%20Payment%20Revolution1_b37fc319-e15f-46c8-b2f9-c0d4c8327285.pdf.

Harris, Ron. 1994. "Avon Is Calling, and It's a Jungle Out There: Brazil: Women Find Independence Doing Big Business in the Amazon." *Los Angeles Times*. August 29. Accessed on June 9, 2014. http://articles.latimes.com/1994-08-29/news/mn-32556_1_big-business.

Hoene, Christopher, Christopher Kingsley, and Matthew Leighninger. 2013. "Bright Spots in Community Engagement: Case Studies of U.S. Creating Greater Civic Participation from the Bottom Up." National League of Cities. April. Accessed on June 19, 2014. www.knightfoundation.org/media/uploads/publication_pdfs/BrightSpots-final.pdf.

Hoffman PR. n.d. "Handwashing Could Save One Million Children's Lives Each Year." Accessed on September 15, 2015. www.hoffmanpr.com/press-release/handwashing-could-save-one-million-childrens-lives-each-year.

Hower, Mike. 2013. "Adidas Helps Indonesian Suppliers Save Nearly 5,000 Tons of CO2." Sustainable Brands. September 9. Accessed on August 15, 2014. www.sustainablebrands.com/news_and_views/supply_chain/adidas-helps-indonesian-suppliers-save-nearly-5000-tons-co2.

Langridge, Kathryn. 2015. "The Changing Shape of Capital Markets in Emerging Economies." Manulife Asset Management. May 11. Accessed on April 22, 2016, www.manulifeam.com/ca/Research-and-Insights/Documents/2015-May-The-changing-shape-of-capital.

Lee, Hau L. 2010. "Don't Tweak Your Supply Chain—Rethink It End to End." *Harvard Business Review*. October. Accessed on April 22, 2016. https://hbr.org/2010/10/dont-tweak-your-supply-chain-rethink-it-end-to-end/ar/1.

Lipsky, John. 2007. "Developing Deeper Capital Markets in Emerging Market Economies." International Monetary Fund. February 2. Accessed on March 24, 2016. www.imf.org/external/np/speeches/2007/020207a.htm.

McKinsey&Company. 2009. "Public-Private Partnerships: Enabling the Private Sector to Enhance Social Impact." December. Accessed on September 9, 2015. http://mckinseyonsociety.com/public-private-partnerships-harnessing-the-private-sectors-unique-ability-to-enhance-social-impact.

Microsoft. 2010. "Driving National Transformation and Competitiveness with ICT." January. Accessed on September 15, 2015. http://download.microsoft.com/download/0/9/6/0961b0ca-af99-4011-95f0-4fa9c86225c6/ictwhitepaper.pdf.

————.n.d. "Microsoft Math." Accessed on August 13, 2015. https://math.microsoft.com/Account/Login?ReturnUrl=%2F.

Nestlé. n.d. (a). "Door-to-Door Sales of Fortified Products." Accessed on March 6, 2016. www.nestle.com/csv/case-studies/allcasestudies/door-to-doorsalesoffortifiedproducts,brazil.

————n.d. (b). "Nestlé Ghana Commits to a Sustainable Cocoa Supply Chain through the Nestlé Cocoa Plan." Accessed on December 11, 2015. www.nestle-cwa.com/en/nestl-ghana-commits-to-a-sustainable-cocoa-supply-chain-through-the-nestl-cocoa-plan.

Olympic.org. 2007. "New Coca-Cola—Beijing 2008 Olympic Composite Logo." January 25. Accessed on March 24, 2016. www.olympic.org/news/new-coca-cola-beijing-2008-olympic-composite-logo/54605.

P&G. 2012. "Tampax and Always Launch Protecting Futures Program Dedicated to Helping African Girls Stay in School." November 12. Accessed on December 25, 2015. http://news.pg.com/press-release/pg-corporate-announcements/tampax-and-always-launch-protecting-futures-program-dedicat.

Porter, Michael E. and Mark R. Kramer. 2006. "Strategy and Society: The Link between Competitive Advantage and Corporate Social Responsibility." *Harvard Business Review*, 84 (12): 78–92.

————. 2011. "The Big Idea: Creating Shared Value." *Harvard Business Review* 89 (1/2): 62–77.

PYXERA Global. n.d. "Dow Supports Sustainable Agriculture in Ghana." Accessed on December 25, 2015. http://pyxeraglobal .org/case-studies/leadership-action-ghana-community-development-project-supports-hydroponics.

Rangan, Kasturi V., and Mona Sinha. 2011. "Hindustan Unilever's 'Pureit' Water Purifier." *Harvard Business Review*: Case 511-067.

Reck, Jennifer and Brad Wood. 2003. "What Works: Vodacom's Community Service Phone Shops." *World Resources Institute*. August. Accessed on May 29, 2014. http://pdf.wri.org/dd_vodacom.pdf.

Rosenbluth, Hal F. and Diane McFerrin Peters. 2002. *The Customer Comes Second: Put Your People First and Watch 'em Kick Butt.* New York: HarperCollins.

Sheth, Jagdish N. and Mona Sinha. 2015. "B2B Branding in Emerging Markets: A Sustainability Perspective." *Industrial Marketing Management* 51: 79–88.

Simanis, Erik. 2009."At the Base of the Pyramid." *The Wall Street Journal*. October 26. Accessed on January 1, 2015. www.wsj.com/ articles/SB10001424052970203946904574301802684947732.

Sisodia, Raj, David B. Wolfe, and Jag N. Sheth. 2007. *Firms of Endearment: How World-Class Companies Profit from Passion and Purpose.* Upper Saddle River, NJ: Wharton School Publishing.

Statista. n.d. "Annual per Capita Consumption of Coca-Cola Company's Beverage Products from 1991 to 2012, by Country (in servings of 8-fluid ounce beverages)." Accessed on March 6, 2016. http:// www.statista.com/statistics/271156/per-capita-consumption-of-soft-drinks-of-the-coca-cola-company-by-country.

Tonaton.com. 2014. "Popular Water Purifiers in Ghana." August 29. Accessed on March 24, 2016. http://tonaton.com/blog/popular-water-purifiers-ghana.

Williams, David K. 2013. "Collaborative Marketing Is the Next Big Thing." *Forbes*. June 18. Accessed on January 5, 2015. www.forbes.com/sites/davidkwilliams/2013/06/18/collaborative-marketing-is-the-next-big-thing.

The World Bank. 2015. "What are Public Private Partnerships?" October 15. Accessed on April 29, 2016. http://ppp.worldbank.org/public-private-partnership/overview/what-are-public-private-partnerships.

World Health Organization. n.d. "Nestle's Commitments to Every Woman Every Child." Accessed on March 24, 2016. www.who.int/pmnch/topics/part_publications/pmnch2011_summ_nestle.pdf.

Zhang, Feng. 2008. "Corporate Social Responsibility in Emerging Markets: The Role of Multinational Corporations." The Foreign Policy Centre. March. Accessed on May 29, 2014. http://fpc.org.uk/fsblob/919.pdf.

10 —————————————————

Connecting the Dots

Emerging markets are the brave new frontiers for companies looking to grow and expand their global presence, but competing successfully in these markets requires companies to make a significant change in their marketing strategy. The first step we have advocated for this journey is to adopt the 4 A's framework that compels a business to answer four fundamental questions from a customer perspective: What do consumers find *acceptable* in this market? What is *affordable* for these consumers? What will increase consumers' *accessibility* to products and services? What efforts are required to increase consumers' *awareness* (Sheth and Sisodia 2012)? Traditionally, marketing strategy has been dominated by the 4 P's—product, price, place, and promotion—not to mention, the various other P's, such as people and processes, that have been added subsequently to the marketers' tool kit. The 4 A's perspective moves the focus from the toolkit to customer outcomes. This is more than a semantic difference because centering on the expected customer benefits requires the creative and possibly joint use of the marketing mix (product, price, place, promotion, people, processes, etc.) to create acceptability, affordability, accessibility, and awareness for consumers.

Although the 4 A's framework can be applied to any market, we believe its power to create transformative change is best illustrated in emerging markets. In the previous chapters we described how companies have enhanced *acceptability* by creating *functional fusion* and *cultural fusion*. Both of these require a holistic consideration of the offering—that is, the product or service in relation to the local market's social, cultural, and physical needs, and the environmental context. Both these strategies result in products that are not only localized but also unique hybrids, reflecting features and requirements of their countries of origin as well as of the emerging market(s) to spur rapid adoption. *Affordability* requires simultaneous evaluation of two P's, pricing and product, to overcome economic and noneconomic obstacles to purchase by *democratizing the offer* for lower/middle income groups or by *upscaling the offer* for all income groups. *Accessibility* requires consideration of two P's, place and processes, either by *managing reach*—that is by building infrastructure, or by leveraging existing distribution methods. Companies can also *reinvent reach*—that is, adopt modern technology and new methods for providing enhanced access. *Awareness* requires a joint evaluation of three P's—product, promotion, and people—for *building product awareness and brand identity,* but also for going beyond a customer-centric view to find ways to benefit many other constituencies by *engaging stakeholders.*

In this last chapter we connect the dots between the 4 A's framework and our eight strategies to demonstrate how they work toward overcoming the challenges that marketers face in emerging markets. We draw your attention back to the foundational premises about emerging markets that we began discussing in Chapter 1: These markets are highly heterogeneous. They face chronic shortages of resources and have inadequate infrastructure. Sociopolitical governance structures such as religion, government, nongovernmental organizations (NGOs) and community, rather than businesses, play defining roles in consumption. Competition in these markets comes more from non-consumption or consumption of unbranded or homemade options rather than from large, local, or international companies or brands (Sheth 2011). The fundamental outcome desired by implementing these strategies is conversion of nonusers to users in order to grow the market rather than simply grab market share from competitors. Table 1 provides a snapshot of the way in which these strategies specifically help companies in overcoming one or more emerging market challenges.

Overcoming Emerging Market Challenges

As we describe each challenge we draw your attention to the specific strategies that help overcome that challenge. In addition, we recall select examples from those chapters to demonstrate how the strategy helped the company overcome that challenge.

Market Heterogeneity

As countries develop, they move from agriculture to manufacturing and eventually to services. Typically, most emerging markets tend to be dominated by agriculture or manufacturing, though some may be outliers, like India, which has a larger service than manufacturing sector. Emerging markets are highly fragmented and are dominated by small, local businesses. They typically have large populations, most of which are at the base of the pyramid (BoP), but as their economies prosper, the middle class grows rapidly. These markets also have a growing affluent class, and are home to millions of millionaires. Although emerging markets house numerous megacities, the majority of the population often remains in rural areas, and there are stark contrasts between urban and rural consumption. Even urban areas have populations ranging from the very wealthy to the very poor. These countries not only differ from each other in terms of culture, faith, economic well-being, climate, traditions, and a host of factors, but many countries also exhibit high diversity within their borders. For example, India has over 20 official languages and hundreds of dialects. Languages, and even food preferences and climate, vary among and even within its 29 states. Thus, the needs and wants of emerging market consumers are highly diverse. For overcoming such high market heterogeneity, we propose bringing to bear the power of all 4 A's.

To create acceptability, companies can use functional and cultural fusion strategies that often result in hybrid innovations that reflect heterogeneous needs and wants. An example of *creating functional fusion* is when companies adapt their products for climatic variations such as the homes that Habitat for Humanity builds in different countries. They use modern technology as well as local material and designs. For example, in Thailand they build homes on stilts that are often partially constructed with bamboo. Similarly, *overcoming infrastructural constraints* or *incorporating local essence* (ingredients, employees or suppliers) also results in fusion products, such as the Vespa scooter adapted for the Indian physique with narrower and lower seats. *Considering genetic difference* spurred Marico to create a new product, savory oats, that transformed the breakfast category in India where the population is predisposed to cholesterol and diabetes issues, while also adhering to the traditional preference for hot, savory, homemade breakfasts. For

Table 1: Breakout Strategies to Address Emerging Market Challenges

4 A's	Break-Out Strategies	Challenges of Emerging Markets		
		Market Heterogeneity	Socio-Political Governance	
ACCEPTABILITY	**CREATING FUNCTIONAL FUSION**			
	Adapting to Climate	✓		
	Considering Genetic Differences	✓		
	Overcoming Infrastructural Limitations			
	Incorporating Local Essence	✓		
	Aligning to Regulatory Requirements		✓	
	DESIGNING CULTURAL FUSION			
	Incorporating Traditions	✓		
	Using Local Languages	✓		
	Considering Social Norms		✓	
	Respecting Faith		✓	
	Understanding Sensory Preferences	✓		
AFFORDABILITY	**DEMOCRATIZING THE OFFER**			
	Reducing Economic Barriers to Purchase	✓		
	Overcoming Noneconomic Barriers to Purchase	✓		
	Achieving Reverse Innovation	✓		
	Extending Product Value	✓		
	Developing Creative Financing	✓		
	UPSCALING THE OFFER			
	Adding or Changing Packaging	✓		
	Positioning	✓		
	Enhancing Services and Benefits	✓		
	Reversing the Brand Lifecycle	✓		
	Leveraging the Country or Origin			

	Unbranded Competition	Shortage of Resources	Inadequate Infrastructure
			✓
	✓		
	✓		
	✓		
	✓		
	✓		
		✓	
		✓	
		✓	
	✓	✓	
		✓	
	✓		
	✓		
	✓		
	✓	✓	
	✓		

Table 1: Breakout Strategies to Address Emerging Market Challenges *(continued)*

4 A's	Break-Out Strategies	Challenges of Emerging Markets		
		Market Heterogeneity	Socio-Political Governance	
ACCESSIBILITY	**MANAGING REACH**			
	Adapting to Traditional Channels	✓		
	Navigating Indigenous Channels	✓		
	Developing Channel Partnerships		✓	
	Building for Access			
	Managing Channel Ownership			
	REINVENTING REACH			
	Modernizing Retail	✓		
	Setting Up E-Commerce	✓		
	Accessing Self-Service Technologies	✓		
	Enabling Payments	✓		
	Providing Financing	✓		
AWARENESS	**BUILDING PRODUCT AWARENESS AND BRAND IDENTITY**			
	Establishing Product Knowledge	✓		
	Leveraging Sources of Communication			
	Developing Appropriate Messaging	✓		
	Using Traditional Channels of Communication	✓		
	Leveraging New and Unconventional Media	✓		
	ENGAGING STAKEHOLDERS			
	Educating Consumers and Markets	✓	✓	
	Involving Communities and Leaders	✓	✓	
	Engaging Employees		✓	
	Co-opting Suppliers		✓	
	Developing Partnerships with Public, Private, and Nonprofit Companies	✓	✓	

	Unbranded Competition	Shortage of Resources	Inadequate Infrastructure
			✓
			✓
			✓
			✓
		✓	✓
			✓
			✓
			✓
			✓
		✓	✓
	✓	✓	
	✓		
	✓		
	✓		
	✓		
	✓		
		✓	✓
		✓	✓
		✓	

designing cultural fusion, we encourage companies to *incorporate the country's traditions*, like Maver did when it created a lemon-flavored powdered flu medication in Chile that combined Western medication with the traditional hot lemonade Chileans used for treating the flu. Similarly, being mindful of sensory preferences led Kentucky Fried Chicken (KFC) to innovate many hybrid menu items for China. Language also promotes the creation of hybrid products, like *Slumdog Millionaire*, the Bollywood-Hollywood fusion movie. Often product acceptability is dictated by social norms and religion.

All of the strategies we recommended for creating affordability are geared toward addressing the economic heterogeneity that exists in emerging markets. *Democratizing the offer* by reducing the price without compromising on features calls for innovation, like Glaxo-SmithKline did for pneumococcal vaccines in Latin America—it created a different version of its vaccine for low-income countries at a lower price point. Often such innovations find a market for similarly deprived populations in other parts of the world, including in developed countries—a process called reverse innovation—as GE found for its portable electrocardiogram device. Along with *reducing economic barriers*, companies must also *overcome noneconomic barriers* created due to issues related to awareness, access, or social norms. *Extending value* by increasing the life of a product involves creating secondary or used markets for reaching out to diverse socioeconomic groups. Companies also need to think out of the box to *provide financing* to people, like the Chit Funds system in India. These markets also have an aspiring middle class and a large affluent class, so companies need to consider *upscaling their offer* by using *packaging and positioning* creatively. For example, the Ford Motor Company positioned itself on an innovation platform to upscale its offer in the Middle East. Similarly, airlines from that region, such as Emirates and Etihad Airways, are creating high-end luxury experiences for affluent customers. However, upscaling can pertain to nonluxury categories as well. Packaging and branding commodities, such as dates from Morocco, elevated the product in terms of quality and price. Companies must be mindful that even the most mundane consumption in developed countries can be an upscaled experience for people who have never used such a product or service before, such as a basic, no-frills cell phone or even good quality healthcare.

Market heterogeneity is an important consideration for providing accessibility as well. For example, the *managing reach* strategy takes into consideration *traditional and indigenous distribution* mechanisms such as tiny neighborhood stores, souks, or even pushcarts. Often captive infrastructure and manufacturing must be set up like Shark Design Studio had to *build its own access* in India. Similarly, halaal *certification* was another example of managing reach by expanding access. Companies also need to *reinvent reach*, such as by *modernizing retail*. *E-commerce* websites like Alibaba in China or even websites for second-hand products like OLX classifieds are becoming popular ways of expanding reach. Along with traditional *self-service technologies* like ATMs, mobile-based systems are *enabling payments* and spurring m-commerce in countries like Thailand, and in large parts of Africa and Asia. On the other hand, creating *access to financing* is illustrated by the microfinance industry in countries across Asia, Africa, and Latin America. Thus, both managing and reinventing reach involve meeting needs for a broad spectrum of people.

Creating awareness by *building brand identity* in emerging markets often requires *establishing product awareness*, depending on the characteristics of the target audience, such as urban/rural, socio-economic status, and so on. For example, the low financial literacy levels in Uganda spurred MasterCard to educate consumers before it was able to promote microfinance and banking. Building a brand identity comes thereafter. Selecting the source of communication, as Lux did with its long-standing celebrity-focused communication, and selecting an aspirationally focused message are good ways to build a brand across a wide spectrum of audiences. Media choices must also have a wide range. *Traditional channels of communication*, like wall paintings for rural areas, must often be combined with *new (or even unconventional) media*, such as social media websites for the young, urban population. More importantly, building awareness in emerging markets requires much more than just considering the fourth P, promotion, which tends to be customer-centric. Instead it requires taking products and people into account as well, because awareness needs to include all stakeholders in emerging markets.

Engaging stakeholders involves *educating consumers and markets*. The Coca-Cola Company had to not only educate consumers about drinking its beverage cold instead of at room temperature in China, but it also had to educate Chinese consumers on the importance of being fit and healthy to counter associations of its product with health challenges like obesity. Companies must find ways not just to to *engage communities and opinion leaders* but also *engage their own suppliers and employees*, like Dow Chemical Company does with its Leadership in Action program that it conducts in many parts of the world. For its program in Ghana, Dow partnered with governments, universities, and NGOs to develop sustainable farming initiatives. *Public-private partnerships* help improve the lives of billions of people, like Unilever has done with its Sustainable Living Plan, which addresses issues such as water contamination and hygiene. Thus, companies have to be creative in creating awareness among a whole host of stakeholders, including but not limited to consumers or investors, and they have to address issues that go beyond just their own product or brand.

Sociopolitical Governance

Emerging markets are characterized more by the influence of religion, government, business groups, NGOs, and the local community than they are by competitive forces. Navigating regulatory requirements can be challenging but truly making a difference can mean partnering with lawmakers to reform or build systems, which is described as one of our functional fusion strategies for creating acceptability. The *functional fusion* strategy speaks to *managing regulatory requirements* whereas the *cultural fusion* strategy takes two major sociopolitical forces into *consideration—society/social norms and faith*, as illustrated by Sula Vineyard and Islamic banking respectively. For expanding access by leveraging existing governance structures in these markets, companies must *manage reach* as described in our strategy of *channel partnerships*. For example, E Health Point partnered with community members to gain buy-in for its telemedicine service in India. Most critically, companies will find themselves creating awareness by *engaging multiple stakeholders such as consumers, communities, leaders, employees, suppliers, and other companies— public, private, as well as nonprofit*—as described in Chapter 9. In that chapter, one of the stories we shared was of Nestlé, which partnered with many government agencies, civil society organizations, and local associations to address the issue of child labor in the Ivory Coast.

Unbranded Competition

Emerging markets have large segments of the population who use unbranded goods—estimated at more than 60 percent of consumption. About 50–65 percent of jewelry, alcohol, luggage, appliances, and small electronics/appliances are unbranded. Furthermore, traditionally, demand for many goods, such as food or clothing, and services, such as child care or even counseling, is limited because household members make these goods or provide these services. To tap into unbranded markets, companies must often first create *product awareness* by providing their potential consumer with knowledge, and only then can they create *brand identity* by using *sources of communication* and targeted messages that resonate with the local people from a social and cultural perspective. This is exemplified by IKEA; in China, it crafted its aspirational *messaging* based on romance. Both *traditional as well as new/unconventional media* may need to be deployed in a creative fashion to reach the intended audience, as described earlier in ways to address market heterogeneity.

Educating multiple stakeholders is a big part of what builds a brand. Often, education must start at the origin of the value chain—farming, for example—and then proceed upward, extending even to the customer. Esquel's education initiative, *co-opting suppliers* as part of its *stakeholder engagement* strategy, helped promote sustainable farming in China. Strategies for creating affordability included *upscaling an offer* by *packaging, positioning, and enhancing services and benefits*, all of which add to the brand image. Often companies start off by creating affordable products as part of *democratizing the offer* so they can initiate consumption of brands into the consumer psyche. For example, when companies *extend product value* by building or participating in active secondary markets, like sales of second-hand goods, they gain the opportunity to introduce nonusers to product and brand benefits at a significantly lower price, which may eventually lead to a purchase in the primary market. Later companies can scale upward with more value-added, pricier products; this is described as *reversing the brand lifecycle*. For example, Sundrop oil, in India, introduced branding to a commodity category but eventually *upscaled* to enter the ready-to-cook market. Further, multinationals from the developed world can *leverage their country of origin*, which gives their brands a premium and good-quality image associated with higher prices that nonusers of the product category or users of unbranded products can aspire toward.

Shortage of Resources

Emerging markets face chronic shortages in production, consumption, and exchange. Skilled labor may be limited since large segments of the population may lack education, which leads to production constraints. There may also be demand constraints if consumers have low education and hence low income, or if they do not consume a product or consume unbranded products. Moreover, the exchange mechanisms may also be constrained due to process or infrastructural issues, or even if the supply chain is broken or has many middle men. *Democratizing the offer* for creating affordable solutions requires companies to improvise in order to address resource shortages; to do so, they *reduce economic barriers* for lower income groups, such as by offering smaller pack sizes, like single serving sachets, or by offering a subscription model, like Sistema Ser/CEGIN did when providing medical care for poor women. Companies like Capitec Bank in South Africa *overcame noneconomic obstacles* to purchase by simplifying the loan application process and waiving previously required documentation for poor applicants. Often such inventions spur *reverse innovation* when the rest of the world can also adopt those products. Encouraging secondary markets to extend product value by offering *creative financing* options is another way of addressing resource shortage challenges. *Managing reach* via *channel ownership* is another way of creating accessibility by overcoming resource shortages like Grupo Los Grobo did when they partnered for land access instead of opting for land ownership. Companies can also *reinvent reach* by *providing financing*, as seen by the rise of the microfinance industry. Lack of education and hence lack of awareness, is an important factor that impedes consumption of products and/or brands. So companies in emerging markets often need to first *educate consumers* about products and potentially also *educate communities, employees, and suppliers*. Navigating such resource constraints often becomes easier with *partnerships such as with NGOs, governments, or even other companies*. For example, Procter & Gamble partnered with the United Nations to educate schoolgirls in Africa on health, hygiene, and puberty and provide them with related products. Thus, *engaging stakeholders* is a central part of addressing resource constraints.

Inadequate Infrastructure

Emerging markets suffer from little or poor infrastructure. Shortages of electricity, water, transportation, telephone service, and Internet access hamper daily life and business as usual. A company's ability to overcome logistical issues such as connectivity due to poor quality roads or lack of storage facilities requires them to be great at improvising in order to create accessibility. When discussing *functional fusion*, one of the ways we described was designing products that can handle infrastructural constraints such as lack of water or power outages. Being open to *managing reach* via *traditional and indigenous channels*, experimenting with different models of *channel ownership*, and even *building infrastructure* are important cultural and organizational shifts that many companies have successfully navigated, as described earlier. For instance, consider how Living Goods used Avon's door-to-door distribution method to sell affordable healthcare in Uganda. *Reinventing reach* is another critical strategy for overcoming infrastructural challenges. Providing technology-based *payment methods* or *financing options* addresses shortages of banks and other financial inclusion challenges. Alternately, using a new-to-the-company method of reaching customers expands access, like the South African Revenue Service (SARS) used mobile vans to reach current and potential taxpayers, thereby easing and simplifying the tax payments process. Even building awareness via *co-opting suppliers* and *engaging employees* are ways of *engaging stakeholders* to fill infrastructural and resource gaps.

The Way Forward

Thus, companies doing business in emerging markets will need to move away from traditional marketing thought, such as market orientation, relationship marketing, and customer satisfaction, and instead think about market development and converting nonusers to users (Sheth 2011). We wrote this book because we believe the time has come for companies to realize that competing in emerging markets means that they can no longer think about simply setting a low or high price, but instead they need to dwell on what consumers can "afford," which may be a shampoo sachet or a luxury car. It is no longer enough to create awareness with content, messages, and media in ways that we have been used to doing in the past. Moreover, stakeholders, especially the community, must be managed along with brands. To win hearts and minds, we need to move past merely localizing global offerings to create value through fusion, both cultural and functional. Finally, delivery in emerging markets entails using existing distribution mechanisms creatively and even creating new ones. Gearing up to compete in emerging markets will be a transformative experience for consumers and companies, as well as the market. Our strategies are anchored to both conceptual reasoning about the benefits to customers, along with practical experiences of companies that illustrate how these strategies are successfully used. Thus, more than anywhere else in the world, emerging markets compel marketers to break out of an inward-looking mindset and create an outward perspective of what their offerings really mean to customers and other stakeholders.

In addition to helping overcome the key challenges of emerging markets, our strategies are also resilient enough to deal with another notable feature of competition in emerging markets—constant change. Emerging markets are and will be highly diverse, varying in cultures, languages, faith, histories, traditions, consumption patterns, and preferences. So the strategy for each country will have to be customized to its cultural and socioeconomic reality. Furthermore, these markets will also evolve over time. The emerging markets of today may gain the status of developed markets, while those that we consider frontier or developing markets may become the emerging markets of the future. What companies learn from the current emerging markets may not easily be replicated in the next major markets, like Africa and the Arab world. When the countries that are considered developed today, underwent industrialization, they shared many similarities, such as the same religion, Christianity. This is not true in current and future emerging markets.

Our eight strategies are broad enough to allow for innovation and customization but this will require deep insights not just into consumers, but also all stakeholders. Traditional surveys, data analytics, and large-scale quantitative studies may not work for this purpose because there has not been enough research conducted in these markets. Moreover, there may be no preexisting databases to draw upon or the data might be proprietary. Letting go of one's own cultural myopia is essential for learning about other cultures, and so to truly understand what emerging market customers value, managers must take on experiential learning using ethnographic approaches and immersion experiences, such as customer safaris—where consumers are observed in their natural living and working environment. By developing competencies for generating such deep insights, multinationals will become better equipped to cross boundaries in search of more markets.

In adopting these strategies, multinationals cannot assume that their actions will always be welcomed. There are already many instances of pushback from customers, communities, and even countries because multinationals or even large domestic corporations are often seen as greedy and self-centered. For example, when Coca Cola tried tapping into Chinese consumers' preference for tea, juice, and herbal products rather than soda, they moved to acquire a Chinese juice company, China Huiyuan Juice Group Limited, in a 2.5 billion USD offer—the biggest foreign acquisition at that time. However, Coca-Cola faced tremendous consumer opposition. Finally, China's ministry of commerce struck down the deal on the grounds that it would hurt smaller, domestic companies and limit consumer choice (Tucker, Smith, and Anderlini 2009). Similarly, relations between African countries and their Chinese trading partners who have been investing heavily in the continent are facing issues; for example, a Chinese oil company was shut down by the Niger government due to accusations of environmental negligence (Nossiter 2013). Thus, managing regulators, consumers, and indeed all stakeholders is a balance that companies must achieve in emerging markets, while keeping in mind that, due to rapid and global communication, their reputation precedes their market entry. It helps to be mindful of the fact that many emerging markets have been erstwhile colonies, and the advent of multinationals may be reminiscent of a best-forgotten colonial past. Thus, multinationals may be subject to a higher level of scrutiny than local companies who are a part of the social fabric.

Along with all the challenges we described in this book, companies must also deal with issues of corruption, a problem endemic to many emerging markets where either laws do not exist or are not adequately enforced. Further, adjusting to local norms may require companies to strike a balance between what may be acceptable in their own home countries compared to the local markets. For example, culturally acceptable practices such as gift-giving, which is considered a courtesy in many countries, may be perceived as a bribe by headquarters. And corruption does not just pertain to bribes. It includes all manners of social ills, such as child labor, bonded labor, human trafficking, environmental destruction, poor education standards, and even terrorism.

Impact on Multinationals

Competing in emerging markets makes multinationals more flexible and helps them build new skills and competencies. Learning to provide value to consumers who have severe resource constraints is the key trigger for "frugal innovation," which can then help the company target new markets in other parts of the world, including their home country. On the other hand, at least for the near future, multinationals continue to pursue their existing *glocalization* strategy where developed world products are localized in order to be sold in less-developed countries. But the goals and resource requirements of the two strategies are in conflict (Immelt, Govindarajan, and Trimble 2009). Our breakout strategies can help companies balance these markedly differently strategies and thereby determine the scope and success of their operations in emerging markets.

Impact on Local Companies

Emerging markets root global brands in the local milieu while at the same time they internationalize local brands to prepare them for the global marketplace. Domestic companies go through a transformation as they learn to collaborate or compete with multinationals on their home turf. The engagement between domestic and foreign companies can be at various levels as competitors, joint venture partners, franchisees, suppliers/vendors, and so on. Local companies imbibe new strategies, technologies, and processes, and managerial talent moves between local companies and multinationals. Although multinationals lag in their knowledge of local markets and consumers, they bring with them significant competitive advantages, such as a breadth of experience and expertise, technology, process-driven orientation, and a portfolio of powerful brands. As local companies compete or engage with multinationals, they learn, shore up their competencies, and gain confidence. Many become ambitious and start stepping outside their national boundaries to become what is now known as emerging market multinationals (EMMs). These companies are now changing the face of global competition (Sheth 2011). It is widely predicted that emerging economies will transform from being the world's factories to global marketers, much like what Korea and Japan have accomplished (Kumar and Steenkamp 2015). EMMs like the Tata Group from India and Huawei from China are already demonstrating this.

EMMs have many skeptics in the developed world. Shelly Lazarus, chairman of Ogilvy & Mather, asked this about Chinese brands: "Is Lenovo a brand? No. Is Haier a brand? No. They are brand names that aspire to be brands. But they [their Chinese owners] have to understand that branding is about the relationship with people both intellectually and emotionally. They have to have a consistent proposition they put in front of people." (Wang 2008). EMMs have a challenge ahead of them in facing such doubts about how they will establish their brands globally and overcome perceptions about inferior quality (Temporal 2001). However, given the nimbleness with which they have learned to survive and flourish in their home countries, we believe EMMs are here to stay and will find a way to compete. Thought leaders and experts are already proposing strategies for how EMM brands can transform or even disrupt markets (Chattopadhyay, Batra, and Ozsomer 2012) and ways in which multinationals should gear up to face these new competitors (Guillen and Garcia-Canal 2012).

Mindful Consumption

We caution companies to use the 4 A's judiciously and in a way that it does not lead to uninhibited consumption, which causes social and environmental ills. Emerging markets are already fragile and cannot bear the costs of overconsumption. We can already see the severe environmental fallout of rapid industrialization and consumption in countries like India and China. Companies can and must reign in the kind of excesses that overconsumption has wrought on the developed world. They need to create affordable solutions for consumers, set prices in a way to control demand at sustainable levels, and use advertising and communication in ways that curb excess aspirational consumption. Sheth, Sethia, and Srinivas (2011) urge businesses to pursue sustainability goals, but from a customers' perspective. They conceptualize mindful consumption as a confluence of a mindful mindset—that is, caring for self, community, and nature—and mindful behavior—that is, tempering the three modes of consumption: acquisitive, repetitive, and aspirational. Companies can manage this by way of their promotion and communication as well as by changing their offering—for example, they can create products that are durable, amenable to re-use, can be used multiple times potentially even by multiple users, and can be shared, upgraded, and repaired easily. Sustainable innovations are ways in which companies create new products, processes, or practices, or can modify existing ones in order to reduce the impact of the firm's activities on the natural environment (Varadarajan 2015). Along with innovating sustainably, companies have to educate, persuade, and inspire consumers to value such products and services. Further, even their branding activities impact local cultures (Cayla and Arnould 2008) and there is growing concern that not enough is known about the impact of marketing activities in the public sphere. This is an even greater knowledge gap in emerging markets. Thus, we urge practitioners and researchers to work toward acquiring deeper insights about these countries, their markets, and their consumers in order to rethink their mission, vision, and strategies for a truly global presence.

In this book we have drawn on the marketing strategies and tactics of dozens of companies from a number of emerging markets, and we have shared stories of their successes in navigating the competitive landscape by adopting different aspects of the 4 A's framework (acceptability, affordability, accessibility, and awareness) and the strategies we propose. Although the ultimate success of a company in any country depends on a host of factors, some of which may contribute to their success while others may detract from it, we chose to share with the readers those select aspects that exemplified our framework and strategies, rather than provide an in-depth look at the sum total of any company's performance in each country. The strategies can be viewed as a managerial toolkit, and Table 1 (at the beginning of this chapter) illustrates especially well what emerging market challenges a specific strategy can address. For managers, the first task will be to define and prioritize their objectives in terms of the challenge(s) to be addressed. Then scrolling vertically along the table will help them drill down deeper into specific business strategies and tactics to deploy. Competing in emerging markets will be a thrilling, transformative experience for companies, consumers, markets, and also for the business of marketing. We hope that our insights will inform and inspire all those who are or will be a part of this emerging landscape.

References

Cayla, Julien, and Eric J. Arnould. 2008. "A Cultural Approach to Branding in the Global Marketplace." *Journal of International Marketing* 16 (4): 86–112.

Chattopadhyay, Amitava, and Rajeev Batra, with Aysegul Ozsomer. 2012. *The New Emerging Market Multinationals: Four Strategies for Disrupting Markets and Building Brands.* New York: McGraw-Hill Education.

Guillen, Mauro, and Esteban Garcia-Canal. 2012. *Emerging Markets Rule: Growth Strategies of the New Global Giants Brands.* New York: McGraw-Hill Education.

Immelt, Jeffrey R., Vijay Govindarajan, Chris Trimble. 2009. "How GE Is Disrupting Itself." *Harvard Business Review.* October. 56–65.

Kumar, Nirmalya, and Jan-Benedict E.M. Steenkamp. 2015. *Brand Breakout: How Emerging Market Brands Will Go Global.* London, U.K.: Palgrave Macmillan.

Nossiter, Adam. 2013."China Finds Resistance to Oil Deals in Africa." *The New York Times.* September 17. Accessed on February 13, 2016. www.nytimes.com/2013/09/18/world/africa/china-finds-resistance-to-oil-deals-in-africa.html.

Sheth, Jagdish N. 2011. "Impact of Emerging Markets on Marketing: Rethinking Existing Perspectives and Practices," *Journal of Marketing* 75 (4): 166–182.

Sheth, Jagdish N., Nirmal K. Sethia, and Shanthi Srinivas. 2011. "Mindful Consumption: A Customer-centric Approach to Sustainability." *Journal of the Academy of Marketing Sciences* 39: 21–39.

Sheth, Jagdish N., and Rajendra S.Sisodia. 2012. The 4 A's of Marketing: Creating Value for Customers, Companies, and Society. New York: Routledge.

Temporal, Paul. 2001. *Branding in Asia: The Creation, Development and Management of Asian Brands for the Global Market*. Singapore: John Wiley & Sons.

Tucker, Sundeep, Peter Smith, and Jamil Anderlini. 2009."China Blocks Coca-Cola Bid for Huiyuan." *Financial Times*. March 19. Accessed on February 10, 2016. www.ft.com/intl/cms/s/0/5c645830-1391-11de-9e32-0000779fd2ac.html#axzz44ywq30rK.

Varadarajan, Rajan. 2015."Innovating for Sustainability: A Framework for Sustainable Innovations and a Model of Sustainable Innovations Orientation." *Journal of the Academy of Marketing Sciences*. Accessed on January 14, 2016.

Wang, Jing. 2008. *Brand New China: Advertising, Media, and Commercial Culture*. Cambridge: Harvard University Press. 21.

About the Authors

Dr. Jagdish N. Sheth has been the Charles H. Kellstadt Professor of Marketing in the Goizueta Business School at Emory University in Atlanta, Georgia (U.S.), since 1991. Prior to his present position, he was on the faculty of the University of Southern California (USC), the University of Illinois, Columbia University, and the Massachusetts Institute of Technology (MIT). Professor Sheth is well known for his scholarly contributions in consumer behavior, relationship marketing, competitive strategy, and emerging markets. He is the past president of the Association for Consumer Research (ACR) and Division 23 (Consumer Psychology) of the American Psychological Association (APA). He is also a fellow of the APA. He is the recipient of all of the top four academic awards bestowed by the American Marketing Association (AMA). His academic publications include more than 300 hundred papers and several books, including *The Theory of Buyer Behavior* coauthored with John A. Howard; *Marketing Theory: Evolution and Evaluation* coauthored with David Gardner and Dennis Garrett; *Consumption Values and Market Choices* co-authored with Bruce Newman and Barbara Gross; and *Customer Behavior* coauthored with Banwari Mittal and Bruce Newman. He has also published several professional books including, *The Rule of Three, Clients for Life, The Self-Destructive Habits of Good Companies, Chindia Rising,* and *Firms of Endearment*. All of these have been translated into multiple languages. His latest publication is *The 4 A's of Marketing*. He lives in Atlanta with his wife, Madhu.

Email: jag@jagsheth.com

Dr. Mona Sinha is assistant Professor of marketing at the Michael J. Coles College of Business at Kennesaw State University in Georgia (U.S.). Dr. Sinha holds a PhD from Texas A&M University and has worked as a post-doctoral research fellow at Emory University. Her work experience in India is in brand management and sales. She also worked at the Harvard Business School India Research Center where she wrote several case studies on India. Her teaching interests are in international marketing and consumer behavior. Her research on emerging markets, sustainability, and consumer fairness/social justice has been published in several academic journals and in a book chapter. She has been the recipient of awards for outstanding performance at Harvard Business School and for teaching excellence at Texas A&M University. She lives in Atlanta with her husband, Sridhar, and daughter, Nuri.

Email: msinha1@kennesaw.edu

Dr. Reshma Shah is associate professor in the practice of marketing at the Goizueta Business School of Emory University in Atlanta, Georgia (U.S.). Her marketing insights and strategies have helped companies like Delta, GE, IBM, Solvay, The Coca-Cola Company, Turner Broadcasting, and UPS, among many others, improve their marketing return on investment (ROI). Her articles have appeared in several academic journals in the areas of marketing alliances and brand extensions and she is the coauthor of a bestselling book on social media. She is also the recipient of the Distinguished Educator Award at Emory University. She lives in Atlanta with her husband, Hitesh, and her two daughters, Anya and Maya.

Email: Reshma.shah@emory.edu

Contributors

Dr. George Kofi Amoako is a senior lecturer and head of the Marketing department of the Central Business School at Central University in Accra, Ghana. He earned his bachelor's degree from Kwame Nkrumah University of Science and Technology in Ghana, an MBA in marketing from the University of Ghana, a PhD from London Metropolitan University (U.K.), and is a chartered marketer from the London School of Marketing. He has consulted for public sector and private organizations both in Ghana and in the U.K. George has published extensively in internationally peer-reviewed journals and has presented many papers at international conferences in Africa, Europe, and Australia.

Dr. Kwaku Appiah-Adu is professor of strategy at Central University, in Accra, Ghana, dean of the Business School, and the principal strategic adviser of Oxford Policy Management's Oil and Gas Programme, Ghana. Previously, he was head of policy for the Office of the President; chairman of Ghana's Oil and Gas Technical Committee; and advisory board member of the United Nations initiative on continental shelf delineation. Earlier, Kwaku worked with PricewaterhouseCoopers, and the universities of Cardiff and Portsmouth. He has authored several books and over 100 papers. Kwaku has been elected to the ANBAR Hall of Excellence for Outstanding Contribution to the Literature and Body of Knowledge.

Dr. Yaping Chang is professor and director of the Marketing department at the Management School of Huazhong University of Science and Technology in Wuhan, China. He has been awarded a government special allowance for his outstanding contributions in academics and service to industries. He teaches marketing management and strategy management for MBA/EMBA courses. His research interests include international marketing, online marketing, and corporate social responsibility. He has completed 42 consulting projects for various governments and companies. He has served as a long-term strategic consultant for companies in the high-tech industry including Unisplendour Corporation Limited (UNIS) under the Qsinghua UnisGroup.

Dr. Sanjaya Singh Gaur is professor and head of marketing at Sunway University Business School. He is also a director on the board of the Bank of India (New Zealand) Limited. With 25 years of academic and professional experience, he is a well-published scholar, trainer, and an accomplished professor. His research spans micro and macro aspects of business. The research settings in his empirical work include Malaysia, India, China, Germany, and New Zealand. Dr. Gaur has also been a consultant to many companies including GlaxoSmithKline, Advanced Medical Optics (AMO), Johnson & Johnson, HSBC, Kotak Mahindra Prime Limited (KMPL), Ranbaxy Laboratories, RFCL, Geologistics India, SGS, and Godrej & Boyce.

Dr. Amaleya Goneos-Malka received her PhD and two post-doctoral fellowships in marketing management from the University of Pretoria, South Africa, and she specializes in the field of marketing to young adults in the context of a postmodern society. She has published several academic and professional articles and has presented her work at leading international conferences. She has been an integral part of the African marketing and communication industry, working with the world's leading marketers, brands, financial institutions, and government departments, and she has won several prestigious local and international awards. Currently, she holds the position of head of digital wealth for Standard Bank.

 **Dr. Balakrishna Grandhi** is the dean of the Executive MBA (Dubai, Singapore, and Sydney), professor, and head of marketing at the SP Jain School of Global Management. He has consulted for firms like Frost & Sullivan, Phillips, Du Telecom, Maersk Logistics, Dunia Finance, Swarovski, and Landmark Retail, Dubai. His professional interests include strategic marketing, business-to-business marketing, product portfolio strategies, and marketing metrics and audit. He is a member of the American Marketing Association (AMA) and the Chartered Institute of Marketing (CIM) in the U.K. He is also the country director for the EuroMed Research Business Institute (EMBRI) in the United Arab Emirates (UAE).

 **Dr. Rodrigo Guesalaga** is a senior lecturer at the School of Management at Cranfield University (U.K.) and is director of the Key Account Management Research Club and the Sales Director's Programme. He is also a visiting professor at the University of Miami (U.S.) and Pontificia Universidad Católica (Chile). His main area of expertise (teaching, research, and consulting) is on marketing strategy, sales management, service quality, and cross-cultural management. Rodrigo obtained a PhD in marketing from Emory University (U.S.) and has published several articles in international journals. As a consultant, Rodrigo has worked with companies in several industries, such as print media, retailing, healthcare, automotive, wood manufacturing, education and entertainment, and financial banking.

 **Tomás Kidd** is a researcher at Torcuato Di Tella University's (Buenos Aires, Argentina) Inclusive Business Think Tank (also known as ENI Di Tella for its acronym in Spanish). His articles have been published in European as well as Asian academic journals. Professionally, he has worked for a number of microfinance nongovernmental organizations (NGOs) in Buenos Aires, Argentina. His research experience and interests are in the areas of inclusive businesses, emerging markets, and poverty alleviation. Currently, he is working on his master's degree in public and social policies at Pompeu Fabra University in Barcelona, Spain.

 **Dr. Jaqueline Pels** is professor of marketing at Torcuato Di Tella University's Business School, in Buenos Aires, Argentina. Her research experience is in the areas of inclusive business, emerging economies, marketing theory, and relationship and networking marketing. She is director of the Inclusive Business Think Tank (ENI-Di Tella). Her publications have appeared in leading international journals including the *Journal of the Academy of Marketing Science, Marketing Theory*, the *Journal of Business and Industrial Marketing*, the *European Journal of Marketing*, and the *Journal of Relationship Marketing*, among others. She has served on the editorial boards of the *Journal of Marketing, Marketing Theory*, the *Journal of Business and Industrial Marketing*, and others.

 **Anudeep Raghuthaman** has over 10 years of corporate and academic experience. His professional experience scales customer experience management, go-to-market strategy, and brand management. He has a keen interest and expertise in customer journey mapping, brand architecture and positioning planning, brand and corporate strategy alignment, competition analysis, promotion planning, and marketing tie ups. He currently heads the Customer Service and Digital Marketing department for Dollar Rent a Car in the UAE and Oman.

 **Dr. Vera Rebiazina** is an associate professor of the Strategic Marketing department, at the National Research University Higher School of Economics in Moscow, Russia. She holds a PhD in economics from the Graduate School of Management, Saint-Petersburg State University, in Saint-Petersburg, Russia. Her research interests include marketing, marketing strategies in emerging markets, innovation marketing, e-commerce, and relationship marketing. She is a member of the American Marketing Association (AMA), the European Marketing Academy (EMAC), and the Global Alliance of Marketing & Management Associations (GAMMA). She has been a consultant for leading companies such as L'Oréal, Nokia, Nielsen, and Sberbank.

Dr. Meghna Rishi has over a decade of experience in research, training, and consulting. She is marketing faculty and a member of the research team at the Centre for Marketing in Emerging Economies at IIM Lucknow, Noida campus in India. She is also visiting faculty at the Institute of Management Technology in Ghaziabad and at the University of Rajasthan in Jaipur. She has been a consultant to the government of India, the Department of Public Enterprises (Ministry of Heavy Industries) and the Uttar Pradesh Coir Board. Her research has been published in journals such as the *Journal of Consumer Marketing, Worldwide Hospitality and Tourism Themes,* the *Journal of Services Research,* and the *Emerald Emerging Markets Case Study Collection.* She has received five international awards for her research work.

Dr. Piyush "Pi" Sharma is professor of marketing at Curtin University, in Perth, Australia, and has over 25 years of experience in industry and academics. He has served as associate professor (marketing), director (Asian Centre for Branding & Marketing), deputy program director (HKMBA), and associate dean (internationalization), all at the Hong Kong Polytechnic University (PolyU). He serves as an associate editor for the *Journal of Business Research* and the *Journal of Services Marketing,* and is a member of the editorial review board for the *Journal of the Academy of Marketing Science.* He works with companies on topics such as cross-cultural consumer behavior, branding and marketing strategy, organizational transformation, and leadership. His research is published in journals such as the *Journal of International Business Studies,* the *Journal of the Academy of Marketing Science,* the *Journal of Service Research,* and the *Journal of Business Research.*

Jyothsna Appaiah Singh is a doctoral scholar at University of Gloucestershire, in the U.K. working on her thesis entitled "Emotional Labour in Service Relationships." Serving as a researcher for DP World (Jafza, Dubai), she contributes to strategic research initiatives for the organization (investor sentiment, churn prediction, and customer lifetime value management). She has coauthored research work for leading journals in *Emerald* and the *Journal of Food Products Marketing*. As a director of a family-owned business—Coorg Heritage Inn Pvt. Ltd. (CHIPL, India)—she believes in steering sustainable growth through ethical business practices.

Dr. Rahul Singh is an associate professor of strategic management and emerging markets at the Birla Institute of Technology in India. He teaches and conducts research in strategic management, emerging markets, cross-cultural management, and sustainability. He has over two decades of teaching, research, and consulting experience in India, France, Austria, and Finland with companies and agencies such as the Confederation of Indian Industry (CII), the European Union, the Bank of International Settlements (BIS), the Steel Authority of India Limited(SAIL), United States Agency for International Development (USAID), and Ferragamo. He has published in journals such as the *Journal of Business Research,* the *Journal of Brand Management,* the *International Journal of Emerging Markets,* and the *Journal of Global Scholars of Marketing Science.*

Dr. Jun Yan is an associate professor in marketing at the Management School of Huazhong University of Science and Technology in China. She teaches internet marketing, marketing research, and marketing engineering for undergraduate and MBA programs. Her research interests include online marketing, mobile advertising, and marketing ethics. She has published over 30 articles in international journals and conferences. She serves as a consultant for several service companies in banking, telecommunication, and tourist industries in China.

Index